正确的饮食带给您：

健壮的身体·清晰的思考
灵敏的头脑·愉快的心情
充沛的活力·饱满的精神
平和的性情·悦人的性格
集中的注意力·旺盛的生命力
健全的下一代

林光常深深祝福您，并为您祈祷。

林光常 *21*天 排毒养生餐

DAY 21

林光常◎著

Dr.Luke Lin's Guide to Toxin-free Living:
A pharmacopoeia of meal plans with tips on maintaining sound dietary habits and a wholesome lifestyle.

Translated by Lynne Mallinson

国际文化出版公司

作者序

在耗时年余，整理搜集大量资料、整合各方资源与人才之后，终于推出这本中英对照的健康排毒食谱。

销售突破五十万册的《无毒一身轻》自出版以来，因为健康意识的抬头，我感觉到最受读者垂询与关注的，首推排毒餐食谱，其次则是《无毒一身轻》英文版本。因此《林光常21天排毒养生餐》的出版，可说是众人引颈期盼许久。在世茂出版社的支持下，此次不仅呈现出完全客制化的作品，体现读者的所需所想，同时更圆满解答了一般人该如何吃出健康的疑问。

许多研究指出，环境荷尔蒙是影响人体健康的因素之一，而且随着进口食物的大量倾销，人们越来越不清楚自己吃的食物来源如何，许多疾病也逐步全球化。根据卫生部门的统计，由于饮食受到日渐西化及精致化的影响，台湾人在动物性脂肪类的食物摄取量过高，已经造成糖尿病、心血管疾病等慢性病的病患比例，有逐年升高的状况。

而我所推广的〝健康排毒餐〞的制作，皆以汆烫、水煮、炖、蒸或者生食等避免高温的烹调方式处理，保留了食物最原始的美味与营养，不仅吃的人健康，烹调的过程也能免于油烟之害，堪称实践最透彻的排毒健康餐点。

〝健康排毒餐〞选用食材最重要的几项要点是，避免摄食鱼肉蛋奶等动物性蛋白质、蔬果食材讲究当地与当季盛产、根茎蔬果强调连皮完整，连如何饮用及选择好水都大有学问。

由于选用是当季当地盛产的食材，所以不必担心食物的进口来源，而当季当地即表示这些食材正值盛产，价格便宜亦本质优良，兼顾排毒养生又不必花大钱，可说是一套最经济实惠的养生餐点。正是因为以最自然的方式调养身体，让居家养生变得这么轻松而简单！

食用当季当地盛产的蔬果对于身体是最健康的，若消费者都力行排毒养生，相对地，便能带动本土农作物的发展市场，来十个WTO也不怕。

这次在书中，我除了紧扣这几个原则之外，并首度加上食用排毒餐的正确知识，包括：排毒餐前该做的准备、吃排毒餐注意事项、排毒餐Q＆A，及许多一般人容易疏漏，却是我苦口婆心一再叮咛的要点。像是很多人常会问我，遵守排毒餐原则的饮食很难持久，怎么样调适比较好？所以我就特别在书中告诉您，如何渐进式的食用排毒餐；食用到哪一个阶段应暂停；如果真的很想吃肉的时候又该怎么办？这些大家最想问的问题都在书中一一解答。

想要拥有健康人生，首先要有健康的认知，而健康的生活，从正确的饮食开始。众所周知，一日之计在于晨，当然，健康的一天更是从健康的早餐开始。因此，迈向健康人生，您可选择的步骤：

一、确保早餐一定是健康排毒餐，即便只吃百分之五十，都有一定的助益。

二、改变饮食顺序比改变饮食内容简单易行，所以，无论如何，一定要注意饮食的顺序。尤其午晚餐，一定要空腹时吃水果，先喝汤，吃生菜，再吃熟菜、杂粮米饭和地瓜，最后肚子还有空间才吃动物性蛋白质，而且鱼比肉优选。

三、如果非吃肉不可，一定要信守"八大原则"，才不致于让肉成为身体的负担。

四、健康排毒餐不只是一种饮食方法，更是一套健康的生活模式，故可循序渐进，逐渐走向健康之路，已经有病痛者，建议连续四个月三餐都吃健康排毒餐，再加力行"健康每日七件事"，尚未生病者，每年至少连续二十一天三餐都吃健康排毒餐，之后，仍要保持早餐吃排毒餐，午晚餐则要尽量避免中太多毒。

五、利用休假日来进行阶段排毒，也是好方法。

六、您现在可以立即进行的健康行动是，起床后，刷牙前，生饮七合好水。

七、书中所列二十一天食谱，绝大多数都可以互相替换任意选择搭配，请不要拘泥文字，更重要的是其中精义。随着季节与地域的不同，请自行更换，只是一定要记得，当地当季盛产、食物比例和完整摄食三大原则。

同时，为了方便更多英语读者，这次特地在书末附上全文英译，为世界各地的读者排除语言障碍，力行排毒全球化，让全世界更健康！

由于所学有限，难免疏漏，尚祈各位先进不吝指教，甚幸，甚幸！

Contents 目录

Life

Health

导论

附注：书中所选用的菜品及香料都是台湾地区的称谓及特产，大陆地区读者可用类似材料代替。

何谓健康排毒餐

许多人都会这么想："不生病就是健康"，然而，就是这样错误的健康观念，往往让人在不知不觉中让健康的身体被啃蚀掉。而造成不健康的最大主因，就是不正确的饮食观念及生活习惯。

其实，现代人身处在强大竞争压力的生活中，为了寻求平衡，让口腹之欲不断扩大，在长期接触各式高脂肪、高胆固醇、高钠、低纤维、低碳水化合物、化学添加物之后，使人们的免疫系统功能开始失调或衰退，进而罹患各种慢性病或导致疾病入侵。而发达的医学科技，只让我们不断地陷于药剂使用，却忽略了根本的错误饮食习惯、不良生活习惯问题。

而健康排毒餐，就是摄取身体需要的所有养分，排除对身体有负担、有伤害的物质，让身体保持健康的饮食方法。根茎类生食熟食比例是配合人体阴阳平衡法则，和糙米、地瓜、五谷米的五行原理来组合成一套有弹性有规则的健康饮食方式。身体排毒的方法有许多，但用高纤低油低脂低糖低盐的方式，以最普及化的地瓜、糙米、生鲜蔬果做排毒食材，不但安全、经济易实行，接受度高，且改变体质效果显著。排毒是净化体质必经的过程，以自然饮食排毒无强迫性，负担少，无刺激的方式进行，不但能养生无形中也得到自愈的结果。也就是说，当我们都把身体内的毒素清除掉，身体就能得到全然的健康，自然能免除疾病的威胁。

排毒餐设计制作重点

1.颜色平衡→五色平均分配，单色多色平衡。

2.属性平衡→阴阳、酸碱、凉热、分解合成、收缩与膨胀。

3.质感平衡→根、茎、叶、瓜、果、谷、豆轮替变换。

4.口感平衡→酸、甜、咸、辛、苦浓淡皆有。

5.营养平衡→蛋白质与淀粉比例适当分配。

排毒餐的特色

1. 食材种类的选择：当地、当季、盛产之蔬果，洗净连皮(易消化咀嚼)食用。食材选择有弹性，变换容易，方便获得，价格稳定，符合人与天地连结的自然法则，对体质改善或代谢，比较能持续进行。

2. 食材份量比例原则：一份水果、二份蔬菜、一份地瓜、一份五谷饭。1：2：1：1份量恰当可维持体内酸碱平衡和基本均衡的营养，让身体在净化、排毒的同时，仍能满足所需养分，保持体力和正常的运作。

3. 吃食物的顺序：汤、果、菜、豆、藻、米、地瓜。先饮流质，再食生纤维、蔬果，后食蛋白质与淀粉熟食，是配合体内消化系统分解吸收的速度与时间进食，食物单纯有秩序的吸收，一者减少身体负担，二者让其它系统能同步运作，进行分解合成功能，身体可以顺畅代谢排毒。

4. 改善的水质：喝好水，每日三千毫升，水在体内占百分之七十，对身体新陈代谢有颇大影响。WHO警告，百分之八十的疾病与水源不洁有关。有足够的好水在体内，可以加速体质的净化，缩短排毒时间，减少康复过程中好转反应所带来的不适，平衡身体的压力。

5. 改善生活品质：饮食改善，让身体有足够的本钱和时间去修复和自愈，运动、睡眠、作息的改善，让身体在空间上得到适当的休息和准备，身体会在适当的时机告知身体健康状况和自我进行净化治愈的功能，提供正确的讯息和反应，减少生活中的压力和冲突，发挥所需的工作效益。

6. 体质改善：身体在安全适当饮食改变下，会自然进行排毒与更新的变化，进而改善体质或得到自我治愈和修复的结果，大多数慢性疾病和饮食不平衡者，都可以利用排毒餐饮食原则，简易轻松实施体质调整，提升免疫力、觉察力和敏锐度。随个人体质和实施方法，正确性持续性得到不同的改善效果。

健康进食的主张

● 早餐的办法

1份水果＋2份蔬菜＋1份地瓜＋1份糙米

说明：

1. 水果的选择，以当地、当季、盛产为原则，凡是进口水果或是非当季的冷藏品皆不宜。
2. 蔬菜选择时，除保持当地、当季、盛产的原则之外，并以根、茎、花、果四大类为主。
3. 地瓜的选择，以黄肉比红肉为佳，并需连皮一同食用。若为慢性病患，可以食用两份。
4. 食用糙米时，可以在其中添加小红豆、紫米、薏仁、黄豆等各种五谷杂粮。
5. 若本地不产地瓜，则以马铃薯替代。

● 午.晚餐的办法

60~65％五谷杂粮＋25~30％蔬菜类＋10~15％豆类和海藻类＋5~10％汤

说明：

1. 烹调方式以蒸、煮、烫、炖为主，尤其以蒸最好。
2. 五谷杂粮的比例最好为五谷类占百分之七十，杂粮占百分之三十。
3. 蔬菜类最好保持1/2～3/4的生食，让身体可以吸收足够的酵素。
4. 蔬菜中的叶菜类和芽菜类虽佳，但较不适合病人在康复期食用。
5. 癌症患者或是尿酸过高与肾脏病患，则尽量不吃豆类等蛋白质。
6. 汤可尽量用海带或紫菜等蔬菜熬煮。
7. 于两餐之间食用水果。并记得不要同时吃两种以上的瓜类水果，
   以免容易引起腹泻。
8. 每天生饮好水三千毫升以上。
9. 午晚餐需要搭配二至三道的熟食，请根据本书P144～P150熟菜菜单
   自行选择组合。

十二大禁忌食物

慢性病人在进行头四个月健康排毒时，为什么需要慎选摄取的饮食？因为不当的饮食摄取，会让身体一面排毒，却又一面"中"毒。以下这些禁忌的食物，就是非常容易造成身体二次伤害的食物：

1. 鱼虾蟹等海鲜

因为水域的污染日益严重，让生长于水中的生物也间接受到污染，尤其含有大量的重金属，更是会对人体的肾脏造成伤害。

2. 肉

肉类除了容易让人体转为酸性体质之外，还因为在动物生长的过程中，为了加速产量而注射许多抗生素、荷尔蒙，而这些药剂会存留于肉中，在食用后自然就会对身体造成伤害。

3. 蛋

蛋是高度浓缩的蛋白质，使我们的身体很难消化吸收，而且含有复杂的荷尔蒙，让人体对此引发过敏反应。

4. 奶

牛奶中的钙在杀菌的产程中，会转为无机钙，不但无法为身体补充钙，还可能提升体内结石的机率。而牛奶中的蛋白质，在体内经消化分解后，会产生一种属于强酸的"氨素"，于是造成身体为了平衡酸碱，而将骨骼中属于碱性的钙质溶出，让钙消耗更多。

5. 油

经过油处理的食物，不论是油炒还是油炸，在体内的消化时间需要四至十二小时，对身体造成很大的负担。而且油脂容易使动脉硬化，让血管失去弹性，且造成血脂肪的累积，严重妨害血液的输送。

6. 盐

食用含盐高的食物，等于吃进了很多的钠。当体内的钠含量越高，相对地会让钾含量降低，而让身体严重的酸化，让细胞容易罹癌。

7. 糖

精致的糖在进入身体消化时，会释放出身体内的钙及维生素B。而且摄取糖之后，会使血液的浓度增加，让精力降低，增加疲劳感。

8. 味精

味精是常用的调味料之一，可刺激味蕾，增添食物鲜味。不过，它加热后产生的成分不易排出体外，对中枢神经系统、视神经都有影响，长期食用会导致口干舌燥、易头晕、注意力不集中、容易疲劳、掉头发等反应。

9. 酱油

酱油中同样含有高量的钠，且会影响血压的状况。

10. 所有精致与加工食品

精致的加工食品是没有营养而且无能量的食物，因为它们会在精制的过程中，损失极多的营养成份。

11. 含咖啡因的食品

因为咖啡因会刺激神经系统，使精神兴奋、心跳加快、血压上升、活力充沛。但咖啡因也有加强止痛的效果，在长久使用之后会使身体上瘾，进而对健康造成危害。

12. 含酒精食品、冰品类

酒精对身体的损害是严重的，它会产生的不良影响包括：诱发头痛、损害肝脏、影响中枢神经、增加致癌风险、促进心血管疾病发生机率。而冰品很容易伤肾，对女性尤其不宜。

健康选食10大原则

1. 重五谷

未经加工的五谷杂粮含有丰富的营养素以及纤维素，尤其纤维素有预防便秘、缓解腹泻、预防大肠直肠癌的发生等优点，是精致加工的食品所无法提供的。而且五谷对脾脏有相当的助益，能够让脾胃的消化吸收功能更健全。而在摄取五谷时亦需挑选适合的谷物，就是生长的地域要符合当地性，即要分别挑选生长在长江以南（含东南亚）的谷物，如糙米、红米、小米、薏仁等，或是生长在长江以北（含美加地区）的谷物，如大麦、小麦、燕麦、荞麦等。

2. 结种子的蔬菜

蔬菜含有丰富的β-胡萝卜素、叶酸、维生素C、维生素E及纤维素，若每天摄取足够的蔬菜，能提供身体足够的营养素，保持身体健康，帮助身体免受感染以及抵御疾病。蔬菜根据食用的部位可以分为：叶菜类、花芽茎类、种籽及豆荚类、瓜果类、根茎、球茎及块茎类、海藻类、坚果及干豆类，可以运用不同的搭配，供应身体一切所需。

※挑选参考原则

1. 球茎类→紫元白菜、白元白菜、大头菜、花椰菜。形状完整、外表光泽、紧密结实、有重量感、底部坚硬、无变色空心、腐烂、颜色无枯黄斑点、纤维质无老化、内部无变色、清炒时有微甜，外部颜色鲜明。

2. 根茎类→芦笋、芹菜、牛蒡、胡萝卜、甜菜、白萝卜、菜心、嫩茎莴苣、茭白、竹笋、生姜、莲藕。外表光滑、质地细、颜色无过暗或太白、形状直、有重量感、无空心或块斑、皮薄、内外颜色平均一致、根部无过多纤维、外部无裂开、有香味耐久煮。

3. 块茎类→马铃薯、芋头、地瓜、凉薯、马蹄、慈菇、百合、山药。形状完整、无发芽、皮薄干糙、有光泽有重量感、结实无裂开或缺损、纹路明显、无皱缩纹或变色、不腐烂。

4. 叶菜类→根部不长须根、全株完整、叶不变黄或腐烂、颜色鲜明、斑点少、有光泽、无过分肥大或过长现象、不开花、茎部无裂开、叶柄结实而鲜嫩多汁，放室温下一日，在浸水中仍保持完整和翠绿色，有清香味或淡甜味。

3 有核的水果

新鲜的水果含有丰富的维生素和矿物质，尤其是维生素A、C，还有纤维素、天然糖分以及水分。而且水果不仅营养丰富，还有味道鲜美、极容易被消化吸收的优点，尤其连皮一同打成果汁饮用，只需要半小时就能被身体完全消化吸收。而且需谨记，有籽有核的水果才拥有能量，千万不要选择科技的新产品，譬如无子葡萄、无子西瓜等等，否则反而会对健康有害。

※挑选参考原则

水果类→表面光泽、果肉饱满多汁、结实完整有脆度、有重量感、外形无过分肥大、有香味、甜度适当、室温下放数日仍有香味，放水中浸泡，沥干后无快速腐烂现象，颜色无太鲜艳或太淡。

4.当地出产

所谓当地的食物，就是同一纬度或泛指同一个气候带所生产的食物。这是因为地区不同，人们摄取的食物也会不同，因为所有在当地生产的食物，刚好是解决当地所特有疾病的最好药物。譬如说，生活在热带地区的人，就不适合摄取产自寒带地区或温带地区的食物。

5.当季盛产

所有的农产品，都依不同的季节种植及采收，所以我们也需照着食物的节奏与定律摄取，才是符合人体的自然律动。而且当季所生产的食物，刚好就是解决·在这个季节最容易发生疾病的最好药物。这是因为食物会记录温度，植物本身会记载当地当季的气候、温度、湿度、太阳的照度以及宇宙的射线，还有整个土壤的变化，这些讯息一旦被食物记录之后，人吃了这些食物，自然就能帮助人去适应这个气候季节的变化。所以老是吃进口食物、过季的或提早早熟食物的人，身体一定不好。

至于如何判别当季盛产的蔬果，就是市场上的贩售量最丰富，而且价格最便宜的蔬果。不过即使是盛产的蔬果，仍须符合当地的原则才是。

6.成熟的食物

每一种植物都有一定的发育时期，但商人为了尽快获得利益，提早采收，而使用许多化学肥料、农药、荷尔蒙等，进而让这些不健康的化合物随着食物进入我们体内，严重影响健康。

7. 完整食用

食物的每一个部分都具有不同的营养成分，要一起食用才能发挥最大的效果，所以在食用蔬菜及水果时，一定要完整食用，千万不要因为口感差，觉得不好吃，就把外皮、叶子通通去除。这样的吃法即使摄取很多蔬菜水果，但因为吃错了，身体依旧会一样的差。

8. 熟食水煮

最好的烹调方式，就是水煮，就是运用蒸、炖、烫来料理食物。在2003年10月，有一篇西班牙国家科学委员会的报告指出，研究发现使用蒸的方式，能够把食物的营养保存得完整。

相对的，会让身体遭受最大伤害的烹调方式，就是油炸。这是因为当食物经过油炸后，会成为高脂肪的食物，当脂肪摄取过多，便容易使血管内囤积脂肪，增加心血管疾病的发生机率。而且，过多的脂肪还会引发肥胖，以及让新陈代谢不正常，诱发疾病，增加肝脏分解工作的负担。

9. 部分生食

在每一餐里，最好有百分之五十以上的蔬菜和水果维持生食。因为蔬菜与水果中的酵素和维生素在烹调的过程中，容易被破坏或流失，大大降低摄取量，甚至引发消化问题。只要一旦恢复生食，可以改善耗损的身体功能，减缓老化速率，让精力充沛。

10. 禁食

健康的禁食不但可以让负担过重的消化器官有休息的时间，还可以帮助排除身体的毒素，尽快的调整体质。禁食的进行是从一天开始，然后慢慢增加到三至七天，而禁食期间不要吃任何东西，只要喝好水即可，再配合呼吸调整、轻松劳动和灌肠，自然可以让身体更健康。

排毒餐前的准备

●所有的料理皆以一人份为设计准则。不过若为手术后患者、消化道功能差者或儿童，水分与食材可自行减量或稀释，由少渐增调整浓度与水量。

●如果一时无法接受排毒餐的饮食原则，可以依照循序渐进的方式，慢慢改变，譬如先从早餐开始做起。

●全部的料理并无调味料的配置，若不习惯的人，可以自行用天然食材、健康调味食品、健康防癌高汤等来添加菜肴风味。

●烹调时如一定要使用油，请务必选用冷压橄榄油。水都要用好水，包括洗涤、浸泡用水。

●炒菜时若用不沾锅，请勿用含铁氟龙成分的材质。

●对健康的正常人来说，若午、晚餐因生食过多而无法满足饱腹感，可以另增2～3种熟食，但烹调方式以水炒、水煮、氽烫、蒸、炖、卤为主。午晚餐需要的熟食，请根据P144～P150的菜单自行选择组合。

●地瓜洗净表层泥土后，以蔬果解毒机浸泡20分钟，对半斜切，放电饭锅中蒸20分钟即可。

●在烹调前，所有的蔬菜及水果必须以蔬果解毒机洗净。

●两种不同颜色之根茎蔬菜，同水果洗净，连皮连籽，放果汁机中均匀打细。若无法打细或咀嚼不易则勿食，以免难消化；若直接生食，必须充分咀嚼或切细再吃。

●蔬果及水分比例依体质不同、年龄(老人或儿童)差异，弹性调整浓度份量。

　水果一份150～200克　　蔬果两种50～100克　　水分100～200毫升

　参考搭配食材如下：苹果+元白菜+胡萝卜　　葡萄+甜菜+牛蒡　　菠萝+青椒+紫元白菜

　　　　　　　　　　香蕉+小黄瓜+甜菜　　番石榴+西洋芹+西红柿

食材容量换算

1杯=240毫升=16大匙　　　1大匙=15毫升=3小匙　　　1小匙=5毫升

1/2小匙=2.5毫升　　　　1/4小匙=1.25毫升.

DIY健康防癌高汤

材料

带须玉米	300克
白萝卜	250克
胡萝卜	200克
西红柿	200克
黄豆芽	160克
白萝卜叶	150克
金针花	100克
牛蒡	70克
姜	30克
昆布	20克
香菇	5朵
好水	5000毫升

做法：

1. 将所有材料依比例及所需份量备妥，洗净后连皮一同切块，放进锅中。
2. 锅中倒入好水后，以大火煮滚。
3. 转小火续炖煮2小时后熄火，滤出汤汁即可作为烹调汤底。
4. 最好的状况是现煮现喝。若要一次煮多量高汤储存备用，可在汤汁待凉后，装入保鲜盒或冰块盒中，放进冷冻库中保存。

▲ 材料

▲ 成品

DIY健康美味粉

材料：

黑芝麻	等量
白芝麻	等量
卵磷脂	等量
啤酒酵母	等量
松子	等量

做法：

1. 先将黑芝麻、白芝麻、松子磨成粉。
2. 把全部材料搅拌均匀。装于密封罐中保存即可。
3. 食用前再依照所需份量挖取。

▲ 材料

▲ 成品

DIY健康沙拉酱

材料

蜂蜜	1小匙
柠檬	1颗
橄榄油	1大匙

▲ 材料

做法

1. 先将柠檬榨汁。

2. 将所有材料一同放在大碗中。用打蛋器或搅拌器搅和均匀至滑润的黏稠状即可。

3. 装于保鲜盒中，置于冰箱中冷藏。保存时间约为1星期。

4. 也可于色拉酱中添加新鲜水果泥一同搅拌。创造不同风味。

▲ 成品

蔬菜节约烹调法

- 高汤烫菜，会有自然甜味，使高汤的味道更丰富，减少糖、盐用量。
- 汆烫后的蔬菜汤汁，可放入高汤中或留作蔬菜拌饭。
- 高汤若有余，可用来煮饭，增加香甜感。
- 蔬菜用小火干炒后再放调味料，可增加甜味，减少调味料的用量。
- 将坚果放至汤中煮，可减少烹调时的用油量。
- 用胶质高的食材烹调后，留汁加水即可烫青菜，不必另外勾芡。
- 用天然甜味食材放入高汤中，可省略加糖步骤，汤味更好。
- 将蔬果去皮去籽的部分放入锅内，小火慢煮，即成高汤，含有综合的营养成分和丰富的味道。

可使用的调味食品

天然食材 – 柠檬、昆布、香菇、九层塔、葱、姜、蒜、辣椒、玉米

健康食品 – 葡萄干、竹盐、米醋、红糖、蜂蜜、枫糖、纳豆、味噌、米酒、松茸精

暖性香料 – 芥菜、肉桂、紫苏、红花、红辣椒、黑白花椒、山葵、茴香、八角、姜、豆蔻、香菜、月桂、罗勒、香椿、刺葱

勾芡食材 – 秋葵、葛粉、藕粉、海藻（石花粉）、马铃薯、玉米粉（米、豆类打浆沉淀之粉）、淀粉蔬菜、皇宫菜、过猫菜、川七、麻薏菜、芋头茎

甜味食材 – 水果、水果干、甘草、糖蜜、牧草、甜菊叶、蔬菜酵素、菠萝皮、蔬果（球茎、根类、瓜类）、菇类

油脂食材 – 椰子、酪梨、种子、坚果、橄榄、杏仁

杂粮糙米饭

材料：

糙米	70%
五谷（莲子、薏仁、枸杞、小米、小红豆、红枣）	30%

食用的注意事项：

1. 烹煮前须先将糙米泡水4小时（冬季6-8小时），五谷泡水1小时。水要用好水，不可用自来水。

2. 入锅前可以加少许竹盐，两滴油或备长炭煮，可增加米的适口度，减少米的粗涩感，增加耐放时间。

3. 饭后不要立即吃其它点心或饮料，会导致消化不良，并影响排毒效果。

4. 若为夏天，或是儿童、体质燥热者，应以单一谷物，譬如糙米、胚芽米，来搭配地瓜。

5. 若为冬天，或是体质虚寒者，可选择多种淀粉类食物搭配。

6. 若位于温、寒带地区者，可于糙饭中添加大米、小麦、燕麦、荞麦。

7. 谷麦合食，虽然淀粉含量较多，但摄食偏酸，不宜长期多食。

8. 若胃酸过多者，而常有饥饿感，可以选择碱性配法，譬如将糙米与纳豆搭配食用。

9. 白米适合碱性体质，可在腹泻时，煮粥作为调养止泻用。

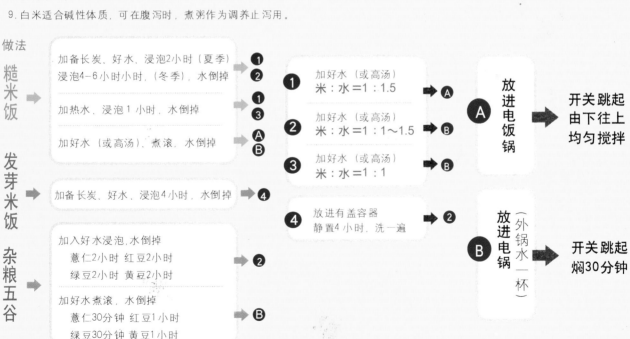

做法

糙米饭

加备长炭、好水，浸泡2小时（夏季） ❶
浸泡4-6小时小时（冬季），水倒掉 ❷

加热水，浸泡1小时，水倒掉 ❶ ❸

加好水（或高汤），煮滚，水倒掉 Ⓐ Ⓑ

❶ 加好水（或高汤）
米：水 = 1：1.5 → Ⓐ

❷ 加好水（或高汤）
米：水 = 1：1～1.5 → Ⓑ

❸ 加好水（或高汤）
米：水 = 1：1 → Ⓑ

Ⓐ 放进电饭锅 → 开关跳起 由下往上 均匀搅拌

发芽米饭

加备长炭、好水，浸泡4小时，水倒掉 → ❹

❹ 放进有盖容器
静置4小时，洗一遍 → ❷

Ⓑ （外锅水一杯）放进电锅 → 开关跳起 焖30分钟

杂粮五谷

加入好水浸泡，水倒掉
薏仁2小时 红豆2小时
绿豆2小时 黄豆2小时 → ❷

加好水煮滚，水倒掉
薏仁30分钟 红豆1小时
绿豆30分钟 黄豆1小时 → Ⓑ

快乐蔬果沙拉

材料　番石榴·········200克
　　　　紫元白菜·······30克
　　　　玉米粒·········1大匙

做法　①将番石榴洗净后，切成小块备用。
　　　　②把紫色元白菜一片片剥开洗净后，切成小块备用。
　　　　③准备一锅沸水，将玉米粒投入，氽烫至熟后捞起放凉。
　　　　④最后将所有材料放入盘中即可。

附注　若将以上食材打成果汁，可加入适当柠檬、蜂蜜、黑白芝麻，酵母B群、卵磷脂、松子（或腰果），以及植物综合酵素、全然谷粉、钙源或植物种子纤维等，效果更佳。

芝麻地瓜球

材料　黑芝麻·········3大匙
　　　　地瓜···········60克

做法　①把熟黑芝麻倒进盘中备用。
　　　　②将地瓜放进电饭锅内，蒸至全熟松软。
　　　　③从电饭锅中取出地瓜，放进大碗中待凉后，用大汤匙捣成泥。
　　　　④将双手洗净，取适量地瓜泥于掌心揉捏成丸状。
　　　　⑤把地瓜丸放在铺满黑芝麻的盘子中滚动，使地瓜丸的表面沾满黑芝麻即可。

附注　若黑芝麻是生的，可以倒在烤盘上，以低温烘烤即可。

薏仁糙米饭

材料　薏仁···········1杯
　　　　糙米···········3杯
　　　　好水···········6杯

做法　①将薏仁与糙米倒入电饭锅内锅中，再倒入好水浸30分钟。
　　　　②再将内锅放入电饭锅中，外锅加水1杯，煮至跳起再焖10分钟即可。

＊光常的叮咛＊

解决农药残留的好方法

　　想要安心的生吃蔬果，必须要先排除农药残留的问题，除了慎重地挑选不使用化学肥料、农药的新鲜蔬果外，亦可以通过三个解决的方案来避免：

1. 自己种，这是从根本上解决问题的办法。

2. 找农民请他种。

3. 借助O₃臭氧，即OZONE蔬果解毒机。在挑选机器时必须符合臭氧的释放量一小时是在200到250毫克之间，尤其不要超过300毫克以上，否则反而伤害身体。并且一定要是符合德国标准制造或拥有德国专利的机器，因为德国技术标准达到了全世界最高。

三菇抗老汤

材料　干香菇 —— 5朵　　杂粮面包 —————— 2片　白芝麻　1小匙
　　　　金针菇 —— 30克　健康防癌高汤或好水 —— 250毫升　姜丝　　少许
　　　　灵芝菇 —— 30克　树薯粉 ———————— 1小匙

做法　①将干香菇预先泡软，切丝备用。
　　　　②把金针菇及灵芝菇洗净备用。
　　　　③高汤中投入姜丝煮沸，放入干香菇、金针菇及灵芝菇。
　　　　④树薯粉调水搅匀，等汤再次沸腾时倒入，勾芡成糊状。
　　　　⑤把汤填装入碗中，把面包放至汤上，撒上白芝麻即可。

排毒蔬菜棒

材料　小黄瓜 —— 1条　　白萝卜 —— 50克
　　　　胡萝卜 —— 80克　梅汁 ———— 1大匙

做法　①将小黄瓜、胡萝卜及白萝卜洗净后，切成长条状。
　　　　②白萝卜丝以梅汁渍10分钟，与其它材料拌匀即可。

附注　若觉得生食白萝卜仍有辛辣味，可以先冲洗5分钟来降低辛辣味。

凉拌海带根

材料　海带根 —— 50克
　　　　蒜头 —— 2颗

做法　①将蒜头磨成泥，备用。
　　　　②海带根洗净后过滚水汆烫沥干，与蒜泥拌匀即可。

附注　亦可另加芝麻粒、香油、姜泥、芹菜末、味噌，来做变化。

＊餐间水果－苹果＊

苹果素有"一天一苹果，健康不生病"之称，这是因为苹果内含各种有机酸，对排毒很有帮助。而其中的果胶具有调理肠功能作用，果糖则可以消除疲劳。除此之外，苹果还含有大量的抗氧化物，能防止自由基对细胞的伤害。而且苹果所含的钾还可以与体中多余的钠离子结合，如果多吃苹果就可以协助盐分的排除，降低血压。

黄豆糙米饭

材料　黄豆　0.5杯
糙米　3.5杯

做法
①黄豆在前一晚先泡好水，或事先泡好水6小时。
②糙米事先泡好水4小时。
③把黄豆与糙米浸泡的水倒掉后，放进电锅内锅中，倒入6杯好水。
④再将内锅放入电锅中，外锅加水1杯，煮至跳起再焖10分钟即可。

明日叶豆腐汤

材料　明日叶　50克
嫩豆腐　1块
胡萝卜　30克
健康防癌高汤或好水　300毫升
竹盐　少许

做法
①将明日叶洗净后，切成约5公分长的小段备用。
②把嫩豆腐切成约3公分长的小块备用。
③把胡萝卜切成薄片备用。
④在锅中将高汤煮沸，投入胡萝卜及豆腐，等再次煮沸后放入明日叶、竹盐，待煮沸即可熄火。

苦瓜紫菜卷

材料　苦瓜　100克
元白菜　30克
海苔　3片

做法
①将苦瓜剖开洗净后，切成薄片用热水汆烫1分钟，再用梅汁渍30分钟。
②把元白菜洗净后，切成细丝备用。
③让海苔在桌上摊平，放上元白菜丝及苦瓜片，以手卷起即可。

早餐 · Breakfast ·

清肝蔬果汁

材料　苹果 ——————— 200克
　　　小黄瓜 —————— 60克
　　　胡萝卜 —————— 50克
　　　好水 ——————— 300毫升

做法　①将苹果、小黄瓜、胡萝卜切成小块后，放进果汁机中。
　　　②再把好水倒入果汁机中，一同搅拌打匀即可。

附注　①亦可加入适当柠檬、蜂蜜、黑白芝麻、酵母B群、卵磷脂、
　　　　松子（或腰果），以及植物综合酵素、全然谷粉、钙源或植
　　　　物种子纤维等，效果更佳。
　　　②蔬果汁饮完半小时再吃地瓜饭，对于胃肠消化不良的人来
　　　　说，若食用的时间太近较容易导致胀气。

地瓜枸杞饭团

材料　地瓜 ——————— 60克
　　　枸杞 ——————— 2大匙
　　　糙米 ——————— 2杯

做法　①将糙米倒于电锅内锅中，以清水冲洗，加入3杯好水。
　　　②把地瓜外皮冲洗后，切成约1公分的小块，拌进糙米中。
　　　③把内锅放进电锅中，外锅倒半杯好水，煮约20分钟至全熟。
　　　④待稍凉后以饭勺将饭与枸杞拌匀，挖取适量填装至饭团模型中，
　　　　稍微压挤成型即可。

附注　若地瓜饭无法一次吃完，建议将地瓜与糙米分开蒸煮，吃前再拌在
　　　一起，可以增加地瓜饭的新鲜保存时效。

＊ 光常的叮咛 ＊

小心食品添加物

　　因为食品化学及加工技术的快速发展，现代生活中充斥着种类繁多的各种加工食品，各处可见的零食、调理包、快餐等等，都添加了大量的食品添加物。所谓食品添加物，即是让食物在制造、包装、运送、贮存等过程中，为了着色、调味、防腐、增添香味、安定品质、防止氧化…等用途，而添加于食品中的物质。

　　而食品添加物中除糖、盐、酒、醋等可算天然添加物外，其它大多是由化学合成的。也就是说，食品添加物只是为了延长食物保鲜的时效，或让食物的色香味更诱人而已，对健康完全没有好处，而且食品添加物会影响人体健康，也有致癌的危险。所以，即使有法律规范食品添加物，但为了避免化学毒素进入身体，还是能避免就尽量避免。

紫米烤饭团

材料　紫米————2杯
　　　枸杞————2大匙

做法　①将枸杞、紫米装入电锅内锅中，以清水冲洗后，加入3杯好水。
　　　②把内锅放进电锅中，煮约20分钟至熟即可。
　　　③待饭稍凉后，以饭勺挖取适量，以手或饭团模型捏制成三角饭团。
　　　④平底锅用小火烧热，把饭团放置于锅面上，烤至表面稍硬。
　　　⑤翻转饭团，至饭团两面皆稍微干硬即可。

山药昆布汤

材料　山药————30克　青葱————————1根　姜丝————10克
　　　海带————30克　健康防癌高汤或好水　250毫升　竹盐————少许

做法　①将山药切成长条片状，海带泡开，备用。
　　　②青葱洗净后切成碎葱花，备用。
　　　③高汤倒入锅中加海带、姜丝煮至沸腾，投入山药、竹盐，再煮至沸腾即熄火。
　　　④起锅后装至碗中，撒上葱花即可。

三彩沙拉

材料　南瓜————60克　豌豆仁——1大匙　味噌————1小匙
　　　白花菜——60克　芝麻酱——1小匙

做法　①将南瓜切成约5公分大小的块状。
　　　②白花菜洗净后，切成小朵备用。
　　　③备一锅滚水，把南瓜、白花菜投入烫至熟，再放入豌豆仁烫一分钟，即捞起放凉。
　　　④把所有材料摆放置碗中，拌上味噌、芝麻酱即可。

附注　若食用豌豆仁容易胀气，可以用青花菜替代。

＊餐间水果－香蕉＊

　香蕉也是要连皮吃的水果。香蕉的果肉对脾胃帮助甚大，而皮则是对心脏很好，所以完整的摄取不仅可以维持食物的酸碱平衡，也可以兼顾心脏脾胃。且香蕉的糖质不但能补充能量，且富含的食物纤维可刺激肠管蠕动，使粪便畅通。而香蕉中亦含有丰富的钾，可以平衡体内过多的钠，防止血压上升，降低心血管病的发生。

午餐 · Lunch ·

小米煎饼

◎ 材料　小米 —— 1大匙　全麦面粉 —— 150克
　　　　玉米粒 —— 50克　好水 —— 50毫升

◎ 做法　①小米先浸好水30分钟，或用热水
　　　　　浸10分钟。
　　　　②将玉米粒切碎或磨泥，与小米、
　　　　　面粉、好水拌匀，使之揉成面团。
　　　　③把面团搓成圆球状，以擀面棍擀
　　　　　成圆饼状面皮。
　　　　④平底锅以小火热锅，将面皮放入
　　　　　锅中，煎至表面呈现金黄色即可。

香菇串

◎ 材料　新鲜香菇 —— 7朵　姜泥 —— 1/2小匙
　　　　蒜头 —— 2颗　酱油 —— 1/2小匙

◎ 做法　①将香菇洗净后去除蒂头，以竹签
　　　　　从中心点穿过，依序串起香菇。
　　　　②把香菇串放进烤箱中，以120℃
　　　　　烤约5分钟。
　　　　③蒜头剥除外皮后，在磨泥器表面
　　　　　来回搓成蒜泥，与姜泥、酱油拌
　　　　　匀成酱料。
　　　　④从烤箱中取出香菇串，食用前沾
　　　　　取酱料即可。

高纤什锦沙拉

◎ 材料　海带丝 —— 50克　乌醋 —— 1小匙
　　　　剑笋 —— 50克　酱油 —— 1小匙
　　　　玉米粒 —— 1大匙　麻油 —— 1/2小匙

◎ 做法　①把乌醋、酱油、麻油拌匀成酱料。
　　　　②准备一锅沸水，依序将海带丝、
　　　　　剑笋、玉米粒投入汆烫至熟。
　　　　③捞起放凉后，一同摆放至盘中，
　　　　　最后撒上玉米粒，淋上酱汁即可。

罗宋汤

◎ 材料　元白菜 —— 50克　洋葱 —— 50克
　　　　四季豆 —— 10支　胡萝卜 —— 30克
　　　　大西红柿 —— 80克　竹盐 —— 适量
　　　　健康防癌高汤或好水 —— 1000毫升

◎ 做法　①把元白菜一片片剥开洗净，四季
　　　　　豆洗净对切。
　　　　②大西红柿洗净后，切成4片备用，
　　　　　洋葱、胡萝卜切成约1公分的丁
　　　　　块。
　　　　③将高汤倒入锅中煮沸，放入大西
　　　　　红柿煮沸后，再放入胡萝卜、洋
　　　　　葱煮15分钟。
　　　　④再放入元白菜、四季豆煮约15分钟，
　　　　　最后加入竹盐即可。

早餐 · Breakfast ·

香蕉

◎ **材料**　香蕉 ———————— 1根

◎ **做法**　将香蕉剥皮后，直接食用即可。

◎ **附注**　①食用时可沾取少许肉桂粉。
　　　　　②香蕉最好在皮表面已出现黑点时食用。
　　　　　③香蕉若要连皮吃，须挑选有机无农药的香蕉。
　　　　　④香蕉有润肺、清肠胃、通便的功用。

地瓜饼

◎ **材料**　地瓜 ———————— 60克
　　　　　地瓜粉 ——————— 150克
　　　　　竹盐 ———————— 1/2小匙

◎ **做法**　①地瓜表面洗净后，放进电锅中蒸至熟软。
　　　　　②将地瓜从电锅取出放于大碗中，去皮后用大汤匙捣成泥。
　　　　　③在大碗中加入地瓜粉、竹盐，混匀成面团。
　　　　　④把面团分别搓揉成直径约5公分大的圆球，并用擀面棍压整
　　　　　　成圆饼状。
　　　　　⑤平底锅以小火热锅，将圆饼放进锅中，至两面呈金黄色即可
　　　　　　起锅。

◎ **附注**　地瓜若要连皮吃，须挑选有机无农药的地瓜。

糙米蔬菜粥

◎ **材料**　糙米 ———————————— 1/2杯
　　　　　西红柿 ————————————— 60克
　　　　　小黄瓜 ————————————— 50克
　　　　　健康防癌高汤或好水 ————— 500毫升

◎ **做法**　①把西红柿、小黄瓜洗净后，切成约1公分的小丁块。
　　　　　②在锅中倒入高汤及糙米，煮至熟软即熄火。
　　　　　③将西红柿丁、小黄瓜丁倒入锅中，与糙米粥搅拌均匀即可。

◎ **附注**　亦可加入坚果或核桃5粒，或马铃薯50克切丁与糙米同煮。

*** 光常的叮咛 ***

要喝好水

　水的补充对于健康很重要。除了每天要喝足3000毫升的水，在一天之中，有三个时段一定要喝水：早上起床后、下午三点钟左右、晚上七至九点钟。另外当处于七、八月份的夏季时节，身体水分的需求量更是大幅增加。

　每早起床后，就马上生饮1260毫升的好水，效果非常好。但是有肾脏病、心脏病、肝硬化的病患，仍需依照医师指示喝水。另外在医学上有种说法叫做"危险四点钟"，因为心脑血管爆发大多在凌晨四点，此时血浓度、黏度都最高，若在睡前喝200毫升的水，可以帮助人体的血浓度降低。

　并且，喝的是否是好水同样重要。因为水不仅能解渴，还能提供人体必须的矿物质和微量元素。所以，好水必须有条件：保留原始的矿物质；没有氯、杂质、重金属；酸碱值为微弱碱性的7.4～8之间；要能符合生饮的标准；必须有含氧；好水的分子整齐且密度高；运用一台不使用电的滤水器。

杂粮馒头

🌀 **材料** 松子 1大匙 小米 1大匙 酵母 4克 泡打粉 3克
黑芝麻 1大匙 全麦面粉 150克 黑糖 1/2小匙 好水 150毫升
枸杞 1大匙 中筋面粉 200克

🌀 **做法** ①把全麦面粉、中筋面粉、泡打粉置于大碗中，一边慢慢加入混合酵母的好水，
一边揉捏成面团。
②将小米先用热水泡10分钟后，与松子、黑芝麻、枸杞、黑糖一同倒入大碗中，
均匀混入面团。
③面团放至阴凉处，待醒面20分钟。
④将面团揉成圆形，放进电饭锅中蒸30分钟即可。

拌什锦

🌀 **材料** 茭白笋 1支 黑木耳 20克 香菜 1株 酱油 1小匙
金针菇 20克 辣椒 1支 乌醋 1小匙 麻油 1/2小匙

🌀 **做法** ①将茭白笋、黑木耳洗净过水汆烫后，与辣椒一同切成细丝备用。
②香菜洗净后，切成约1公分小段。
③备一锅滚水，将金针菇过水汆烫至熟软，捞起备用。
④取一大碗，将所有材料投入拌匀即可。

黄豆芽汤

🌀 **材料** 黄豆芽 50克 健康防癌高汤或好水 1000毫升
青蒜 1根 竹盐 少许

🌀 **做法** ①将青蒜洗净后，切成碎段。
②黄豆芽洗净后，投入煮沸的高汤中，煮约15分钟至熟软便熄火。
③将汤起锅装碗后，撒下青蒜段、竹盐即可。

✳ 餐间水果－葡萄 ✳

葡萄是对肾、内分泌、泌尿生殖系统都很好的食物，但必须连果肉、皮、籽一起食用。更含有各种具防老抗病效果的多酚类，其最营养的部分，就是皮上那层白色的"葡萄多酚"，即是很好的抗癌元素之一。而葡萄中的葡萄糖和铁质，则可以恢复体力、预防贫血。另外葡萄亦能帮助清除肝、肾、肠、胃、心血管的废物毒素。

午餐 · L u n c h ·

黑白饭

◎ 材料　薏仁————————1杯
　　　　白果————————9粒
　　　　紫米————————1杯
　　　　糙米————————1杯

◎ 做法　① 将薏仁浸好水2小时，糙米浸好
　　　　　水4小时，白果浸热水至微软。
　　　　② 把所有材料倒于电锅内锅中，加
　　　　　入5杯好水。
　　　　③ 将内锅放至电锅中，外锅加水半
　　　　　杯，煮约20分钟即可。

西红柿海苔沙拉

◎ 材料　大西红柿———————200克
　　　　海苔————————2片
　　　　松子————————1大匙

◎ 做法　① 将大西红柿洗净后，分别切成4
　　　　　片，置于盘中。
　　　　② 把海苔片剪成细丝，撒在西红柿
　　　　　片上。
　　　　③ 最后将松子撒于盘中即可。

素味汤

◎ 材料　玉米笋————————4支
　　　　四季豆————————5支
　　　　胡萝卜————————30克
　　　　健康防癌高汤或好水——250毫升

◎ 做法　① 将玉米笋、四季豆洗净后，切成
　　　　　对半备用。
　　　　② 胡萝卜洗净后，切成薄片备用。
　　　　③ 于锅中把高汤煮沸，先投入胡萝
　　　　　卜煮至微软后，再放玉米笋、四
　　　　　季豆。
　　　　④ 待再次煮至沸腾，在起锅前放入
　　　　　竹盐即可。

健康蔬果汁

🌀 **材料**　　葡萄 —————— 60克
　　　　　　西洋芹 ————— 60克
　　　　　　山药 —————— 40克
　　　　　　好水 —————— 300毫升

🌀 **做法**　　①将葡萄洗净后，备用。
　　　　　　②把西洋芹剥开洗净后，切成小块备用。
　　　　　　③准备山药，须连皮刷洗干净，去除斑点。
　　　　　　④最后将所有材料放入果汁机中，打匀即可。

🌀 **附注**　　若将以上食材打成果汁，可加入适当柠檬、蜂蜜、黑白芝麻、酵母B
　　　　　　群、卵磷脂、松子（或腰果），以及植物综合酵素、全然谷粉、钙源
　　　　　　或植物种子纤维等，效果更佳。

地瓜蔬菜色拉

🌀 **材料**　　地瓜 —————— 100克
　　　　　　核桃 —————— 1大匙
　　　　　　红甜椒 ————— 20克
　　　　　　西洋芹 ————— 30克
　　　　　　梅汁 —————— 1小匙

🌀 **做法**　　①将地瓜切成3公分大小块状，红甜椒切片。
　　　　　　②备一锅滚水，投入地瓜块煮至熟软，捞起备用。
　　　　　　③西洋芹洗净后取中段约20公分长，切成约3公分的小段。
　　　　　　④将地瓜块、红甜椒、核桃、西洋芹铺在盘中，淋上梅汁即可。

糙米饭

🌀 **材料**　　糙米 —————— 2杯
　　　　　　健康防癌高汤 — 2杯

🌀 **做法**　　①糙米以好水浸泡4小时，将水滤除。
　　　　　　②将糙米、高汤倒入电锅内锅中，把内锅置于电锅中，外锅加好水
　　　　　　　半杯，煮约20分钟即可。

＊ 光常的叮咛 ＊

地瓜的重要性

　　千万不要小看地瓜，它可是排毒餐里最重要的一个部分，也就是说，你什么都可以不吃，但一定要吃地瓜！

　　这是因为地瓜不但高纤低脂，还拥有非常丰富完整的矿物质、维生素及胺基酸，几乎涵盖了人体大部分需要的成分。根据日本癌症医学研究所列举排名前20项的抗癌食物中，熟地瓜为第一名，生地瓜则为第二名，可以看出地瓜的营养价值对于人体健康的贡献。并且，黄瓤的地瓜会比红瓤的能量更高。

　　地瓜的烹调可以是用蒸的或烤的，当在气温15℃以下的时候，可以烤来

吃；在15℃以上的时候，则用蒸的。不过千万别忘了，吃地瓜的时候一定要连皮吃。

营养盖饭

🌀 **材料**　西洋芹———1支　　南瓜—————————50克　　竹盐———少许
　　　　　洋菇———3朵　　糙米—————————1杯
　　　　　玉米粒——1大匙　健康防癌高汤或好水——120毫升

🌀 **做法**　①将糙米倒入电锅内锅中，以清水稍微冲洗后，倒入1又1/2杯好水。
　　　　　②把内锅置于电锅中，外锅加好水半杯，煮约20分钟即可装碗备用。
　　　　　③西洋芹洗净后，切成约3公分小段备用。
　　　　　④洋菇洗净后对半切，南瓜切成约3公分小块。
　　　　　⑤平底锅热锅后，投入高汤、西洋芹、洋菇、玉米粒、南瓜、竹盐。
　　　　　⑥待所有材料煮至熟软，即可起锅淋在饭上。

长豆菜卷

🌀 **材料**　长豆———50克　　芝麻酱———适量
　　　　　莴苣———30克

🌀 **做法**　①长豆切成约10公分的长段，过滚水汆烫至熟，备用。
　　　　　②将莴苣叶展开，放入3根长豆及少许芝麻酱，再将莴苣叶卷起即成菜卷。
　　　　　③依此做法，陆续完成所有菜卷即可。

香菇海带汤

🌀 **材料**　干香菇—————30克　　姜丝———10克
　　　　　海带芽—————30克　　竹盐———少许
　　　　　健康防癌高汤——500毫升

🌀 **做法**　①先将干香菇泡水至软，备用。
　　　　　②高汤于锅中煮沸，放入香菇、海带芽、姜丝、竹盐，煮沸滚约10分钟，即可熄火起锅。

＊ 餐间水果—桃子 ＊

　　桃子汁多味美，除含有较多的糖类、维生素及脂肪外，还含丰富且易于人体吸收的有机酸，可以促进食欲及消化液的分泌，而纤维及果胶，可以增加肠胃蠕动，帮助消化。另外，桃子中所含的矿物质也相当多，像铁对造血功能有很大的助益，而钾则可以利尿消肿。

午餐 · Lunch ·

小米饭

◎ **材料** 小米 —————— 1杯
糙米 —————— 1杯

◎ **做法** ①将糙米、小米倒入电锅内锅中，以
清水稍微冲洗后，倒入3杯水。
②把内锅置于电锅中，外锅加水半杯，
煮约20分钟即可。

开胃沙拉

◎ **材料** 海带丝 —————— 30克
大黄瓜 —————— 60克
洋葱 —————— 30克
红辣椒 —————— 半匙
麻油 —————— 1/2小匙
乌醋 —————— 1小匙
酱油 —————— 1小匙

◎ **做法** ①将大黄瓜、洋葱、红辣椒洗净后，切细丝备
用。
②海带丝过热水汆烫，沥干备用。
③取一大碗，放进所有材料，搅拌均匀即可。

豆腐强身汤

◎ **材料** 豆腐 —————— 1块
芥菜 —————— 50克
胡萝卜 —————— 30克
健康防癌高汤或好水 —— 250毫升
竹盐 —————— 少许

◎ **做法** ①将芥菜洗净后，切约3公分小段备用。
②豆腐切小块，红萝卜切丝，备用。
③准备一个小锅将高汤煮沸，投入胡
萝卜煮软后，再依序放入豆腐、芥
菜。

补血蔬果汁

◉ **材料** 红葡萄 ············· 15颗
西洋芹 ············· 30克
胡萝卜 ············· 50克
好水 ·············· 200毫升

◉ **做法** ①将西洋芹、胡萝卜洗净后，切成小块。
②把所有材料放进果汁机中，搅拌均匀即可。

◉ **附注** 身体不能吸收纤维质者，可在饮用蔬果汁前先滤渣，或以榨汁的方式吸收原汁。

地瓜红枣糙米饭团

◉ **材料** 地瓜 ·············· 60克
红枣 ·············· 2大匙
糙米 ·············· 1杯

◉ **做法** ①地瓜洗净后，切成约1公分的小块备用。
②在电饭内锅中放进糙米、红枣，以清水冲洗后，加进地瓜及2杯好水。
③将内锅放进电锅中，蒸约45分钟后取出待凉。
④以饭勺挖取适量于手掌中，搓揉成一口大小的圆形饭团。
⑤可依个人食量制作数量不等的饭团。

❋ 光常的叮咛 ❋

吃排毒早餐的最佳时间

　　排毒早餐什么时候吃，所产生的效果会最好呢？早上六点半到七点半之间吃的效果最好。更进一步的解释，则是对慢性病患来说，是在早上六点半到七点之间吃；而对一般保健者来说，是在早上六点到七点半之间吃。这是为什么呢？因为这跟我们身体器官的运作时辰有关，上帝创造我们这个身体很奇妙，每一个器官都有它特定发挥的时间，个体照着个体的功用，彼此相助。而早上五到七点正是大肠经的时间，也就是大肠蠕动最激烈的时间。

　　所以养成规律饮食的习惯之后，当排毒早餐一吃完，就会让人想上厕所，消除不顺畅的排便困扰。

清润冷汤面

⊙ 材料　健康高纤面　　80克　　健康防癌高汤或好水——300毫升
　　　　海带芽　　　　30克　　味噌　　　　　　　　1小匙
　　　　白芝麻　　　　1大匙

⊙ 做法　① 将高汤倒至碗中。
　　　　② 备一锅滚水，将面条均匀放入水中，用慢火煮6分钟后放进海带芽。
　　　　③ 待再次滚后即熄火，将面条及海带芽捞起放进碗中，再放入味噌、撒上白芝麻即可。

蒜泥烫苋菜

⊙ 材料　苋菜　　　　50克　　竹盐　　　少许
　　　　蒜头　　　　80克　　姜泥　　　10克
　　　　麻油　　　　1/2小匙

⊙ 做法　① 将苋菜洗净后，放进滚水中汆烫。
　　　　② 捞起苋菜沥干后，切成约7公分长段。
　　　　③ 把蒜头去皮后切成块丁，与麻油、竹盐、姜泥一同与苋菜拌匀即可。

有味菜

⊙ 材料　雪菜　　　30克　　红辣椒　　　　　1根
　　　　毛豆　　　30克　　冷压橄榄油　　　5滴

⊙ 做法　① 雪菜洗净后切成约1公分小段，备用。
　　　　② 备一锅滚水，投入毛豆汆烫，再放入雪菜烫1分钟，捞起沥干。
　　　　③ 辣椒切丁，与雪菜、毛豆、橄榄油搅拌均匀即可。

＊餐间水果-西瓜＊

　　西瓜是所有瓜果中含汁量最丰沛的，在夏日来一片冰凉多汁的西瓜，不但可以消暑解渴，还能补充流失的水分。吃西瓜的时候要注意，要将红色果肉与白色内层、籽一起打果汁喝。而且西瓜所含的营养丰富，不但包含人体大部分所需的营养成分，包括糖类、维生素、有机酸及矿物质，在西瓜汁中还含有一种利尿元素，可以增加肾脏的机能。

补气紫米卷

◎ 材料　紫米 ⋯⋯⋯⋯2杯
　　　　粽叶 ⋯⋯⋯⋯2片

◎ 做法　①粽叶洗净，剪成10公分长的叶片数段备用。
　　　　②将紫米放进电锅内锅洗净后，再加入3杯好水，蒸煮至熟。
　　　　③待饭稍凉，以饭勺挖取适量放于粽叶上，将粽叶卷起即成紫米卷。
　　　　④依个人需求完成数个紫米卷。

清肺萝卜丝

◎ 材料　白萝卜 ⋯⋯⋯⋯50克
　　　　柳橙 ⋯⋯⋯⋯1颗

◎ 做法　①取柳橙放在磨皮器上，磨下柳橙皮备用。
　　　　②将取皮后的柳橙对切开，榨出柳橙汁。
　　　　③白萝卜洗净后，切成细丝。
　　　　④把白萝卜丝、柳橙皮、柳橙汁放进大碗中，搅拌均匀即可。

烩什锦

◎ 材料　健康防癌高汤或好水 ⋯⋯⋯80毫升
　　　　海带根 ⋯⋯⋯⋯30克
　　　　黄甜椒 ⋯⋯⋯⋯1/2颗
　　　　红甜椒 ⋯⋯⋯⋯1/2颗
　　　　树薯粉 ⋯⋯⋯⋯10克
　　　　姜 ⋯⋯⋯⋯20克

◎ 做法　①将黄甜椒、红甜椒洗净后，切成细丝备用。
　　　　②以磨姜器把姜磨成姜泥，备用。
　　　　③将高汤煮沸后，先加入海带根煮至沸腾，起锅前放甜椒，最后以树薯粉调水勾芡即可。

西红柿玉米汤

◎ 材料　大西红柿 ⋯⋯⋯⋯1颗
　　　　玉米 ⋯⋯⋯⋯1根
　　　　青豆仁 ⋯⋯⋯⋯1大匙
　　　　健康防癌高汤或好水 ⋯1000毫升

◎ 做法　①西红柿洗净后，切成薄片备用。
　　　　②玉米去皮洗净后，切片备用。
　　　　③将高汤倒于锅中煮沸，放入西红柿、玉米，待再次煮沸放入青豆仁，即可熄火。

◎ 附注　玉米剥皮时，需保留玉米须不要去除，并一同煮汤。

早餐 · Breakfast ·

降压蔬果汁

- **材料**　胡萝卜 —————— 60克
　　　　西洋芹 —————— 60克
　　　　苹果 —————————— 100克
　　　　好水 —————————— 200毫升

- **做法**　①以好水冲洗食材，若再以蔬果解毒机处理则更佳。
　　　　②把材料切成小块后，与好水一同放入果汁机中打成果汁

- **附注**　另可加入适当柠檬、蜂蜜、黑白芝麻、酵母B群、卵磷脂、松子（或腰果），以及植物综合酵素、全然谷粉、钙源或植物种子纤维等，效果更佳。

地瓜浓汤

- **材料**　地瓜 —————————— 2颗　　竹盐 —————— 少许
　　　　健康防癌高汤或好水 —— 500毫升　　姜 ————— 3片

- **做法**　①将1颗地瓜切块，与高汤500毫升一同装于果汁机中，搅拌均匀。
　　　　②将另1颗地瓜洗净后，切细丝备用。
　　　　③将高汤与地瓜汁一同倒于锅中煮沸，再加入地瓜丝、竹盐、姜片，以小火煮滚约10分钟即可。

蔬菜米汉堡

- **材料**　生菜 —————————— 50克
　　　　西红柿 —————— 1颗
　　　　糙米 —————————— 2杯

- **做法**　①将糙米装于电锅中，内锅加好水3杯，外锅加好水1杯，煮至开关跳起。
　　　　②西红柿切片，莴苣切丝，备用。
　　　　③将平底锅以小火热锅，用饭勺挖取适量糙米饭，分别煎成两块米板。
　　　　④将一片米板置于盘中，取2片西红柿、适量莴苣置于其上，再将另一片米板盖上即可。

＊光常的叮咛＊

排毒中的身体反应

　有些人在开始食用排毒餐的数天后，会出现好像有副作用一般不舒服，其实，这正是来自于身体机能好转的"好转反应"。也就是因为摄取排毒餐之后，食物中的各式营养素开始进入人体，而身体在得到这些均衡的营养素之后，细胞开始活化以排除毒素废物所产生的现象，而这种现象在中医则称为"暝眩反应"。

　一般而言，病的愈重，好转反应也就愈强烈。每个人产生好转反应的时期、时间长短与出现的反应皆不同，在出现好转反应的期间，千万要坚持下去，不要半途而废。

常见的反应现象

头痛　目眩　发热　关节痛
呕吐　呼吸困难　痘痘增加
拉肚子　虚弱　多尿　皮肤敏
感　不想动　神经紧张　易发
脾气　消极　忧郁

干拌高纤健康面

◎ **材料** 高纤健康面————80克   味噌————1小匙
黑芝麻————1小匙   丝瓜————1条

◎ **做法** ①将高纤健康面均匀放入滚水中，用慢火煮约6分钟后，捞起备用。
②丝瓜去皮后，切成小块，放入滚水中，汆烫至熟捞起。
③把高纤健康面、丝瓜、黑芝麻、味噌于大碗中搅拌均匀即可。

开胃沙拉

◎ **材料** 菠萝————50克   香菜————1株   梅汁————1小匙
豌豆荚————30克   红甜椒————1颗   梅醋————1小匙

◎ **做法** ①菠萝去皮、红甜椒洗净后，切成约1公分大小的块状备用。
②豌豆荚洗净，过滚水烫后，捞起沥干，切成小段备用。
③香菜洗净后，切成小段备用。
④取一大碗，将所有材料放入，搅拌均匀即可。

◎ **附注** 菠萝皮的酵素与矿物质含量特高，可打果汁饮用。

润肠秋葵汤

◎ **材料** 秋葵————50克   健康防癌高汤或好水————500毫升
海带结————30克   竹盐————少许
胡萝卜————30克

◎ **做法** ①秋葵洗净后，对半斜切备用。
②胡萝卜洗净后，切成薄片备用。
③取一锅子，倒进高汤煮沸后，放入海带结、胡萝卜待再次滚沸，于起锅前加入
秋葵、竹盐即可熄火。

❋ 餐间水果─梨 ❋

梨吃起来的口感清脆多汁，素有"百果之宗"的美誉。自古以来，梨就被用作清
心润肺的药膳水果，具有化痰止咳的助益，而梨皮则对肝脏有益，可降肝火、清肝
毒。更别说梨含有多种有机成分、矿物质及纤维素，不但能降低胆固醇，还可刺激
肠壁，解除便秘症状。

补脾糙米糕

⊙ **材料** 紫米 ——1杯 白糯米 ——1/2杯
松子 ——1/2杯 冷压橄榄油 ——1小匙
生花生 ——1/2杯 竹盐 ——少许

⊙ **做法** ①紫米、白糯米洗净后，以好水浸
泡约1小时。
②再均匀拌入松子、花生，并加入
2杯好水，分别盛进小碗中。
③将小碗移入电锅中，外锅加水1
杯蒸至开关跳起。
④把已蒸熟的米糕取出，加入橄榄
油、竹盐拌匀成团状即可。

抗癌清炒菜

⊙ **材料** 包心菜芽 ——50克
白花菜 ——100克
冷压橄榄油 ——1大匙
竹盐 ——少许

⊙ **做法** ①将包心菜芽、白花菜洗净后，切
成小块。
②取一平底锅，以中火热锅后，投
入白花菜，并加入1/2杯水，
③再放包心菜芽，盖上锅盖焖煮约
3分钟，熄火起锅前拌入橄榄油、
竹盐即可。

双色萝卜汤

⊙ **材料** 胡萝卜 ——50克
白萝卜 ——50克
芦笋 ——50片
味噌 ——2小匙
健康防癌高汤或好水 ——1000毫升

⊙ **做法** ①将胡萝卜、白萝卜切片，芦笋切
小段，备用。
②把高汤倒进锅中，煮沸后投入胡
萝卜、白萝卜。
③待再次煮沸，放入芦笋、味噌，
搅拌均匀后即可熄火。

DAY 7 早餐 · Breakfast ·

甜心蔬果沙拉

材料
莴苣 ———————— 120克
红甜椒 ———————— 50克
玉米粒 ———————— 50克

做法
①将莴苣一片片剥下洗净后，以手剥成小片，置于盘内。
②红甜椒去子洗净后，切成细丝装盘。
③玉米粒以热水汆烫后，撒于盘中即可。

附注
①玉米亦可生食。
②若将以上食材打成果汁，可加入适当柠檬、蜂蜜、黑白芝麻、酵母B群、卵磷脂、松子（或腰果），以及植物综合酵素、高纤谷粉、钙源或植物种子纤维等，效果更佳。

滋润养生汤

材料
生酪梨 ———————— 60克　　健康防癌高汤或好水 ———————— 3000毫升
地瓜 ———————— 60克　　竹盐 ———————— 少许

做法
①将生酪梨、地瓜切成小丁，备用。
②取一锅子将高汤煮沸，投入生酪梨、地瓜，待再次滚沸加竹盐，即可熄火。

附注 若买到熟酪梨，则不必待煮熟，只须在起锅前放入汤中即可。

健康馒头

材料
腰果 ———————— 1杯　　酵母粉 ———————— 5克
葡萄干 ———————— 1/2杯　　泡打粉 ———————— 3克
中筋面粉 ———————— 200克　　好水 ———————— 180毫升
全麦面粉 ———————— 50克　　高纤谷粉 ———————— 50克

做法
①腰果压碎，成细小颗粒。
②取一大盆，放入全麦面粉、中筋面粉、泡打粉与酵母粉，加好水搅拌搓揉。
③再将腰果、葡萄干、高纤谷粉倒入盆中，搓揉均匀成面团。
④以湿布覆盖盆上，置放约1小时20分钟，待面团发起。
⑤将面团再揉成长条形，切小段，放入电饭锅内蒸约15分钟即可。

＊光常的叮咛＊

吃饭 要细嚼慢咽
赢得 好脑力

吃饭时记得每一口要咬三十下，千万不要狼吞虎咽。这是因为越咬越健康！越咬越年轻！越咬牙齿会越好！可以试着作一个实验：把手放到太阳穴上，然后咬动，会发现太阳穴在动。这就是因为在咀嚼的时候，让脑部也有在运动，加强大脑活化，让小孩脑筋发育好，让长者远离老年痴呆症。

而且，咀嚼时嘴中会产生大量的唾液，而唾液里面不但有酵素消化酶，帮助胃的吸收，还拥有很强的消毒功能，可以杀减食物中的致癌物质。

咀嚼亦有助于压力的宣泄，因为透过咀嚼食物的过程，能够解放身体里的庞大压力，带来身心的快感和满足。

防癌薏仁汤饭

🌀 **材料**　莴苣————30克　　薏仁——————————1/2杯

　　　　香菇————5朵　　糙米——————————1杯

　　　　海苔————2片　　健康防癌高汤或好水——2000毫升

🌀 **做法**　①莴苣洗净后，切丝备用。海苔切丝备用。

　　　　②香菇泡软洗净后，切成细丝。

　　　　③取一锅子，倒入高汤、香菇、薏仁、糙米，用大火熬煮至沸腾后，改以小火炖40分钟。

　　　　④起锅盛碗后，撒上莴苣、海苔即可。

补钙珊瑚菜

🌀 **材料**　珊瑚草——————10克　　好水————200毫升

　　　　黄豆——————1大匙　　味噌————少许

　　　　薄荷叶——————2片

🌀 **做法**　①珊瑚草先用温水泡软，切段备用。

　　　　②薄荷叶洗净后，切丝备用。

　　　　③黄豆先浸泡好水4小时，以大火滚后捞去浮起的黄豆皮，再用中火煮至熟软成泥。

　　　　④将珊瑚草、黄豆泥、薄荷叶搅拌均匀即可。

解热白玉汤

🌀 **材料**　苦瓜————————50克　　健康防癌高汤或好水——250毫升

　　　　菠萝————————50克

🌀 **做法**　①菠萝去皮后，与苦瓜一同切成细长条，菠萝皮另切成大块，备用。

　　　　②把高汤倒进锅中煮沸，先加入菠萝皮熬煮约10分钟，再加入苦瓜、菠萝，煮至沸腾，即可熄火。

　　　　③将菠萝皮捞出去除，其余装碗食用。

＊餐间水果-西红柿＊

　　又比小西红柿好。西红柿不但低热量、高纤维，其中含量丰富的维生素及茄红素对身体更是有非常大的助益。尤其茄红素是强力的抗氧化剂，不但对骨质疏松症有预防的作用，最主要的是它能够延迟老化，并降低癌症的危害。且西红柿含钾量高，同样具有降血压的功能。

马铃薯披萨

◎ **材料**　青椒⋯⋯⋯⋯30克　马铃薯⋯⋯250克
　　　　埃及豆⋯⋯⋯1大匙　树薯粉⋯⋯1大匙
　　　　圣女小西红柿⋯50克

◎ **做法**　① 先把埃及豆放入滚水中煮熟，沥干备
　　　　　用。
　　　　② 将马铃薯放入滚水中煮至熟透，捞起
　　　　　放凉。
　　　　③ 用大汤匙将马铃薯捣成泥，并混入树
　　　　　薯粉后，以擀面棍压制成圆形面皮。
　　　　④ 将西红柿切成片，青椒切成丁，与埃
　　　　　及豆一同均匀铺于面皮上。
　　　　⑤ 用叉子沿着面皮周围一圈，轻轻压出
　　　　　痕迹。
　　　　⑥ 面皮放进烤箱，以250℃烤15分钟，
　　　　　至表面成金黄色即可。

减压蔬菜汤

◎ **材料**　紫元白菜⋯⋯⋯⋯⋯⋯50克
　　　　洋菇⋯⋯⋯⋯⋯⋯⋯⋯5朵
　　　　迷迭香⋯⋯⋯⋯⋯⋯⋯少许
　　　　芹菜⋯⋯⋯⋯⋯⋯⋯⋯30克
　　　　健康防癌高汤或好水⋯500毫升
　　　　竹盐⋯⋯⋯⋯⋯⋯⋯⋯少许

◎ **做法**　① 将紫元白菜、芹菜洗净后，切段备
　　　　　用。
　　　　② 洋菇洗净后，切对半备用。
　　　　③ 把高汤倒进锅子中煮沸，放入紫元
　　　　　白菜、芹菜、洋菇，至再次沸腾即
　　　　　熄火。
　　　　④ 最后起锅前趁热拌入迷迭香、竹盐
　　　　　即可。

瘦身生菜卷

◎ **材料**　白肉山药⋯⋯⋯⋯⋯50克
　　　　莴苣⋯⋯⋯⋯⋯⋯⋯50克
　　　　梅汁⋯⋯⋯⋯⋯⋯⋯1小匙
　　　　梅醋⋯⋯⋯⋯⋯⋯⋯1小匙

◎ **做法**　① 将山药去皮后，切成细长条放入好水
　　　　　中浸10分钟，再放梅汁、梅醋渍1小时。
　　　　② 把莴苣叶片摘下洗净，备用。
　　　　③ 取一片莴苣叶平放在桌上，把2条山药
　　　　　摆在叶片中间，再把莴苣叶片卷起。
　　　　④ 陆续完成其它生菜卷即可。

开胃西红柿

◎ 材料　西红柿————50克
　　　　梅子————2粒

◎ 做法　将西红柿洗净后沥干，加入梅子一同摆放碗中即可。

暖身地瓜姜汤

◎ 材料　地瓜————120克
　　　　嫩姜————30克
　　　　好水————500毫升
　　　　肉桂粉————1小匙

◎ 做法　①将地瓜切块，嫩姜切丝备用。
　　　　②将一锅好水煮沸后，投入地瓜、嫩姜煮至沸腾，起锅前撒上肉桂
　　　　　粉即可。

多纤卷寿司

◎ 材料　小黄瓜————60克
　　　　牛蒡————50克
　　　　小米————1/2杯
　　　　梅汁————2大匙
　　　　糙米饭————1杯
　　　　寿司海苔————1片

◎ 做法　①小黄瓜纵切成长条，用少许竹盐搓揉，再用好水洗去盐分。
　　　　②牛蒡用刷子清除表皮泥土，用薄刀削成薄片，并过加竹盐的热水
　　　　　汆烫1分钟后，捞起渍梅汁30分钟。
　　　　③取一海苔平铺竹帘上，用饭勺将糙米饭均匀铺在上面。
　　　　④将小黄瓜、牛蒡各2片放置在整片海苔的约2/5处，4/5和5/5为
　　　　　接合处。
　　　　⑤慢慢卷起竹帘，将海苔卷起，直至卷完。

◎ 附注　牛蒡的纤维高，生食对大肠功能不好的人消化不易，可以先用果汁
　　　　机打碎，或事先烫熟，也可以连皮熬汤，以从汤汁中吸取牛蒡含有
　　　　的矿物质。

＊ 光常的叮咛 ＊

食物纤维吃不够
小心大肠癌

　当吃了太多精致食品之后，会使我们严重缺乏纤维素，导致消化道的功能失调。

　所谓纤维素就是存在于植物中，不能被人体消化道的酵素分解吸收，也没有热量或养分的食物成分。但是纤维素却可以促进肠道的蠕动，缩短消化物经过肠道的时间，还可以吸附多种致癌或有害物质，增加胆固醇与脂类的排出，因而大大降低了大肠癌、直肠癌、结肠癌的发生机率。

　而且摄取足够的纤维素，可以延缓胃的排空，增加饱足感，有助于体重控制。还有减少胆固醇和三酸甘油酯的吸收、减少蛀牙的形成等优点。

苗条养生糕

材料　　燕麦粉————1杯　　　葵瓜子————1大匙　　　好水————200毫升
　　　　　绿豆仁————1/2杯　　高筋面粉———1/2杯
　　　　　南瓜子————1大匙　　全麦面粉———1/2杯

做法　　①把绿豆仁、好水一同倒进果汁机中，搅拌均匀。
　　　　　②将全麦面粉、燕麦粉、南瓜子、葵瓜子混合后，慢慢加绿豆水调成面团。
　　　　　③将面团揉捏成直径约5公分的圆饼，摆盘放进电锅内，以1杯好水蒸至开关跳起即可。

高纤牛蒡丝

材料　　牛蒡————50克
　　　　　白芝麻———1匙

做法　　①牛蒡切细丝，用热水氽烫。
　　　　　②与白芝麻拌匀即可。

提神醒脑色拉

材料　　大西红柿——1颗　　　花生粉————1大匙
　　　　　豆苗————30克　　　梅汁————1小匙

做法　　①豆苗洗净后沥干，放进碗中。
　　　　　②大西红柿洗净后，切成数片摆进碗中。
　　　　　③最后撒上花生粉、梅汁即可。

消胀鲜味汤

材料　　海带————30克　　　竹笋——————————30克　　姜片————3片
　　　　　白萝卜———30克　　　健康防癌高汤或好水——500毫升　竹盐————少许

做法　　①海带先用水泡软，切段备用。
　　　　　②白萝卜、竹笋洗净后，切薄片备用。
　　　　　③将高汤倒进锅中煮沸，放进所有材料后，以小火煮沸滚约10分钟，即可熄火。

✳ 餐间水果－猕猴桃 ✳

　酸酸甜甜的猕猴桃含有丰富的维生素C且卡路里低，是众所皆知的事，不过猕猴桃还含有维生素E、精胺酸、多醣体、多酚类、铜、铁等有效的强力抗氧化物质，能预防和对抗癌症及心血管疾病，提升人体免疫力。而且猕猴桃中还含有高量的膳食纤维，可以促进肠胃蠕动，达到体内环保的功效。

午餐 · L u n c h ·

健胃玉米泥

🍶 **材料**　黄豆———30克　马铃薯———120克
玉米———50克　莴苣———30克
味噌———1小匙
胡椒粉———1/2小匙

🍶 **做法**　①备一锅滚水，放入马铃薯煮至熟透，即可捞起放凉。
②再把黄豆、玉米倒进滚水中烫1分钟，捞起沥干备用。
③马铃薯去皮后，以大汤匙捣成泥，再混入黄豆、玉米、味噌、胡椒粉搅拌均匀。
④莴苣洗净后切成丝，铺于盘上，再放置薯泥即可。

心肝保健汤

🍶 **材料**　生地———30克
玉米笋———50克
海带芽———30克
健康防癌高汤或好水———1000毫升
竹盐———少许
乌醋———1小匙

🍶 **做法**　①将玉米笋切半，备用。
②将高汤倒于锅子中煮沸后，放进所有材料煮至沸腾，以小火滚20分钟即可。

碧绿银丝卷

🍶 **材料**　罗美生菜———100克
豆芽———50克
米醋———1小匙
酱油———1小匙
麻油———1/2小匙

🍶 **做法**　①豆芽洗净后，以滚水余烫至熟，即捞起沥干。
②把豆芽与米醋、酱油、麻油一同拌匀。
③将生菜一片片剥下，洗净备用。
④取一片生菜平铺在盘上，取适量豆芽于叶片中间，再将生菜卷起即可。

蔬菜健身沙拉

🌀 **材料**　芦笋 ———— 30克
　　　　南瓜 ———— 30克
　　　　苹果醋 ——— 1小匙
　　　　梅汁 ———— 1小匙

🌀 **做法**　①芦笋洗净后，切长约7公分段备用。
　　　　②南瓜洗净，切一口大小备用。
　　　　③备一锅滚水，将材料投入烫1分钟，捞起沥干后与苹果醋、梅汁拌匀即可。

地瓜消化酥饼

🌀 **材料**　地瓜 ———— 120克
　　　　地瓜粉 ——— 100克
　　　　竹盐 ———— 少许

🌀 **做法**　①把地瓜蒸熟后去皮，趁热压成泥，备用。
　　　　②将地瓜粉、竹盐放入地瓜泥中，拌匀成面团。
　　　　③面团搓成长条，并分成数段，用杆面棍压制成适当的厚片。
　　　　④平底锅先用中火热锅，放进厚片，煎至两面皆成金黄色即可。

杏果润肺糙米粥

🌀 **材料**　杏仁 ———————————— 30克
　　　　薏仁 ——————————— 1/2杯
　　　　猕猴桃 —————————— 1颗
　　　　糙米 ——————————— 1杯
　　　　健康防癌高汤或好水 —— 600毫升

🌀 **做法**　①猕猴桃切成小丁，备用。
　　　　②杏仁放进密封袋中，用刀背或捶肉器敲成碎颗粒。
　　　　③取一个锅子，将高汤倒进煮沸后，再倒入糙米、薏仁，以小火熬煮成粥。
　　　　④熄火后，于粥中加入杏仁、猕猴桃，搅拌均匀即可。

🌀 **附注**　若想增加变化，可以用些水果干拌在粥中。

＊ 光常的叮咛 ＊

要吃当地当季水果

　中医典籍里我们可以看到，中医把人生病的原因归为三类：一个叫内因，一个是外因，一个叫不内外因。内因就是情绪忧思悲恐惊，即情绪会影响到整个身体的病情。外因就是外面气候的变化—风暑湿燥寒火，当人一旦不能适应气候变化就会生病了。第三个不内外因，即是外伤、意外、饮食等等。而大部分的人容易受到外在变化而生病，一个很重要的原因就是，没有吃当地当季的食物。

　所有的蔬果产品，都有不同的种植及采收时节，不过在农业科技的辅助下，现代人可在四季随时品尝到各式蔬果。但是，食物的生长应当是有一定的规则，会随着四季的变化而有所不同，所以人们应当照着大自然的节奏取食，才符合自然律动。

元气黑米粽

材料　紫米————2杯　　香菜——————1株　　棉线————1条
　　　　芋头————1颗　　健康美味粉——2小匙
　　　　腰果———1大匙　　粽叶——————2片

做法　①紫米洗净后泡水1小时，备用。
　　　　②芋头蒸熟后，去皮捣成泥，并均匀拌入腰果。
　　　　③将芋头泥揉捏成长条，切段备用。
　　　　④2片粽叶弯成三角圆锥形，盛入2大匙的紫米，放入芋头泥，再盖上1匙紫米。
　　　　⑤将上端粽叶往下覆盖包住内馅，用棉线绕三圈后打上活结，即可放入电锅中蒸熟。
　　　　⑥香菜洗净后切小段，与健康美味粉一同作为沾料。

附注　可依材料比例一次多作数个。未食用完的粽子可在放凉后立即放入冷冻库中保存。若要食用只要再从冷冻库中取出加热即可。

黄金沙拉

材料　玉米笋————30克　　小黄瓜——————1根
　　　　玉米粒———1大匙

做法　①将小黄瓜切成长条，玉米笋对切。
　　　　②玉米粒、玉米笋以滚水汆烫2分钟，捞起沥干。
　　　　③将所有材料装盘即可。

附注　玉米笋亦可以用秋葵替代。

降压丸子汤

材料　豆腐———1块　　九层塔——————10克　　味噌———1小匙
　　　　紫菜———10克　　健康防癌高汤——1000毫升　　地瓜粉——1小匙

做法　①豆腐放进面粉袋中，用力挤出水分，直到拧不出水为止。
　　　　②取出豆腐与味噌、地瓜泥拌成豆泥，捏成丸子大小，分别放进煮滚的高汤中。
　　　　③最后放进紫菜，待再次沸腾即熄火，并趁热放入九层塔即可。

＊餐间水果－杨桃＊

　　杨桃在传统药用植物学上称为〝五敛子〞，被认为是可以驱暑降火、生津止渴且润喉顺气的一种水果，对呼吸道感染的症状有很好的消除效果。其实杨桃含有丰富的水分、维生素A、B1、B2、C，以及纤维素、糖类、有机酸、微量脂肪、蛋白质等，还可以帮助解决消化不良、胀气打嗝等消化问题。

午餐・Lunch・

晚餐 · Dinner ·

红豆高纤馒头

🌀 **材料**　全麦面粉———50克　　泡打粉————2克
　　　　　中筋面粉——200克　　好水———150毫升
　　　　　酵母粉————3克　　高纤谷粉———50克
　　　　　红豆—————10克
　　　　　温水—————1杯

🌀 **做法**　①红豆先浸好水2小时，加热煮软后一同放进
　　　　　　果汁机中打匀。
　　　　　②取一大盆，放入全麦面粉、中筋面粉、高
　　　　　　纤谷粉、酵母粉、红豆水搓揉均匀成面团。
　　　　　③以湿布覆盖盆上，置放约一小时，待面团
　　　　　　发起。
　　　　　④将面团再揉成长条形，切小段，放入电锅
　　　　　　内蒸约15分钟即可。

🌀 **附注**　可依材料比例增加，一次作数个，未食用完
　　　　　的馒头可在凉后立即放入冰箱保存，若要食
　　　　　用只要取出再蒸过即可。一般来说，冷冻约
　　　　　可保存30天，冷藏约可保存3天。

冬菇竹笙汤

🌀 **材料**　冬菇————————6朵
　　　　　竹笙————————10克
　　　　　健康防癌高汤或好水——1000毫升

🌀 **做法**　①先把竹笙、冬菇泡好水，发透后，将
　　　　　　竹笙切段备用。
　　　　　②将高汤倒于锅中煮沸，放进竹笙、冬
　　　　　　菇，以小火煮约20分钟即可熄火。

三椒色拉

🌀 **材料**　青椒————————30克
　　　　　红甜椒———————30克
　　　　　黄甜椒———————30克
　　　　　核桃————————10克
　　　　　梅汁———————1小匙
　　　　　梅醋———————1小匙

🌀 **做法**　①将青椒、红甜椒、黄甜椒洗净后，切
　　　　　　成细丝置于盘中。
　　　　　②最后摆放上核桃，淋上梅汁、梅醋即
　　　　　　可。

早餐 · B r e a k f a s t ·

西洋梨

🌀 **材料** 西洋梨 ━━━━━ 1颗

🌀 **做法** ①将西洋梨洗净。
②再用蔬果解毒机处理，连皮吃。

蔬菜美白沙拉

🌀 **材料** 青花菜 ━━━━ 50克
白萝卜 ━━━━ 30克
梅子酱 ━━━━ 2小匙

🌀 **做法** ①将青花菜洗净后切成小块，过滚水汆烫后，捞起沥干装于盘中。
②把白萝卜刨丝，置于盘中，淋上梅子酱即可。

益气地瓜饭

🌀 **材料** 地瓜 ━━━━ 60克
糙米 ━━━━ 2杯

🌀 **做法** ①地瓜洗净后，切成细段备用。
②糙米倒于电锅内锅中，以好水冲洗后，加入3杯好水及地瓜。
③将内锅置于电锅中，蒸约20分钟即可。

吃蔬果不剥皮

许多人在作菜时会把蔬果的皮削掉，比如胡萝卜、山药、牛蒡、南瓜、马铃薯、香瓜、水梨等等。但你可能不知道，其实蔬果的外皮是最营养的东西，因为大部分的果肉都是酸性的，而果皮跟蔬菜的皮都是碱性的。也就是说，蔬果的每一个部分都具有不同的营养价值，不论是皮、果肉、根茎或叶子，要一同食用才能酸碱平衡，发挥最大的效果。

*柠檬－柠檬皮中的果胶可以降低胆固醇。

*香蕉－香蕉皮对心脏有益。

*芹菜－芹菜叶含甘露醇具有保健作用。

*柳橙－柳橙皮内的白色部分对呼吸系统有益。

西红柿烩饭

⊙ 材料　糙米————2杯　　玉米笋————3根
　　　　大西红柿　60克　　树薯粉————1小匙
　　　　白萝卜　　40克

⊙ 做法　① 将糙米加入3杯好水后，放进电锅中煮熟。
　　　　② 大西红柿、白萝卜洗净后，切小丁。
　　　　③ 玉米笋洗净后，切约1公分小段备用。
　　　　④ 将平底锅预热，放入大西红柿、白萝卜、玉米笋，加入1/2杯好水，盖上锅盖焖煮。
　　　　⑤ 树薯粉加2大匙好水调匀，倒入锅中勾芡后起锅。
　　　　⑥ 将糙米饭盛碗，淋上烩料即可。

镶香菇

⊙ 材料　豌豆仁——200克　　荸荠——5颗　　香菇——10朵　　竹盐——少许
　　　　绿豆——100克　　海带——10克　　树薯粉——20克　　胡椒粉——1/2小匙

⊙ 做法　① 香菇泡好水，备用。
　　　　② 将已煮熟的豌豆仁及绿豆用刀背压成泥。
　　　　③ 荸荠以刀背拍碎，加豌豆泥、绿豆泥、树薯粉、竹盐、胡椒粉搅拌均匀成馅料。
　　　　④ 将海带切成细丝，拌入馅料中。
　　　　⑤ 在香菇内侧沾上些树薯粉，再将调拌好的馅料挤放在香菇上，并作成微凸状摆放盘中。
　　　　⑥ 将盘子移至电锅内，蒸约十二分钟即可。

补血花菜汤

⊙ 材料　白花菜————50克　　胡萝卜————————30克
　　　　黑木耳————30克　　健康防癌高汤或好水　500毫升

⊙ 做法　① 白花菜洗净后，切小段备用。
　　　　② 黑木耳、胡萝卜切成小片，备用。
　　　　③ 取一锅子将高汤煮沸，依序投入胡萝卜、白花菜、黑木耳，待再次煮沸即熄火。

＊餐间水果–柳橙＊

　　柳橙在食用的时候，最好用刀将外皮切掉，然后让果肉与皮中间白白的囊肉一起进食，这是因为柳橙皮的刺激性太强，不适合食用。而柳橙中丰富的维生素C、锌和叶酸，不但可以降低心血管疾病的发生、加速伤口愈合，还能协助钙质、铁质的吸收，有助于身体保健。并且含有生物类黄酮的抗癌成分，可抑制摄护腺癌细胞的增生。

午餐 · Lunch ·

益气冬瓜汤

材料 枸杞 ———————— 1大匙
当归 ———————— 10克
冬瓜 ———————— 100克
健康防癌高汤或好水 ——— 500毫升

做法 ①将冬瓜连皮一同切成块，备用。
②高汤倒于锅中煮沸，放进当归、冬瓜，以小火炖煮至冬瓜熟透，熄火前再放枸杞即可。

日式山药糙米饭

材料 糙米 ———————— 2杯
山药 ———————— 100克
酱油 ———————— 1小匙

做法 ①糙米装于电锅内锅中以好水冲洗后，加3杯好水。
②将内锅放入电锅内，外锅加1杯好水，煮至开关跳起。
③以饭勺挖取糙米饭装于碗中，将山药磨成泥与酱油拌匀，淋于饭上。

凉爽拌三丝

材料 海带丝 ——— 30克　姜泥 ——— 1小匙
芹菜 ——— 30克　麻油 ——— 1/2小匙
绿豆芽 ——— 30克　乌醋 ——— 1小匙
蒜头 ——— 2颗　酱油 ——— 1小匙

做法 ①海带丝以滚水余烫，捞起沥干后切段，备用。
②绿豆芽洗净后，沥干备用。
③将芹菜洗净后，切段备用。
④蒜头以研磨器磨成蒜泥。
⑤将所有材料混合均匀即可。

健胃沙拉

材料 南瓜 ——— 30克　红甜椒 ——— 30克
嫩豆腐 ——— 1块　梅汁 ——— 1小匙

做法 ①嫩豆腐从盒中取出，置于盘中。
②南瓜、红甜椒切成小丁，混合撒于豆腐上，最后淋上梅汁即可。

开心蔬果汁

- **材料**　葡萄 —————— 15颗
　　　　山药 —————— 50克
　　　　胡萝卜 ————— 30克
　　　　好水 —————— 300毫升

- **做法**　①将山药、胡萝卜连皮切成小块。
　　　　②把所有材料放到果汁机中，搅拌均匀即可。

- **附注**　①亦可加入适当柠檬、蜂蜜、黑白芝麻、酵母B群、卵磷脂、松子
　　　　　（或腰果），以及植物综合酵素、全然谷粉、钙源或植物种子纤维
　　　　　等，效果更佳。
　　　　②体质虚寒者，可于果汁中加姜一片，或肉桂粉少许，或以温水打
　　　　　汁，或加健康美味粉，不但祛寒亦可增加饱足感。

地瓜烤饼

- **材料**　全麦面粉 ———— 150克
　　　　地瓜 —————— 100克
　　　　黑芝麻 ————— 1大匙

- **做法**　①将地瓜蒸熟后，去皮捣成泥。
　　　　②取一大碗将所有材料混合均匀，揉捏成面团。
　　　　③面团搓成长条状，分切成数段，以擀面棍压制成厚圆片，并洒上
　　　　　黑芝麻。
　　　　④将烤箱预热，以200℃烤15分钟即可。

海苔糙米三角饭团

- **材料**　海苔 —————— 2片
　　　　糙米 —————— 2杯

- **做法**　①糙米放进电锅内，加3杯水，蒸煮至熟。
　　　　②把正方形海苔切成4片，备用。
　　　　③将糙米饭取出，放凉后以饭勺挖取适量，置于手中捏成三角形。
　　　　④用1片海苔把饭团包住即可。
　　　　⑤依个人食量制作数个饭团。

＊光常的叮咛＊

牛奶是给牛喝的

　　我们从小被灌输一个观念，即牛奶是非常营养的一种食物，是蛋白质和钙质的重要来源，因此市面上充斥着各式的乳制品。不过，在牛奶或乳制品当中，这些高量的多种蛋白质，不但是造成过敏的重大因素，而且为了消化这些蛋白质，胃会分泌更多胃酸跟酵素来分解，而使得消化性溃疡的症状更恶化。还有许多疾病，譬如慢性鼻窦炎、淋巴腺发炎肿大、慢性中耳炎等等，只要断绝乳制品的摄取，都能获得很大的改善。

　　而牛奶及乳制品可以将流失的钙补充回来，也是一个错误的观念，因为真正的原因在于当摄取的蛋白质越多，骨质中流失的钙也越多。也就是说，若要维持体内钙质平衡，维持骨骼强健，应当要做的是减少每天摄取的蛋白质，而不是增加钙质的补充才对。

洋葱贝果

🌀 **材料** 洋葱———1/2颗 温水———1/4杯 青豆仁———1杯
　　　酵母粉———1/2小匙 全麦面粉———2杯或250克

🌀 **做法** ①酵母粉与温水（约40℃）混合，等待发酵膨起。
　　　②取一大碗，将面粉、酵母水一同混合均匀，成表面光滑的面团。
　　　③拿一块湿布盖于碗上，静置1小时。
　　　④将洋葱刨细丝，均匀混入面团中，把面团分割成4份，再盖布静置5分钟。
　　　⑤把面团搓揉成约25公分的长条形，将两端卷成圆圈状。
　　　⑥备一锅滚水，转小火汆烫面团，即捞起沥干。
　　　⑦将烫好的贝果放在纸上待表面稍干，再入烤箱以200℃烤约15分钟即可。
　　　⑧青豆仁以滚水煮熟捞起后，以汤匙捣成泥，涂在切开的贝果上。

🌀 **附注** 可依材料比例增加，一次作数个，未食用完的贝果可在放凉后，不涂馅直接放入冰箱保存，若要食用只要取出，喷些水再稍微烤过即可。一般来说，常温下则约可保存3天，冷冻约可保存60天。

正点沙拉

🌀 **材料** 生菜———80克 西红柿———100克 青豆仁———30克

🌀 **做法** ①生菜剥开洗净后，切成小片，置于盘中。
　　　②西红柿洗净后，切片放于生菜上。
　　　③玉米以滚水汆烫后，捞起沥干装盘即可。

消脂鲜味汤

🌀 **材料** 蒟蒻卷———6卷 竹笋———50克
　　　香菇———6朵 健康防癌高汤或好水———800毫升

🌀 **做法** ①香菇以热水泡开，在香菇上以刀子轻画十字。
　　　②竹笋去皮后切片，备用。
　　　③高汤装于锅中煮滚，放入香菇、竹笋，以小火煮沸约20分钟。
　　　④最后放入蒟蒻卷，待再次滚沸，即可熄火。

✳ 餐间水果-葡萄柚 ✳

葡萄柚富含有维生素A、C及叶酸、钾等营养素，而红肉的葡萄柚更含有β胡萝卜素及茄红素，可以提高新陈代谢，降低血脂肪，预防心血管疾病。且葡萄柚果肉中含有独特的类黄酮，能有效抑制正常细胞转变成癌细胞。更别说一颗葡萄柚所含的纤维素约为10克，是一般水果的2倍。对于排便有很好的帮助。

DAY
11 晚餐 · Dinner ·

泰式凉面

材料 高纤健康面 ——— 80克　香菜 ——— 1株
　　　芝麻 ——— 1大匙　蒜头 ——— 2颗
　　　柠檬 ——— 1/2颗

做法 ①备一锅滚水，均匀放入面条，滚煮6
　　　分钟，即可熄火捞起面条，置于碗
　　　中。
　　　②香菜洗净后，切成小段备用。
　　　③蒜头以研磨器磨成蒜泥，备用。
　　　④将柠檬对切，榨取出汁，混入香菜、
　　　蒜泥后，淋于面上。
　　　⑤食用前混拌均匀即可。

抗老凉拌菜

材料 豆苗 ——— 50克
　　　海带芽 ——— 30克
　　　黄豆 ——— 30克
　　　健康美味粉 ——— 1大匙

做法 ①豆苗洗净后，沥干置于盘中。
　　　②备一锅滚水，将黄豆、海带芽倒入
　　　后煮至熟软，即可捞起沥干，置于
　　　碗中。
　　　③最后撒上健康美味粉即可。

开胃汤

材料 小白菜 ——— 2株
　　　嫩姜 ——— 20克
　　　白胡椒粉 ——— 1小匙
　　　健康防癌高汤或好水 ——— 1000毫升

做法 ①将小白菜洗净后，切成小段备用。
　　　②嫩姜切成细丝，备用。
　　　③取一锅子将高汤煮沸，放入小白菜、
　　　嫩姜，待再次煮沸即可熄火。
　　　④起锅前拌入白胡椒粉即可。

蔬果沙拉

材料　柳丁 ———————— 1颗
　　　　红甜椒 ——————— 1/2颗
　　　　元白菜 ——————— 50克

做法　①将柳丁去皮，切片备用。
　　　　②红甜椒、元白菜洗净后，切细丝。
　　　　③准备一锅沸水，将玉米粒投入水中，汆烫至熟后捞起放凉。
　　　　④把所有材料装于碗中即可。

附注　①蔬菜可先行经蔬果解毒机处理，再食用。
　　　　②若将以上食材打成果汁，可加入适当柠檬、蜂蜜、黑白芝麻、酵
　　　　　母B群、卵磷脂、松子（或腰果），以及植物综合酵素、全然谷粉、
　　　　　钙源或植物种子纤维等，效果更佳。

地瓜莲子糙米饭

材料　地瓜 ———————— 1颗
　　　　新鲜莲子 —————— 100克
　　　　糙米 ———————— 1杯

做法　①将地瓜切成小块，备用。
　　　　②将糙米装于电锅内锅中，混入地瓜、莲子，加入2杯好水。
　　　　③将内锅放进电锅中，外锅加1杯好水，蒸煮至开关跳起即可。

附注　若采用干莲子，则须先泡好水1小时。

✳ 光常的叮咛 ✳

吃糖会老得快

　糖有一种甜甜的滋味，总是让人无法抵挡诱惑。不过，若长期食糖过量，会使得属于弱碱性的健康体液，受到属于酸性的糖影响，转变为弱酸性或中性，而加速细胞的老化，头发也会受到影响而变白变黄。

　而且，当摄取糖食后，不但会增进胰岛素的分泌，糖还会转为脂肪，影响正常食欲，妨碍维生素、矿物质和其它营养成分的摄取，而容易导致肥胖。

　更严重的是，当糖吃多了，不但会提升胆结石、子宫肌瘤、乳腺癌的罹患率，还会消耗体内的钙，导致骨骼疏松症，亦会刺激胃液分泌，伤害胃黏膜，而引发胃炎或胃溃疡。

高纤健康饭

 材料　糙米———2杯
　　　　松子———1/2杯
　　　　南瓜子———1/2杯

 做法　①将糙米放进电锅内锅中冲洗，加入3杯好水。
　　　　②将内锅放进电锅中，煮约20分钟至开关跳起。
　　　　③将电饭锅打开，趁热拌入松子、南瓜子即可。

开胃沙拉

 材料　黄金西红柿———10颗　　苹果醋———1大匙
　　　　紫元白菜———50克　　梅汁———1大匙
　　　　芦笋———30克

 做法　①将紫元白菜洗净后，切成细丝后用苹果醋、梅汁渍10分钟。
　　　　②芦笋洗净后切对半，过滚水余烫1分钟，捞起装于盘中。
　　　　③最后将西红柿洗净，沥干装盘即可。

轻松鲜味汤

 材料　海带结———50克　　健康防癌高汤或好水———500毫升
　　　　豆皮结———50克　　竹盐———少许
　　　　青葱———20克

 做法　①取一锅子将高汤煮沸，放入海带结、豆皮结、竹盐，待再次煮沸后熄火。
　　　　②将青葱洗净后，切成细丝撒于汤面即可。

＊ 餐间水果－菠萝 ＊

酸酸甜甜的菠萝除了含有丰富的维生素C，它含有的维生素B1也不少，可以与谷胺酸一起作用，让身体减轻疲劳。另外，菠萝果肉中所含有的菠萝酵素，是一种类似木瓜酵素的天然蛋白，除了可以帮助消化，研究更证实，这种酵素对于血块凝结导致的动脉血管栓塞，以及其所引起的心脏病，都具有缓解的作用。

瘦身素包子

🌀 **材料** 竹笋 —— 50克 　香菇 —— 15朵 　全麦面粉 —— 300克
元白菜 —— 50克 　蒜头 —— 3颗 　酵母粉 —— 5克

🌀 **做法**
①蒜头以研磨器磨制成蒜泥。
②将竹笋、元白菜、香菇切成细丝后，加入蒜泥，搅拌均匀成馅料备用。
③将酵母粉与温水搅拌均匀，放置约20至30分钟后，等待至发酵膨胀。
④取一大盆，放入全麦面粉、酵母粉水，以手搓揉均匀成表面光滑的面团。若面团太干无法凝结，可再适量加入好水。
⑤以湿布覆盖盆上，置放约一小时，待面团发起。
⑥将面团再揉成直径约3公分的长条形，切小段，以擀面棍擀成包子皮。
⑦以汤匙挖取馅料，放在包子皮中间，以手指捏起包子皮边缘，将馅料包起。
⑧将包子放入电锅内，蒸约12分钟即可。

🌀 **附注** 可依材料比例增加，一次作数个，未食用完的包子可放凉后，密封放入冰箱保存。只要在食用前取出，再重新蒸过即可。一般来说，冷冻约可保存30天。

凉拌海藻卷

🌀 **材料** 小黄瓜 —— 80克
海苔 —— 1片
白芝麻 —— 1小匙
生菜 —— 60克

🌀 **做法**
①将生菜一片片剥下，洗净之后以手将每片从中间剥成2片，装于盘中。
②小黄瓜切成细丝，放在生菜上。
③把海苔切成细丝，与白芝麻一同撒于盘中。

固肾黑豆汤

🌀 **材料** 黑豆 —— 30克
竹笙 —— 10克
红枣 —— 30克
健康防癌高汤或好水 —— 1000毫升

🌀 **做法**
①竹笙、红枣泡水至发开后，将竹笙切段。
②高汤倒于锅中，把黑豆、竹笙、红枣放入，以小火滚沸约20分钟，至黑豆熟软即可。

柳丁

◎ **材料**　柳丁————————250克

◎ **做法**　将柳丁洗净后，切片即可。

◎ **附注**　记得要连白色部分一起吃。

补气红枣汤

◎ **材料**　地瓜————————60克
　　　　　红枣————————30克
　　　　　好水————————600毫升

◎ **做法**　①红枣泡水1小时，备用。
　　　　　②地瓜切成小丁，备用。
　　　　　③将好水倒入锅中煮沸，加入红枣，以中火煮滚后，再加入地瓜，
　　　　　　续煮20分钟即可。

海苔饭团堡

◎ **材料**　大黄瓜————————50克
　　　　　山药————————50克
　　　　　糙米————————2杯
　　　　　小米————————1/2杯
　　　　　海苔————————2片
　　　　　苹果汁————————2大匙
　　　　　竹盐————————少许

◎ **做法**　①将大黄瓜、山药切片后，用苹果汁、竹盐浸20分钟。
　　　　　②把糙米、小米放进电锅内锅中，加好水3杯，进电锅煮熟。
　　　　　③海苔摊开，以饭勺挖取适量糙米饭，均匀平铺在海苔上。
　　　　　④在饭的1/2处放上大黄瓜、山药，并把另一半海苔覆盖上即可。

＊光常的叮咛＊

不再胃痛的感觉真好

　现代人的生活步调快，加上工作压力大，饮食习惯不正常，让胃痛成了现代人最常见的困扰之一。而从中医的角度来看，凡是阻碍了气在脾胃的运转流动，都会出现胃痛的症状。

　不过只要遵循排毒餐，恢复健康的生鲜饮食，不仅可以清洁肠胃道，让肠胃蠕动正常，消除恶心、胀气、便秘等不适症状，恢复消化吸收的正常功能，还能从食物中完全摄取各式营养素，尤其是维生素A及C，对于加速胃壁粘膜的复原及修补有最佳的效果。

　另外也要学着解除压力，让身心放轻松，并让生活作息遵循自然规律来进行，才能彻底挥别胃痛。

浓汁马铃薯

⊙ **材料**　马铃薯————60克　　青椒————————50克
　　　　　洋菇————10朵　　地瓜粉——————1小匙

⊙ **做法**　①将马铃薯以滚水煮至熟软，切片装盘。
　　　　　②洋菇、青椒切成小片，备用。
　　　　　③平底锅以小火热锅，放入洋菇、青椒及少许的好水，拌炒均匀。
　　　　　④地瓜粉以好水调匀，倒入锅中勾芡，即可起锅淋在马铃薯上。

活力沙拉

⊙ **材料**　菠菜————50克　　海苔————1片　　味噌————1小匙
　　　　　苹果————60克　　芝麻————1小匙　苹果醋————2小匙
　　　　　核桃————30克

⊙ **做法**　①将菠菜切成小段，过滚水汆烫1分钟，捞起置于盘中。
　　　　　②苹果切片后，与拍碎的核桃、芝麻一同摆于菠菜上。
　　　　　③最后将海苔撕成小片放上，最后淋上味噌、苹果醋即可。

墨西哥豆泥汤

⊙ **材料**　斑豆————100克　胡萝卜————50克　健康防癌高汤或好水————500毫升
　　　　　西洋芹————50克　西红柿————50克　竹盐——————————少许
　　　　　　　　　　　　　　　　　　　　　　　胡椒粉—————————少许

⊙ **做法**　①斑豆先泡好水1小时，将水倒掉，备用。
　　　　　②将西洋芹、胡萝卜、西红柿切小丁。
　　　　　③备一锅滚水，投入斑豆以小火煮30分钟后，捞起压成泥状。
　　　　　④把高汤倒入锅中煮沸，投入西洋芹、胡萝卜、西红柿滚后，再加入斑豆泥、竹
　　　　　　盐、胡椒粉续煮10分钟即可。

＊餐间水果－莲雾＊

　　莲雾属于热带水果之一，饱含丰富的水分，对人体有清凉解热的作用。且因为低热量、高纤维的特质，加上含有利尿成分，对于消除水肿、控制体重也有很好的帮助。在传统食疗上更认为莲雾有安神的效果，能够轻松消解因为天气炎热造成的烦躁。

午餐 · L u n c h ·

DAY 13 晚餐 · Dinner ·

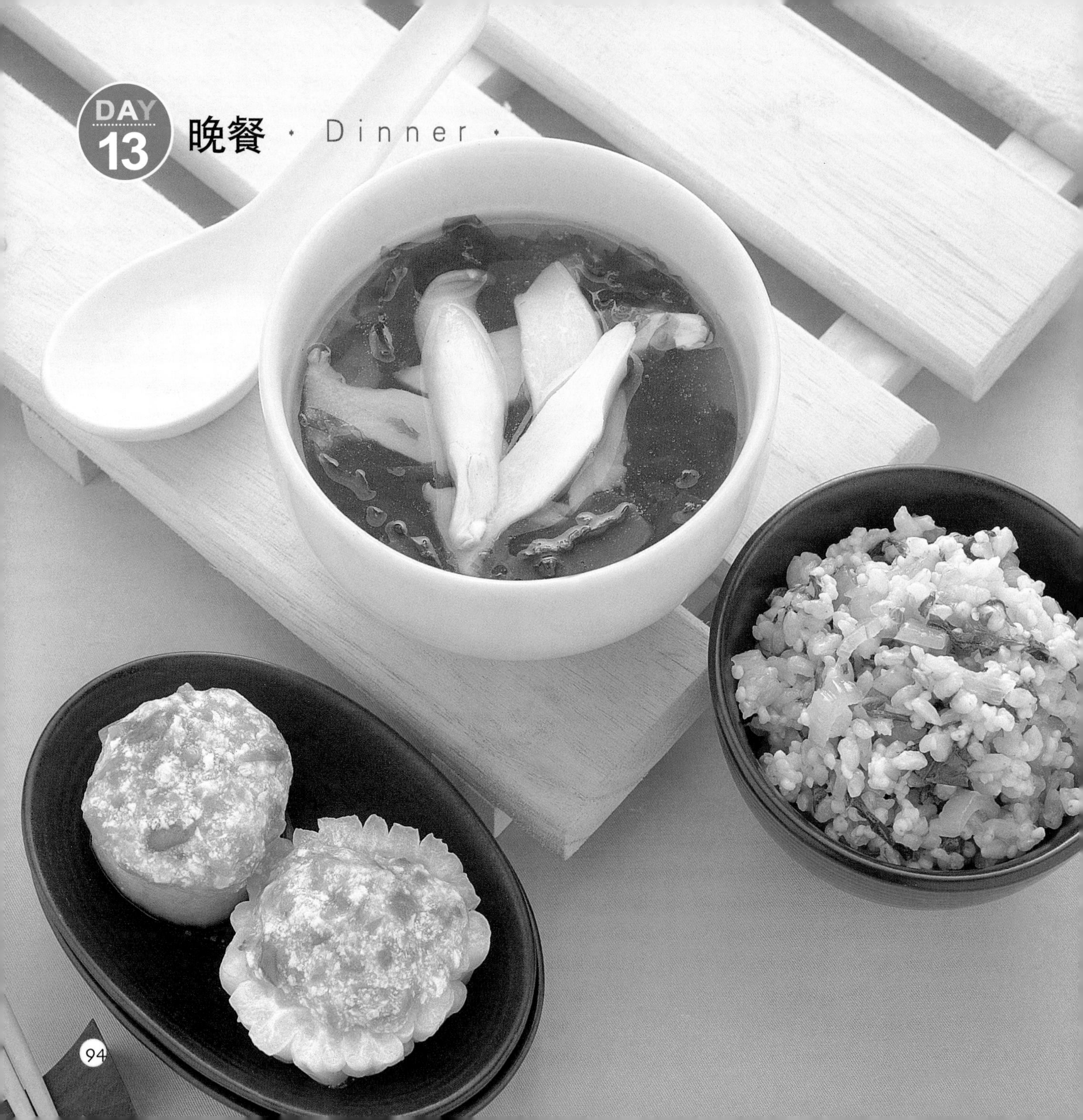

健康菜饭

⊙ **材料**　油麦菜 ⋯⋯⋯ 80克　小米 ⋯⋯⋯⋯⋯ 1杯
　　　　　葱 ⋯⋯⋯⋯⋯ 1根　健康防癌高汤 ⋯ 3杯
　　　　　糙米 ⋯⋯⋯⋯ 1杯

⊙ **做法**　①将葱、油麦菜切碎段，备用。
　　　　　②平底锅以小火热锅，放入葱、油麦菜
　　　　　　略拌炒，盛起。
　　　　　③糙米、小米泡水半小时后，将水滤
　　　　　　掉，加入高汤、葱、油麦菜拌匀。
　　　　　④放入电锅中，外锅加1杯水煮至开关
　　　　　　跳起即可。

双瓜镶豆腐

⊙ **材料**　大黄瓜 ⋯⋯⋯⋯⋯⋯⋯⋯ 30克
　　　　　苦瓜 ⋯⋯⋯⋯⋯⋯⋯⋯⋯ 30克
　　　　　青豆 ⋯⋯⋯⋯⋯⋯⋯⋯ 1大匙
　　　　　豆腐 ⋯⋯⋯⋯⋯⋯⋯⋯⋯ 1块
　　　　　胡萝卜 ⋯⋯⋯⋯⋯⋯⋯⋯ 30克
　　　　　地瓜粉 ⋯⋯⋯⋯⋯⋯⋯⋯ 1匙
　　　　　胡椒粉 ⋯⋯⋯⋯⋯⋯⋯⋯ 少许
　　　　　竹盐 ⋯⋯⋯⋯⋯⋯⋯⋯⋯ 少许

⊙ **做法**　①将胡萝卜切成小丁。
　　　　　②豆腐放入大碗中捣烂，放入青豆、
　　　　　　胡萝卜、地瓜粉、胡椒粉、竹盐，
　　　　　　拌匀成馅料。
　　　　　③大黄瓜、苦瓜各切下约2公分长块，
　　　　　　将中心挖空，填入馅料至稍微鼓起，
　　　　　　摆放盘中。
　　　　　④将盘子移至电锅中，蒸熟即可。

美味紫菜汤

⊙ **材料**　杏鲍菇 ⋯⋯⋯⋯⋯⋯⋯⋯ 50克
　　　　　紫菜 ⋯⋯⋯⋯⋯⋯⋯⋯⋯ 20克
　　　　　健康防癌高汤或好水 ⋯ 350毫升
　　　　　味噌 ⋯⋯⋯⋯⋯⋯⋯⋯ 1小匙

⊙ **做法**　①将杏鲍菇纵切成薄片。
　　　　　②取一锅子将高汤煮沸，放入杏鲍菇、
　　　　　　紫菜、味噌，待再次煮沸即可熄火。

蔬果多C沙拉

◎ **材料**　木瓜—————250克
青椒—————30克
白萝卜—————30克
百香果汁—————1大匙

◎ **做法**　①青椒横切成圈圈，去籽洗净后，沥干装于盘中。
②木瓜去籽去皮，切成块状装盘。
③最后将白萝卜切成细丝，放于盘中，淋上百香果汁即可。

◎ **附注**　若将以上食材打成果汁，可加入适当柠檬、蜂蜜、黑白芝麻、酵母B群、卵磷脂、松子（或腰果），以及植物综合酵素、全然谷粉、钙源或植物种子纤维等，效果更佳。

翠绿蜂蜜糕

◎ **材料**　明日叶—————200克
蜂蜜—————2大匙
地瓜粉—————50克

◎ **做法**　①将明日叶与1杯好水一同放入果汁机中，搅拌均匀。
②把明日叶汁、蜂蜜、地瓜粉于大碗中拌匀，并以擀面棍压制成厚片。
③厚片置于盘中，放进蒸锅中以大火蒸约20分钟。
④待稍凉，即可取出切片。

地瓜糙米粥

◎ **材料**　地瓜—————60克
糙米—————2杯
好水—————1500毫升

◎ **做法**　①将地瓜切细丝，备用。
②糙米与好水装于锅中，以小火炖煮30分钟，再加入地瓜续煮20分钟即可。

五谷杂粮的养生之道

依照传统养生学的观点，五谷能养五脏之真气，在中医的经典中更强调，"天生万物，独厚五谷"，都意味着五谷杂粮最养脾，脾好则胃好身体好。

这是因为未经加工的五谷杂粮类食物除了提供淀粉外，还含有丰富的矿物质、维生素，也是人体重要的食物纤维来源。这些膳食纤维可以吸收毒素、胆酸等致癌物后增快排出，大大降低得到大肠癌的机率，也能吸收油脂、胆固醇，增进健康。

而五谷杂粮中的淀粉是一种广泛存在于碳水化合物中的"抗性淀粉"，这不同于一般淀粉会导致肥胖的结果，相反地这种淀粉因为在小肠中不易被分解消化，能让饱腹感持久，刺激有益菌生长，维持肠道的酸性，又可促进毒素的分解排出，而达到控制体重的作用。

腰果胚芽饼

- **材料** 马铃薯——1颗　腰果——50克　粗胚芽粉——250克
- **做法** ①马铃薯入滚水煮至熟透，捞起去皮，压制成泥。
  ②与粗胚芽粉混合均匀。
  ③一边搅拌一边慢慢加入水及马铃薯泥，使成面团，并用擀面棍压制成饼皮。
  ④取平底锅以小火热锅，将饼皮放入，煎至两面皆成金黄色为止。

海苔百页卷

- **材料** 海苔——1片　皇宫菜——50克　米醋——2小匙
  百页豆腐——1块　味噌——1小匙　白芝麻——1小匙
- **做法** ①将海苔裁剪成宽3公分长10公分的长条片。
  ②百页豆腐切成约厚1公分宽5公分的薄片。
  ③皇宫菜洗净后过滚水汆烫，切成约7公分的长段。
  ④把海苔平铺在桌上，放上一片百页豆腐，再放上皇宫菜，最后将海苔及百页豆腐卷起。
  ⑤将味噌、米醋、白芝麻调匀成酱料，让百页卷沾取后食用。

高纤沙拉

- **材料** 豆苗——50克　胡萝卜——50克　芝麻——1小匙
  沙拉笋——50克　腰果——10颗　味噌——1大匙
- **做法** ①豆苗洗净后沥干，装于盘中。
  ②将沙拉笋、胡萝卜切成细丝，装盘即可。
  ③把腰果磨碎，与芝麻、味噌调匀成酱料，搭配沙拉食用。
- **附注** 沙拉笋为市售真空包装的熟笋，亦可以用当地当季盛产的各式新鲜笋替代

冬瓜姜丝汤

- **材料** 冬瓜——150克　健康防癌高汤或好水——350毫升
  姜——100克　麻油——少许
- **做法** ①冬瓜切块，姜切细丝，备用。
  ②高汤倒于锅中煮沸，把冬瓜、姜投入，以小火煮约10分钟至冬瓜熟烂即可熄火，起锅前滴麻油。

✽餐间水果－芒果✽

　　味道香浓的芒果，属于热带水果。它有着金黄色的果肉，因此含有丰富的维生素A，除了可以美化肌肤，增加抵抗力，也能改善视力，预防眼睛的疾病。而芒果中的维生素C含量也很高，可以协助人体降低胆固醇，预防动脉硬化、高血压，也含有较高的蛋白质及纤维素、果胶，可以帮助消除疲劳，保持消化系统正常。

高纤健康面

⊘ 材料 高纤健康面 ―――――― 80克
　　　　菠菜 ―――――――― 50克
　　　　玉米笋 ――――――― 6根
　　　　海带结 ――――――― 30克
　　　　甜豆 ―――――――― 30克
　　　　健康防癌高汤或好水――500毫升
　　　　麻油 ―――――――― 少许
　　　　竹盐 ―――――――― 少许

⊘ 做法 ①备一锅滚水，放入面条煮沸腾后，转小火续煮约6分钟，即可
　　　　　捞起面条放至碗中。
　　　　②玉米笋切对半，菠菜切段，备用。
　　　　③另取一干净锅子，将高汤倒于锅中煮沸，放入海带结、玉米笋，
　　　　　待煮沸再放入菠菜、甜豆、竹盐。
　　　　④待再次沸腾即可熄火，将汤料倒于碗中，淋上麻油即可。

绿色奇迹沙拉

⊘ 材料 小黄瓜 ――――――― 100克
　　　　生菜 ―――――――― 50克
　　　　苜宿芽 ――――――― 少许
　　　　西红柿 ――――――― 1颗
　　　　健康美味粉 ―――――― 1大匙

⊘ 材料 ①将小黄瓜切片，西红柿切块后，装于盘中。
　　　　②生菜一片片剥下来洗净，切成小片装盘。
　　　　③最后将苜宿芽置于沙拉上，并撒上健康美味粉即可。

⊘ 附注 叶菜、芽菜类生食适合夏季、体质燥热者和正常完全健康者。

清血降压蔬果汁

- **材料**　芹菜——————60克　　梅汁——————1大匙
　　　　　葡萄柚汁———150克　　好水——————200毫升

- **做法**　①将芹菜洗净后切段，备用。
　　　　　②所有材料放入果汁机中，搅拌均匀即可。

- **附注**　①亦可加入适当柠檬、蜂蜜、黑白芝麻、酵母B群、卵磷脂、松子
　　　　　　（或腰果），以及植物综合酵素、全然谷粉、钙源或植物种子纤
　　　　　　维等，效果更佳。
　　　　　②长期喝蔬果汁感到体力衰退、状况不佳、排便多次松散者，表示
　　　　　　排毒周期已过，应暂停吸收过多纤维质，以榨汁方式来喝并补充
　　　　　　植物性蛋白质与脂肪。

地瓜圆

- **材料**　地瓜——————120克
　　　　　地瓜粉————100克

- **做法**　①将地瓜放入电锅中，蒸至熟透。
　　　　　②把地瓜从电锅中取出，去皮捣成泥，再加入地瓜粉。
　　　　　③搓揉成直径约2公分的条状后，每隔2公分切成小块。
　　　　　④备一锅滚水，将地瓜圆放入锅中，煮至浮起后即可捞起。

小黄瓜拌饭

- **材料**　小黄瓜——————3根
　　　　　糙米——————2杯
　　　　　竹盐——————少许
　　　　　橄榄油————少许

- **做法**　①糙米装于电锅内锅中，冲洗后加入3杯好水。
　　　　　②将内锅放至电锅中，外锅加入1杯水，煮至开关跳起。
　　　　　③把小黄瓜洗净后，切成薄片，与竹盐、橄榄油拌入糙米饭即可。

✻ 光常的叮咛 ✻

认识身体的自然时钟

　　人体有一定运作的时间规律与自然法则，若遵循着这生理时钟的运作法则，会大大有助于身体维持或恢复健康。而这其中又有三个时段要特别注意：

1. 早上5点至7点是大肠经的排泄时间，这是把毒素排出的最好机会。

2. 晚上9至11点是三焦经的免疫恢复时间，是身体开始进入休息状态的时间

3. 晚上11点至隔天凌晨3点是肝经、胆经的修复时间，也是养肝造血的关键时段。必定要进入睡眠。

　　如果是体质差的人或是罹病的患者，一并要把握晚上11点至隔天凌晨3点这6个小时的黄金修复时间，养成9点上床睡觉的习惯，让身体快些复原，尽快恢复健康。

酱汁淋面

🌀 **材料**　高纤健康面──80克　　胡萝卜────────30克
　　　　黑木耳────10克　　健康防癌高汤────1000毫升
　　　　豌豆荚────50克

🌀 **做法**　①备一锅滚水，放入面条煮沸腾后，将火转小，续煮约6分钟。
　　　　②用面勺将面条捞起，再用冷水冲淋冷却，沥干放至碗中。
　　　　③将黑木耳、胡萝卜切丝，备用。
　　　　④另取一干净锅子，将高汤倒于锅中煮沸后放入胡萝卜，待再次沸腾放入黑木耳、豌豆荚，
　　　　　煮1分钟即可熄火。
　　　　⑤将汤料直接倒于面上即可。

沙拉

🌀 **材料**　西洋芹────50克　　红甜椒────50克
　　　　玉米────1根

🌀 **做法**　①将玉米切段，过滚水汆烫，捞起沥干后装盘。
　　　　②把西洋芹斜切成段，红甜椒切块，放入盘中即可。

南瓜浓汤

🌀 **材料**　南瓜────150克　　健康防癌高汤或好水──500毫升
　　　　紫菜────50克　　竹盐────────少许

🌀 **做法**　①将南瓜切块后，与高汤一同放于果汁机中，搅拌均匀。
　　　　②取一锅子，把南瓜汁与剩余高汤倒入，煮至沸腾。
　　　　③把紫菜、竹盐投入锅中，煮至紫菜延展开来即可。

＊餐间水果－柿子＊

　橙红色的柿子对人体最棒的地方，就是富含胡萝卜素，维生素A、C，以及钾、磷、铁等矿物质，尤其维生素C的含量比一般的水果都高，加上与维生素A共同作用，可以确实提高免疫力，预防心血管疾病，远离动脉硬化的困扰。除此之外，新鲜柿子不只含碘量高，对利尿也有相当的作用。

山药碗糕

⊙ **材料**
山药 —————————— 200克
糙米粉 ————————— 200克
在来米粉 ———————— 200克
姜泥 ——————————— 20克
健康防癌高汤或好水 ——1000毫升
竹盐 ——————————— 少许

⊙ **做法**
①将山药切约1公分小丁，备用。
②糙米粉、在来米粉加上高汤混合均
　匀成米浆，倒入锅中以小火煮成黏
　稠状。
③放入山药、姜泥、竹盐，搅拌均匀。
④倒入碗中8分满后，放进电锅蒸约30
　分钟即可。

四神薏仁汤

⊙ **材料**
薏仁 ——————————— 1杯
山药 ——————————— 5钱
莲子 ——————————— 1两
芡实 ——————————— 5钱
茯苓 ——————————— 5钱
好水 ————————— 1500毫升

⊙ **做法**
①所有材料放进锅中，以大火煮至沸腾。
②转小火炖煮约1小时，即可熄火。

烩豆腐

⊙ **材料**
嫩豆腐 ——————————— 1块
四季豆 ——————————— 30克
胡萝卜 ——————————— 30克
干香菇 ——————————— 5朵
健康防癌高汤或好水 ——— 100毫升

⊙ **做法**
①将香菇泡热水至发，切丁备用。
②把嫩豆腐切小块，四季豆、胡萝卜切
　丁备用。
③将平底锅以小火预热，倒入所有材料，
　稍微拌炒后即可起锅。

DAY
16
早餐 · Breakfast ·

蔬果清血沙拉

材料　菠萝 ············ 60克
　　　　四季豆 ·········· 30克
　　　　圣女西红柿 ······ 6颗
　　　　竹盐 ············ 少许

做法　①西红柿洗净后，对切装盘。
　　　　②将菠萝去皮，切小块。
　　　　③取一锅加好水煮沸，倒入少许竹盐，把四季豆放入过滚水汆烫，捞起沥干切段即可。

枸杞地瓜泥

材料　地瓜 ············ 2颗
　　　　枸杞 ············ 2大匙

做法　①地瓜洗净去皮后，与枸杞同置碗中，蒸至熟软。
　　　　②把碗取出，将地瓜搅拌成泥，并与枸杞搅拌均匀。

薏仁糙米饭

材料　糙米 ··················· 2杯
　　　　健康防癌高汤或好水 ······ 4杯

做法　将糙米洗净后，加入高汤，一同蒸约30分钟至熟即可。

＊光常的叮咛＊

想吃肉的困惑

很多人无法一下子除去想吃肉的欲望，那么可以依循一些原则，来慢慢改变摄食的习惯：

1. 一天只在一餐吃肉，而且只能吃一种肉。然后慢慢拉长吃肉的间隔时间。
2. 如果非吃肉不可，请一定记得吃鱼。
3. 即使是吃鱼，一周也只能吃1～2次。
4. 必须在晚上六点以前吃！若超过六点以后吃对身体的负担很重，是很大的伤害。
5. 烹调的方式尽可能是水煮、清蒸。
6. 控制在一餐总饮食的15%以内。
7. 最好是在气温15℃以下才吃，因为太燥对身体不好。
8. 在一餐之中最后才吃肉。

全麦高纤锅贴

🔸 **材料**　干香菇————50克　　松子————20克　　全麦面粉————250克
　　　　　元白菜——1/2颗　　葱————50克　　冷压橄榄油———1小匙
　　　　　枸杞————20克　　嫩姜————30克　　高纤谷粉————50克

🔸 **做法**　①把香菇泡热水至发，切丁备用。
　　　　②将元白菜、葱、姜切碎，以纱布包裹拧干去汁，加入枸杞、松子搅拌均匀成馅料。
　　　　③在面粉中加入高纤谷粉、适量的热开水拌匀，再加入适量的冷开水揉成面团。
　　　　④用保鲜膜把面团包起来，等待约15分钟后，搓成直径约3公分的长条状。
　　　　⑤将长条状的面团每隔约2公分切成数小块，以擀面棍压制成圆薄面皮。
　　　　⑥面皮中间放上一匙馅料，把面皮对合包起。
　　　　⑦在平底锅的锅底涂上一层油，热锅后将锅贴排放在锅底，加5小匙的水后，盖上
　　　　　锅盖以小火煮约10分钟，至锅贴表面呈金黄色即可。

🔸 **附注**　可依材料比例增加，一次作数个锅贴，多制作的生锅贴可以密封放入冰箱冷冻库保
　　　　存，只要在食用前取出，然后下锅煎熟即可

梅酱苦瓜沙拉

🔸 **材料**　苦瓜————50克　　梅子酱————2匙
　　　　　紫元白菜———50克

🔸 **做法**　①把苦瓜、紫元白菜洗净后，切丝装盘。
　　　　②在食用前沾取些梅子酱即可。

🔸 **附注**　若担心苦瓜太苦，只要把苦瓜内膜（白色部分）切除干净，或稍微余烫亦可。　　沾

补气血红莲汤

🔸 **材料**　红枣————50克　　莲子————50克
　　　　　黑木耳——30克　　健康防癌高汤或好水——1500毫升

🔸 **做法**　①将黑木耳切片备用。
　　　　②将高汤倒于锅中煮沸，投入所有材料，待煮沸后以小火炖煮约40分钟。

✷ 餐间水果–哈密瓜 ✷

　　肉质松软多汁的哈密瓜，所含的维生素C是苹果的10倍，且维生素A是苹果的50倍，是养分高、热量低的轻食水果。它亦含有叶黄素与玉米黄素，可以帮助人体降血脂、提高新陈代谢，更具有抗发炎、抗癌细胞的功用。在传统中医中亦有记载，"暑日食之，永不中暑"，即在溽热的夏日摄取后，可以达到消暑、利尿的效果。

萝卜糕

🌀 **材料**　白萝卜 ————————— 300克
　　　　　糙米粉 ————————— 300克
　　　　　在来米粉 ——————— 300克
　　　　　香椿 ————————— 20克
　　　　　健康防癌高汤或好水 — 300毫升

🌀 **做法**　①将萝卜刨丝，香椿切细碎，备用。
　　　　　②把平底锅先热锅，放入萝卜丝翻炒
　　　　　　后，盖上锅盖焖煮至熟软。
　　　　　③糙米粉、在来米粉与高汤拌匀，倒
　　　　　　进锅中，再加入香椿，搅拌至浓稠
　　　　　　糊状。
　　　　　④准备一大碗，将米糊倒入，移至蒸
　　　　　　锅中以大火蒸约40分钟。
　　　　　⑤把蒸好的萝卜糕倒扣于盘中放凉，
　　　　　　切片即可。

海带胡瓜汤

🌀 **材料**　海带丝 ————————— 30克
　　　　　胡瓜 ————————— 50克
　　　　　香菜 ————————— 20克
　　　　　健康防癌高汤或好水 — 100毫升
　　　　　味噌 ————————— 1小匙

🌀 **做法**　①胡瓜洗净后，切薄片备用。
　　　　　②取一锅子将高汤煮沸，放入海带
　　　　　　丝、胡瓜、味噌，待再次煮沸即
　　　　　　可熄火。
　　　　　③把香菜洗净后，切碎撒于汤面即
　　　　　　可。

健美沙拉

🌀 **材料**　毛豆 ————————— 30克
　　　　　黄甜椒 ————————— 50克
　　　　　芦笋 ————————— 30克
　　　　　柳橙 ————————— 1颗
　　　　　竹盐 ————————— 少许

🌀 **做法**　①将芦笋切段，与毛豆一同过加竹盐的
　　　　　　滚水汆烫至熟，捞起沥干后摆放盘中。
　　　　　②黄甜椒洗净后，切块装盘。
　　　　　③柳橙切对半,榨汁后淋在色拉上即可。

好气色蔬果汁

○ **材料** 西红柿 —————— 100克   好水 —————— 250毫升
　　　　　 山药 ——————— 30克   梅汁 —————— 1小匙
　　　　　 胡萝卜 —————— 30克

○ **做法** ①把西红柿、山药、胡萝卜切块，备用。
　　　　　 ②将所有材料放入果汁机中，搅拌均匀即可。

○ **附注** ①亦可加入适当柠檬、蜂蜜、黑白芝麻、酵母B群、卵磷脂、松子
　　　　　　（或腰果），以及植物综合酵素、全然谷粉、钙源或植物种子纤维
　　　　　　等，效果更佳。
　　　　　 ②若会胀气者，可将水果与菜汁分开20分钟打汁食用。但菠萝可以
　　　　　　直接和蔬菜一起打，可消胀气助排便。或在蔬果汁中加竹盐少许。

地瓜卷

○ **材料** 全麦春卷皮 ——————— 1张
　　　　　 地瓜 ————————— 100克
　　　　　 芝麻酱 ————————— 适量

○ **做法** ①把地瓜洗净，蒸至熟透后压制成地瓜泥。
　　　　　 ②将春卷皮平铺在桌上，涂抹上芝麻酱，把地瓜泥摆在靠近身体端。
　　　　　 ③把春卷皮卷起来即可。

薏仁糙米球

○ **材料** 糙米 —————— 1杯
　　　　　 薏仁 —————— 1杯
　　　　　 健康美味粉 —— 2大匙

○ **做法** ①事先将糙米泡好水4小时、薏仁泡好水2小时后，装进电锅内锅
　　　　　　中，加入3杯好水。
　　　　　 ②把内锅装至电锅中，在外锅倒入1杯好水，蒸煮至熟。
　　　　　 ③待饭稍凉，倒入健康美味粉搅拌均匀。
　　　　　 ④以汤匙挖取适量置于手掌中，搓揉成丸状即可。
　　　　　 ⑤重复步骤4，依个人所需制作数量。

❋ 光常的叮咛 ❋

来自大海的力量－昆布

　　昆布是营养丰富的海中植物，也是东方人长寿的秘诀之一。它的成分包括了许多对身体非常重要的矿物质，譬如钙、铁、锰、铜、镁、钾、硅等等，还含有大量的碘、蛋白质、矿物质、维生素A、维生素B、维生素C等成分，都极易被人体吸收。

　　所以多吃昆布，可调节细胞的氧化作用，促进身体的新陈代谢，有效消除身体所受辐射，并可保持血液最佳弱碱性，使酸性体质变成碱性。并且因为昆布含有大量的食物纤维，当食入后会在肠内膨胀，渣滓在大肠内则会被各种有益菌类利用，进而对健康有所贡献。

　　不过现今海洋的污染严重，已经影响海带、昆布的品质，若没有把握食物的安全性，可购买市售的活性昆布粉使用。

健康面疙瘩

材料
大白菜	30克
海带芽	30克
南瓜	30克
金针花	30克
全麦面粉	200克
健康防癌高汤或好水	1000毫升

做法
① 在面粉中加入适量温水，搅拌并搓揉成面团。
② 把大白菜洗净后切丝，南瓜切块，备用。
③ 将高汤倒于锅中，以大火煮沸。
④ 以2指在面团上抓取一块小面团，稍微压扁后投于汤中，重复步骤至面团全部用尽。
⑤ 待汤煮沸后，将大白菜、海带芽、南瓜、金针花投入。
⑥ 当汤再次滚沸，即可熄火。

绝配沙拉

材料
四季豆	50克	味噌	1小匙
胡萝卜	50克	芝麻	1小匙

材料
① 将四季豆切斜段，胡萝卜切小块，以滚水汆烫14分钟，捞起沥干即装于盘中。
② 把味噌、芝麻加好水调成酱料，淋于沙拉上即可。

✳餐间水果－枇杷✳

枇杷含有丰富的胡萝卜素及维生素B群，可以保护视力，滋润肌肤，对于促进胎儿发展也有很重要的作用。并且，枇杷除了是作为止咳化痰的良方外，还含有一种称为苦杏仁的成分，是抗癌的有效物质。枇杷中含有适量的有机酸，能刺激消化腺的分泌，对消化有助益。

莲子红豆饭

◎ **材料**　新鲜莲子 —————— 50克
　　　　　红豆 ——————— 1/2杯
　　　　　糙米 ——————— 2杯

◎ **做法**　①事先将红豆泡好水2小时，糙米泡好
　　　　　　水4小时。
　　　　　②把所有材料装于电锅内锅中，加入4
　　　　　　杯好水，蒸煮至电饭锅开关跳起可。

◎ **附注**　如买到干燥莲子，则须事先泡好水2小
　　　　　时。

美颜沙拉

◎ **材料**　青椒 ——————— 50克
　　　　　黄金西红柿 ————— 50克

◎ **做法**　①将青椒横切，洗净后，再横切成圆圈
　　　　　　状装于盘中。
　　　　　②把黄金西红柿洗净，沥干装盘即可。

红凤菜汤

◎ **材料**　红凤菜 ——————— 50克
　　　　　海带 ———————— 30克
　　　　　蒜头 ———————— 1颗
　　　　　健康防癌高汤或好水 —— 350毫升
　　　　　竹盐 ———————— 少许

◎ **做法**　①将红凤菜洗净，切段备用。
　　　　　②把蒜头去皮，切片备用。
　　　　　③取一锅子，把高汤倒入煮沸后，将
　　　　　　海带先投入。
　　　　　④煮沸后将红凤菜、蒜片、竹盐投入，
　　　　　　待再次煮沸即可熄火。

120

蔬果清心沙拉

🌀 **材料**　梨 ——————— 80克
　　　　　红甜椒 ————— 50克
　　　　　青花菜 ————— 150克

🌀 **做法**　①将梨切片，红甜椒切丝，置于盘中。
　　　　　②青花菜洗净后，切成小块，以滚水汆烫，捞起沥干即可装盘。

🌀 **附注**　若将以上食材打成果汁，可加入适当柠檬、蜂蜜、黑白芝麻、酵母B群、卵磷脂、松子（或腰果），以及植物综合酵素、全然谷粉、钙源或植物种子纤维等，效果更佳。

地瓜姜汤

🌀 **材料**　地瓜 ——————— 100克
　　　　　嫩姜 ——————— 30克
　　　　　好水 ——————— 600毫升

🌀 **做法**　①地瓜切成块状，姜切丝。
　　　　　②好水烧开后放入地瓜及姜丝，以小火炖煮20分钟即可。

高纤窝窝头

🌀 **材料**　玉米粉 ——————— 100克　　白芝麻粉 ——————— 30克
　　　　　糙米粉 ——————— 100克　　核桃 ——————— 50克

🌀 **做法**　①将核桃压成细碎，备用。
　　　　　②把所有材料放于大碗中，加入适量温水（约40℃）揉成面团。
　　　　　③将面团分成约鸡蛋大小的数团，捏成椭圆锥形，放置盘中。
　　　　　④将盘子移至蒸笼中，蒸约30分钟即可。

🌀 **附注**　①可依材料比例增加，一次作数个，未食用完的窝窝头可在放凉后，密封放入冰箱冷冻库保存，只要在食用前取出，再重新蒸热过即可。
　　　　　②若喜欢有些甜味，可于面团中加入适量红糖。

＊ 光常的叮咛 ＊

代谢正常靠酵素

　　身体的正常运作是靠无数的代谢反应维持着，而这些代谢反应靠的却是酵素的参与。因为酵素可以帮助调整体质、促进细胞新陈代谢、修护受损部位、加速体内废物的排除等等。

　　当我们的身体因为年龄增加、紧张、压力、疾病或不当饮食等因素，而使得体内的酵素不足时，会造成体内的新陈代谢无法正常运作，产生容易疲劳、体力不继、消化不良、容易胀气、胃口不佳、内分泌失调、肥胖等等病症。

　　为了让体内的酵素正常，最好多吃生鲜的蔬菜水果，除了可以补充醣类、维生素、矿物质外，当然最重要的就是可以补充酵素，尤其像菠萝、酪梨、香蕉、芒果以及芽菜都含有丰富的酵素。如果从食物摄取的酵素不足，亦可以选用市售的全然植物综合酵素来补充。

山药杂粮饭

◎ 材料　山药————70克
　　　　薏仁————1杯
　　　　糙米————1杯

◎ 做法　①事先把薏仁泡好水2小时，糙米泡好水4小时。
　　　　②将山药切成短条状，备用。
　　　　③把所有材料装于电锅内锅中，加入3杯好水，放入电锅，外锅加1杯好水，煮
　　　　　至开关跳起即可。

苗条沙拉

◎ 材料　豆苗————50克　　柠檬————50克
　　　　玉米粒———30克　　蜂蜜————1大匙
　　　　南瓜子———20克

◎ 做法　①把豆苗洗净沥干，装于盘中。
　　　　②玉米粒以滚水汆烫，捞起沥干放于豆苗上。
　　　　③柠檬榨汁后，与蜂蜜淋沙拉上即可。
　　　　④最后撒上南瓜子即可。

鲜味汤

◎ 材料　海带芽———30克　　灵芝菇————————30克
　　　　豌豆荚———30克　　健康防癌高汤或好水———350毫升

◎ 做法　把高汤倒于锅中煮沸，放入所有材料，待再次煮沸即可熄火。

＊餐间水果—番石榴＊

　口感清脆、略带点甜味的番石榴，含丰富的维生素A、C，尤其富含的维生素C可
以说是水果之冠，并且台湾野生红心土番石榴的含量更高，对感冒、头痛、腹痛等
都有很大的帮助。并因为含有丰富纤维质，不但能增加饱足感，而且热量低，对于
想控制体重的人是很好的选择。

脆芹沙拉

🍂 **材料**　西洋芹 ————————— 50克
　　　　剑笋 ——————————— 50克
　　　　腰果 ——————————— 30克
　　　　米醋 ——————————— 1小匙
　　　　酱油 ——————————— 1小匙
　　　　麻油 ————————— 1/2小匙

🍂 **做法**　①备一锅滚水，将剑笋稍微汆烫过，
　　　　　捞起沥干即可。
　　　　②将西洋芹洗净后，切段装盘。
　　　　③把剑笋、腰果直接放于盘中即可。
　　　　④米醋、酱油、麻油拌匀成酱料，
　　　　　淋于沙拉上。

黄豆饭

🍂 **材料**　黄豆 ——————————— 1/4杯
　　　　糙米 ——————————— 1杯

🍂 **做法**　①黄豆预先泡水4小时。
　　　　②糙米稍洗与黄豆放入电饭锅内锅
　　　　　中，加好水4杯。
　　　　③将内锅放进电锅中，外锅加1杯
　　　　　好水，煮至熟。

西红柿豆腐汤

🍂 **材料**　西红柿 ———————————— 80克
　　　　嫩豆腐 ————————————— 1块
　　　　紫菜 ——————————— 50克
　　　　健康防癌高汤或好水 — 350毫升

🍂 **做法**　①将西红柿、豆腐切块，备用。
　　　　②取一锅子，把高汤倒入煮沸，再
　　　　　放入西红柿、嫩豆腐、紫菜，待
　　　　　再次煮沸，即可熄火。

苹果

🍎 **材料**　苹果 ··········1颗

🍎 **做法**　将苹果洗净后，切块即可。

蒸地瓜

🍎 **材料**　地瓜 ··········120克

🍎 **做法**　将地瓜洗净，放于电锅中蒸至熟软即可。

🍎 **附注**　若喜欢地瓜表面有些咬劲，可以再将地瓜放进烤箱中，以140℃烤5分钟。

糙米手卷

🍎 **材料**　海苔 ···········1片
　　　　　糙米饭 ·········1碗
　　　　　芦笋 ··········50克
　　　　　黄甜椒 ·········30克
　　　　　梅醋 ··········1小匙

🍎 **做法**　①将芦笋切成长约7公分的段，过滚水氽烫1分钟。
　　　　　②黄甜椒切丝，糙米饭拌入梅醋，备用。
　　　　　③把整张正方形的海苔对切成三角形，平铺在桌上，三角尖往前方。
　　　　　④先将适量糙米饭铺在海苔靠身体处，再于饭中央放上芦笋、黄甜椒。
　　　　　⑤最后抓起海苔的左右两角，向中卷成甜筒状即可。

＊光常的叮咛＊

摆脱不适当的体重

　我们都知道当身体重量超过标准后，会有更多的慢性病问题，甚至增加罹患癌率。当然，也许有许多人是一生都在跟节食减重这档事奋斗。

　其实，想要摆脱不适当的体重，首先要做的就是让新陈代谢恢复正常，因为只要代谢一旦正常之后，要胖也不容易。而食用健康排毒餐之后，不但不需要挨饿、节食，还可以借由生食中保留的各式营养素及酵素，重新调整、启发新陈代谢的功能，加强排除废物、毒素的效果，平均每月可以让体重减少3至5公斤。让人在减重的过程中，瘦得美丽又健康。

如意汤面

材料　高纤健康面————80克　健康防癌高汤或好水——800毫升
　　　　冻豆腐—————1块　乌醋————————1小匙
　　　　青蒜—————30克　酱油————————1小匙
　　　　甜豆—————50克　麻油————————少许

做法　①冻豆腐切块，青蒜切斜片，备用。
　　　　②备一锅滚水，将面条均匀投入，以小火煮约6分钟。
　　　　③另取一锅子，将高汤倒入煮沸，投入冻豆腐、甜豆，煮至沸腾。
　　　　④将面条捞出，放于汤中，再放入青蒜、乌醋、酱油、麻油，搅拌均匀，即可熄火起锅。

吉祥沙拉

材料　胡萝卜—————————30克
　　　　小黄瓜————————80克
　　　　海带茸————————20克
　　　　姜丝—————————10克
　　　　麻油————————1/2小匙
　　　　乌醋—————————2小匙
　　　　酱油—————————1小匙
　　　　芝麻—————————1小匙

做法　①将胡萝卜切段，小黄瓜切片，装于盘中。
　　　　②海带茸过水氽烫后沥干，装于盘中。
　　　　③把姜丝、麻油、乌醋、酱油、芝麻拌匀成酱料，淋于沙拉上。

※ 餐间水果-酪梨 ※

吃起来没有甜味的酪梨，脂肪含量却是特别的高，比一般水果多了四倍的热量。不过它这糖份低、高热量的特点，却适合成为糖尿病人的食物。虽然酪梨含有丰富的油脂，却都是不饱和脂肪酸，可以控制血脂肪的含量，防止动脉中的胆固醇堆积，有助于维系脑细胞的结构。

有力沙拉

◎ 材料　珊瑚草 ———————— 20克
　　　　生菜 ————————— 20克
　　　　毛豆 ————————— 30克
　　　　杏仁片 ———————— 10克
　　　　柠檬汁 ——————— 1小匙
　　　　百香果汁 —————— 1小匙

◎ 做法　①将生菜剥下，洗净放于碗中。
　　　　②把珊瑚草泡水至发，捞起渍柠檬
　　　　　汁、百香果汁30分钟后，置于生
　　　　　菜上。
　　　　③毛豆过滚水汆烫后，沥干放于碗
　　　　　中。
　　　　④最后洒上杏仁片即可。

芋头饭

◎ 材料　芋头 ————————— 60克
　　　　糙米 ————————— 2杯

◎ 做法　①将芋头切成小丁，备用。
　　　　②把糙米、芋头一同放于电锅内锅中，
　　　　　加入3杯好水，蒸煮至熟即可。

滋补汤

◎ 材料　胡萝卜 ———————— 30克
　　　　干香菇 ———————— 6朵
　　　　枸杞 ————————— 20克
　　　　人参须 ———————— 20克
　　　　红枣 ————————— 15颗
　　　　健康防癌高汤或好水 —— 2000毫升

◎ 做法　①将胡萝卜切片，香菇泡热水至发，
　　　　　备用。
　　　　②把高汤倒入锅中，投入所有材料，
　　　　　以小火熬煮约60分钟，即可熄火。

早餐　·Breakfast·

补肾黑豆浆

材料　黑豆 ········· 2杯
　　　　好水 ········· 6杯

做法　①将黑豆倒进水中，泡约6小时。
　　　　②把黑豆与水一同倒入果汁机中，搅拌均匀。
　　　　③取一块纱布放在锅上，将果汁机中的黑豆水透过纱布倒在
　　　　　锅中，以滤除豆渣。
　　　　④将锅子移到炉上，以小火沸煮10分钟即可。

清净蔬果色拉

材料　苹果 ········· 60克
　　　　玉米笋 ······· 50克
　　　　柳松菇 ······· 30克
　　　　姜 ··········· 10克

做法　①玉米笋洗净后，过水氽烫1分钟捞起，纵切对半装入盘中。
　　　　②将柳松菇滚水氽烫，捞起沥干后放入盘内。
　　　　③用磨泥器将苹果、姜磨成泥，混匀后即为沾料。

地瓜糙米饭

材料　地瓜 ········· 80克
　　　　糙米 ········· 2杯

做法　①将地瓜切小块，备用。
　　　　②地瓜与糙米一同放于电锅内锅中，加入3杯好水。
　　　　③将内锅放进电锅中，外锅加1杯好水，蒸煮至熟即可。

＊光常的叮咛＊

睡眠充足养健康

　睡眠是养成健康的根本基础，如果睡眠不够，不是靠睡更多能够补回来。而且睡眠不足会严重影响五脏运作及免疫功能，降低学习或工作效率，甚至会造成人格特质的改变。

　想要拥有充足的睡眠，提升睡眠的品质也很重要，有7大要点须注意：

　1. 在固定的时间入眠，最好在晚上11点前上床。

　2. 布置舒适的睡眠环境，调整合适的亮度、室温、湿度，及挑选天然材质的寝具。

　3. 运用腹式呼吸，就是鼻子吸气、嘴巴吐气。

　4. 睡前2个小时之内不饮食。

　5. 保持愉快的心情。

　6. 学习裸睡，因为裸睡可以促进全身肌肉伸展，让血液循环更通畅。

　7. 睡前泡个10至20分钟的热水澡，水中可添加一碗粗盐或备长炭更好。

五色烩饭

材料　糙米饭 ——— 1碗　　洋葱 ——————— 30克　　酱油 ——— 少许
四季豆 ——— 30克　　香菇 ——————— 30克
胡萝卜 ——— 30克　　树薯粉 ——————— 1小匙

做法　①将糙米饭装于碗中，备用。
②把四季豆切段，胡萝卜、洋葱切片，香菇切块。
③平底锅以小火热锅，投入四季豆、胡萝卜、洋葱、香菇，再倒入1/2杯好水，稍微翻炒后盖上锅盖焖煮。
④将树薯粉调水和匀，倒于锅中勾欠，加酱油拌匀后熄火，把烩料淋在饭上即可。

凉拌海带丝

材料　海带丝 ——— 50克
姜 ——— 20克
红辣椒 ——— 10克

做法　①将海带丝稍微汆烫沥干后切段，红辣椒切细丝，放进碗中。
②姜以磨泥器研磨成姜泥，倒入碗内，与海带、红辣椒拌匀即可。

退火菜汤

材料　小白菜 ——— 50克　　竹盐 ——————— 少许
青葱 ——— 20克　　健康防癌高汤或好水 ——— 350毫升
姜丝 ——— 20克

做法　①小白菜、青葱洗净后，分别切段备用。
②把高汤倒于锅中煮沸，投入小白菜、青葱、姜丝、竹盐，待再次煮沸即可熄火。

❋ 餐间水果—李子 ❋

　　李子虽然是属于酸度高的水果，但含有丰富的矿物质，如钾、钙、铁，还有苹果酸、柠檬酸及醣类、葡萄糖等，可以促进消化液的分泌，增加肠胃蠕动，有消除疲劳、预防贫血、增进食欲的作用。而且李子亦有大量的食物纤维，是对付便秘的好帮手。

Quiches, cakes & c

DAY 20 晚餐 · Dinner ·

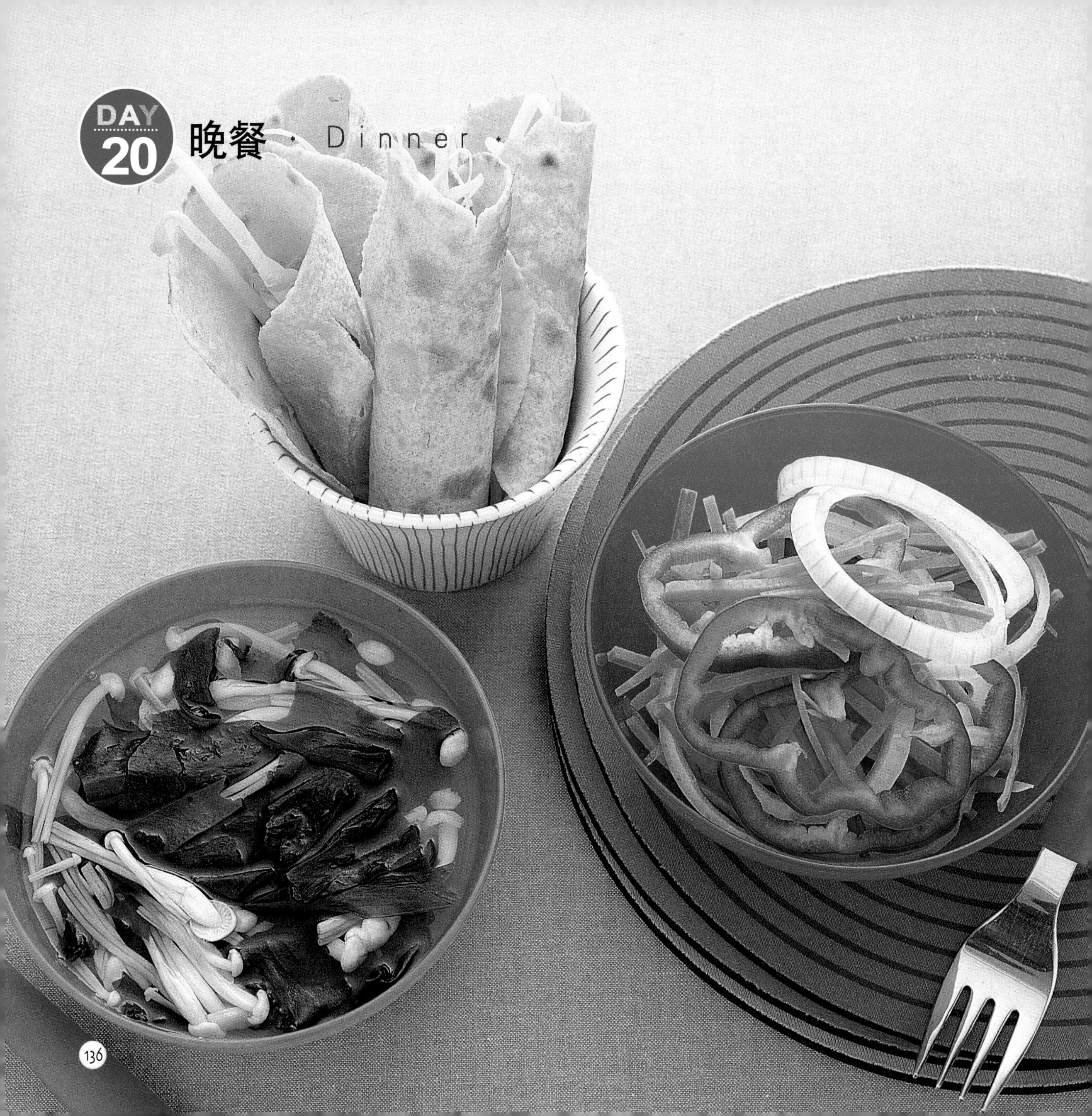

墨西哥卷饼

🌀 **材料**　玉米粉 ⋯⋯⋯⋯⋯ 100克
　　　　中筋面粉 ⋯⋯⋯⋯ 150克
　　　　约60℃温水 ⋯⋯ 125毫升
　　　　豆芽菜 ⋯⋯⋯⋯⋯ 80克
　　　　番茄酱 ⋯⋯⋯⋯⋯ 少许

🌀 **做法**　①将玉米粉和面粉混合，用60℃温水和
　　　　　成面团后，分成每团50克的小块，擀
　　　　　成圆饼状。
　　　　②平底锅先涂少许橄榄油，以小火热锅，
　　　　　放进圆饼煎熟，即成墨西哥玉米饼。
　　　　③将豆芽菜洗净后过滚水汆烫1分钟，
　　　　　捞起沥干。
　　　　④取一片玉米饼平摊在桌上，涂抹上番
　　　　　茄酱后，夹取适量豆芽菜置于饼中央。
　　　　⑤将饼皮左右卷起，把豆芽包裹成卷即
　　　　　可。
　　　　⑥依序完成所有卷饼。

安眠鲜味汤

🌀 **材料**　海带芽 ⋯⋯⋯⋯⋯⋯⋯ 30克
　　　　金针菇 ⋯⋯⋯⋯⋯⋯⋯ 30克
　　　　健康防癌高汤或好水 ⋯ 350毫升
　　　　味噌 ⋯⋯⋯⋯⋯⋯⋯ 少许

🌀 **做法**　高汤倒于锅中煮沸，放入海带芽、金针
　　　　菇、味噌，待再次煮沸即可。

阳光沙拉

🌀 **材料**　胡萝卜 ⋯⋯⋯⋯⋯ 50克
　　　　洋葱 ⋯⋯⋯⋯⋯⋯ 30克
　　　　青椒 ⋯⋯⋯⋯⋯⋯ 50克
　　　　柠檬汁 ⋯⋯⋯⋯⋯ 1/2匙
　　　　蜂蜜 ⋯⋯⋯⋯⋯⋯ 1大匙
　　　　苹果醋 ⋯⋯⋯⋯⋯ 1小匙

🌀 **做法**　①将胡萝卜切丝，洋葱、青椒横切成细
　　　　　圈。
　　　　②把所有材料混合均匀，装于盘中。
　　　　③柠檬汁、蜂蜜、苹果醋拌匀成酱料，
　　　　　淋于沙拉上即可。

早餐 · Breakfast ·

蔬果开胃沙拉

⊙ **材料**　芒果 ———————— 60克
　　　　元白菜 ——————— 50克
　　　　小黄瓜 ——————— 80克
　　　　核桃 ———————— 1大匙

⊙ **做法**　①将元白菜洗净后切丝，铺于盘底。
　　　　②把小黄瓜切片，芒果去皮切块，装于盘中。
　　　　③最后摆上核桃即可。

地瓜芋头泥

⊙ **材料**　地瓜 ———————— 100克
　　　　芋头 ———————— 50克

⊙ **做法**　①将地瓜、芋头放于电锅中，蒸煮至熟烂。
　　　　②把芋头取出，去皮捣成泥后，以汤匙挖取适量至手掌中，
　　　　　搓揉成丸状。
　　　　③依序完成数颗芋头丸。
　　　　④把地瓜取出，去皮捣成泥。
　　　　⑤拿一颗芋头丸，挖取适量地瓜泥包裹在外，再搓揉成圆球。
　　　　⑥陆续将所有芋头丸完全包裹地瓜泥即可。

糙米饭

⊙ **材料**　糙米 ———————— 2杯
　　　　高汤 ———————— 3杯

⊙ **做法**　将糙米、高汤一同放于电锅中，蒸煮至熟即可。

＊光常的叮咛＊

心情不顺畅 身体不健康

情绪对健康的影响很大，而且医学上已经证实，经常开怀大笑有助于免疫力的提升。一个经常批评、责备的人，免疫系统会差，身体自然就不健康。要随时随地让自己的心情顺畅，就要常常做到：喜乐、祷告、谢恩。还有一招"乐乐功"，能让人越笑越快乐，自然保有最自然的健康。

乐乐功三阶级：

1. 心想快乐的事，大笑三声"哈！哈！哈！"。

2. 大笑三声"哈！哈！哈！"，加上两脚一起"咚、咚、咚"踏地三步。

3. "哈！哈！哈！"加上"咚、咚、咚"，再加上两手一起"啪、啪、啪"地拍三次。

全麦蒸糕

○ 材料　枸杞 ——— 60克　　在来米粉 ——————— 300克
　　　　松子 ——— 30克　　全麦面粉 ——————— 300克
　　　　泡打粉 — 15克　　好水 ——————————— 450毫升

○ 做法　① 将在来米粉、全麦面粉倒于大碗中，加入好水，搅拌成面团。
　　　　② 将面团压制成厚圆片，放于盘上。
　　　　③ 将盘子移至电锅中，蒸约5分钟后或待表面稍微变硬，均匀撒上枸杞、松子。
　　　　④ 再盖上锅盖蒸10分钟，取出待凉即可切块食用。

甘味沙拉

○ 材料　大西红柿 ——— 1颗
　　　　青花菜 ——— 60克
　　　　西洋芹 ——— 40克

○ 做法　① 大西红柿切成4片，西洋芹切薄片，备用。
　　　　② 青花菜切小块，过水氽烫1分钟后捞起，沥干备用。
　　　　③ 将所有材料摆放盘中即可。

鲜味汤

○ 材料　皇帝豆 ——— 50克　　健康防癌高汤 ——— 500毫升
　　　　海带结 ——— 30克　　竹盐 ———————— 少许

○ 做法　① 将高汤倒于锅中煮沸后，投入皇帝豆、海带结。
　　　　② 待再次沸腾后转小火，煮约15分钟，至皇帝豆熟软，再加入竹盐调味，即可熄火。

✳ 餐间水果—草莓 ✳

　　含有丰富维生素C的草莓，不但可以增加身体的抵抗力，保护循环系统，而且加上含有鞣花酸、胡萝卜素、花青素等抗氧化物的缘故，可以阻止致癌物的产生，让草莓成为防癌的重要角色。另外，草莓的纤维素含量也相当高，所以对于降低胆固醇、消除便秘、改善高血压都有很好的效果。

DAY 21 晚餐 · Dinner ·

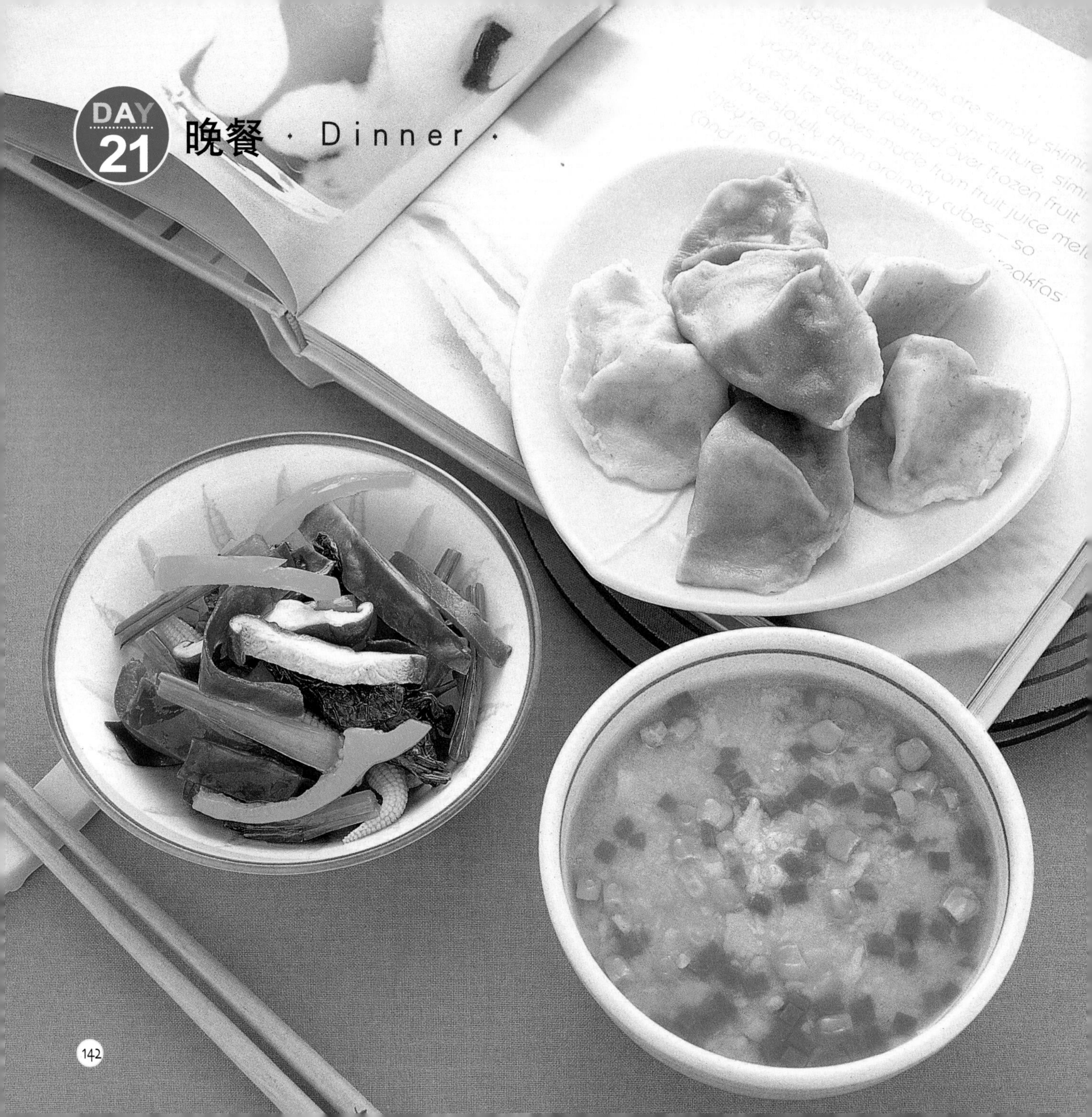

营养水饺

◎ **材料**　低筋面粉 ———— 300克　　菠菜 ———— 100克　　豆干 ———— 50克
　　　　好水 ———— 30克　　胡萝卜 ———— 150克　　姜 ———— 30克

◎ **做法**　①把1/2面粉倒于大碗中，加入适量好水，揉制成面团。
　　　　②菠菜与好水加入果汁机中，搅拌均匀后，以白纱滤除菜渣，成菠菜水。
　　　　③将剩下的面粉拌入菠菜汁，揉成绿色面团。
　　　　④面团搓成长条状，切约2公分小块后，以擀面棍压制成水饺皮。
　　　　⑤将胡萝卜切碎，豆干切小丁，混合均匀成馅料。
　　　　⑥分别把馅料包入水饺皮中，捏制成水饺。
　　　　⑦备一锅滚水，将水饺投入，待再次沸腾后加1杯好水。
　　　　⑧待再次沸腾且水饺浮起，即可，捞起。

◎ **附注**　可依材料比例增加，一次多做数个，未食用的生水饺可密封放入冰箱
　　　　冷冻库保存，只要在食用用前取出，以滚水煮熟即可。

彩色杂烩

◎ **材料**　橄榄菜 ———— 50克
　　　　红甜椒 ———— 30克
　　　　黄甜椒 ———— 30克
　　　　紫元白菜 ———— 30克
　　　　干香菇 ———— 3朵
　　　　橄榄油 ———— 1小匙
　　　　酱油 ———— 1小匙
　　　　米醋 ———— 1小匙

◎ **做法**　①将香菇泡热水至发，切丝备用。
　　　　②把橄榄菜切段，备一锅滚水，一同汆汤橄榄菜、香菇后，捞起沥干装于盘中。
　　　　③红甜椒、黄甜椒、紫元白菜切丝，拌匀后装盘。
　　　　④最后将橄榄油、酱油。米醋拌匀后，淋在盘中即可。

玉米浓汤

◎ **材料**　玉米粒 ———— 30克
　　　　胡萝卜 ———— 30克
　　　　马铃薯 ———— 30克
　　　　健康防癌高汤或好水 ———— 350毫升

◎ **做法**　①将胡萝卜，马铃薯切小丁，备用。
　　　　②取一锅子，将高汤倒入煮沸后，投入玉米粒，胡萝卜，马铃薯，待再次煮沸即可熄火。

01 糖片莲藕

材料：

莲藕	100克
黑芝麻	少许
白芝麻	少许
甘蔗汁	600毫升
米醋	1小匙
好水	200毫升

做法：

1. 把莲藕洗净切薄片，备用。
2. 把甘蔗汁倒进锅中煮沸，放进莲藕片、米醋熬煮。
3. 以小火熬煮约30分钟，至莲藕软熟且汁收干。
4. 起锅装盘后洒上芝麻即可。

02 腐皮西红柿

材料：

豆腐皮	1片
大西红柿	60克
青葱	20克
竹盐	少许
冷压橄榄油	1大匙

做法：

1. 将豆腐皮切约1公分宽条，西红柿切小块，青葱切成葱花。
2. 将平底锅倒入橄榄油后热锅，放入所有材料稍微翻炒后，加入竹盐、1大匙水，盖上锅盖焖煮1分钟。
3. 掀开锅盖，再翻炒均匀即可熄火起锅。

03 豆腐嫩蒸

材料：

嫩豆腐	1盒
青豆仁	10克
香菇	10克
高汤	50毫升

做法：

1. 香菇洗净后切薄片，备用。
2. 将豆腐、高汤放进果汁机中，搅拌均匀。
3. 倒出装于大碗中，铺摆上香菇、青豆仁。
4. 将大碗移至电锅中，蒸约20分钟至全熟即可。

04 爽口拌菜

材料：

黄豆芽	50克
木耳	30克
香菇	30克
米醋	2大匙
辣椒	10克
酱油	少许
麻油	少许

做法：

1. 将木耳切丝，香菇切薄片，辣椒切小段，备用。
2. 备一锅滚水，将黄豆芽、木耳、香菇过水汆烫，捞起沥干。
3. 加入米醋、辣椒、酱油、麻油拌匀，即可装盘。

05 南洋咖哩

材料：

洋葱	50克
马铃薯	60克
胡萝卜	40克
高汤	300毫升
咖哩粉	2大匙
冷压橄榄油	1大匙
酱油	少许

做法：

1. 将洋葱、马铃薯、胡萝卜切块，备用。
2. 取一平底锅倒入橄榄油后热锅，放入洋葱、马铃薯、胡萝卜翻炒至表面略熟。
3. 倒入高汤、咖哩粉、酱油搅拌均匀，转小火沸煮约30分钟即可。

06 金枣萝卜丝

材料：

金枣	3颗
白萝卜	80克
枸杞	1大匙
梅汁	1大匙
香菜	1支

做法：

1. 白萝卜切细丝，香菜切细碎，一同装于碗中。
2. 金枣挤汁后切细丁，与汁一同拌于白萝卜上。
3. 再加入枸杞、梅汁，搅拌均匀后静渍30分钟即可。

07 蔬菜冻

材料：

胡萝卜	30克
青豆仁	30克
山药	50克
蒟蒻粉	50克
健康防癌高汤	100毫升
梅汁	1大匙

做法：

1. 将胡萝卜、山药切小丁。
2. 备一锅滚水，依序将胡萝卜、青豆仁、山药投入汆烫至熟，捞起沥干置于碗中。
3. 把蒟蒻粉倒入碗中，慢慢加入高汤，搅拌均匀至黏稠状。
4. 倒入模型中，放置冰箱冷藏库中静置，食用前取出切块，并淋上梅汁即可。

08 酸甜下饭菜

材料：

西红柿	50克
菠萝	50克
青椒	30克
西红柿汁	1大匙
好水	1大匙

做法：

1. 将西红柿、菠萝、青椒切块备用。
2. 取一平底锅加热，将西红柿、西红柿汁、好水先放入，拌炒均匀，再加入菠萝、青椒翻炒约3分钟即可。

09 简易大阪烧

材料：

面粉	50克
水	50毫升
元白菜丝	100克
海苔粉	1大匙
白芝麻	1大匙
健康美味粉	1大匙
冷压橄榄油	1大匙

做法：

1. 将面粉、水、健康美味粉于碗中拌匀成面糊。
2. 元白菜切细丝后，拌入面糊中。
3. 取一平底锅加热后，倒入橄榄油，并将面糊倒入锅中。
4. 以小火慢煎约5分钟，再翻面煎5分钟。
5. 用竹筷插入中央，取出时若没有面糊沾粘在筷子上，即可熄火起锅。
6. 放入盘中，最后撒上海苔粉、白芝麻即可。

10 综合烩野菇

材料:

香菇	20克
鲍鱼菇	20克
秀珍菇	20克
甜豌豆	30克
姜丝	少许
酱油	1大匙
橄榄油	1大匙

做法:

1. 将香菇、鲍鱼菇、秀珍菇切片,备用。
2. 取一平底锅加热先炒姜丝后,倒入酱油、橄榄油。
3. 投入菇类翻炒,再加入甜豌豆炒1分钟,即可熄火起锅。

11 茄汁马铃薯

材料:

红西红柿	100克
马铃薯	100克
洋葱	30克
大蒜	2颗
高汤	1000毫升

做法:

1. 马铃薯切大块,红西红柿、洋葱、大蒜切小丁,备用。
2. 取一汤锅将所有材料投入,以大火煮至沸腾后转小火,续煮约30分钟即可。

12 炖蔬菜锅

材料:

香菇	3朵
黑木耳	10克
芋头	50克
西红柿	30克
冻豆腐	1块
山东大白菜	100克
高汤	1000毫升
竹盐	少许
乌醋	少许

做法:

1. 白菜切段,黑木耳切丝,芋头、西红柿切块,备用。
2. 将高汤倒入汤锅中加热,以大火煮至沸腾时投入所有材料。
3. 至再次沸腾后转小火,炖煮约30分钟,至所有材料熟烂为止。

13 蔬菜咸派

▼ 材料：

南瓜	200克
苹果	50克
胡萝卜	50克
甜椒	30克
芦笋	30克
松子	1大匙
全麦面粉	200克

▼ 做法：

1. 将面粉慢慢加水，搓揉成均匀面团。
2. 以擀面棍将面团压成面皮，铺于烤盘上。
3. 苹果、胡萝卜、甜椒、芦笋切小块，备用。
4. 把南瓜蒸熟后捣成泥，拌入苹果、胡萝卜、甜椒、芦笋。
5. 混合均匀的南瓜泥倒在面皮上，并用刮刀将表面整平。
6. 烤箱预热180℃，将烤盘放入烤至表面成金黄色即可。

14 味噌萝卜片

▼ 材料：

白萝卜	150克
味噌	2大匙
竹盐	1大匙
米醋	1大匙
红辣椒	1支

▼ 做法：

1. 辣椒切薄片，备用。
2. 将萝卜连皮切薄片后，放至大碗中。
3. 洒上竹盐，静置1天，待萝卜出水。
4. 取出萝卜片后拌上味噌、米醋、红辣椒，再放置一天即可。

15 原味蔬菜串

▼ 材料：

青椒	30克
胡萝卜	50克
马铃薯	50克
菠萝	50克
姜汁	1大匙
酱油	1/2大匙
蜂蜜	1大匙

▼ 做法：

1. 将所有材料切块，装于大碗中搅拌均匀后静置30分钟。
2. 把姜汁、酱油、蜂蜜调匀，即成酱料。
3. 取竹签将材料依序串上。
4. 蔬菜串置于烤盘上，表面刷些许酱料，并不时转面，至表面略呈现烤痕即可。

16 营养珍珠丸

材料:

糯米	50克
紫山药	200克
荸荠	50克

做法:

1. 将糯米事先泡水2小时。
2. 将紫山药放进电锅中蒸至熟透，取出去皮后捣成泥。
3. 荸荠削皮后切成细丁，拌入山药泥中。
4. 把糯米沥干铺于盘中，抓取适量山药泥揉搓成球状，放入盘中滚动，使均匀沾黏上糯米。
5. 把完成的珍珠丸摆放盘中，放入电锅中蒸约半小时即可。

17 脆炒油麦菜

材料:

油麦菜	50克
洋葱	30克
香菇	30克
松子	1大匙
竹盐	少许
橄榄油	少许

做法:

1. 把油麦菜切段，洋葱、香菇切片，备用。
2. 取一平底锅加热，先放入洋葱、香菇，拌炒后再放水、油麦菜、竹盐、橄榄油，翻炒均匀至熟即可。

18 姜汁菠菜

材料:

菠菜	60克
姜	30克
芝麻	1小匙
麻油	1小匙
味噌	少许

做法:

1. 姜磨成泥，与芝麻、麻油、味噌调匀成酱料。
2. 菠菜洗净切段后，入滚水烫熟后沥干，最后淋上酱汁即可。

19 烩白菜

材料:

白菜	100克
腰果	50克
高汤	50克
树薯粉	1小匙
竹盐	少许

做法:

1. 大白菜洗净后，切段备用。
2. 将腰果与高汤一同放入果汁机中，搅拌均匀。
3. 取一平底锅加热，将所有材料放入，煮至白菜熟烂。
4. 起锅前以树薯粉勾芡，放入竹盐拌匀即可。

20 芦笋杂烩

材料:

西洋芹	50克
芦笋	50克
白果	20克
好水	200毫升
酱油	1大匙
橄榄油	1大匙

做法:

1. 西洋芹切斜片，芦笋切段，备用。
2. 取一平底锅，将白果、水一同煮至软，再加入西洋芹、芦笋、酱油、橄榄油，翻炒均匀至熟即可。

21 清蒸茄子

材料:

茄子	100克
蒜头	1颗
味噌	1小匙

做法:

1. 茄子洗净切约5公分长段，排列于盘中。
2. 蒜头去皮研磨成泥，铺在茄子表面。
3. 放上味噌后，将盘子移至电锅中，蒸约20分至茄子熟软即可。

【食物的选择和搭配】

　　短短的九年，健康排毒餐已经风行全球。大部分人吃了都很有效，但也有一些人吃的效果不太明显。为什么？可能是食物的选择与搭配错误。也就是说，有可能食物选错；或食物选对但食物与食物搭配错误；或者搭配正确，但烹饪料理的方式不对，以上三种情形都会影响效果。

圣经上怎么说食物的搭配

　　有一天，我正在为饮食的事情祷告，那一天的灵修，读到的经文就是以西结书第四章九到十六节，谈及食物的选择、配合、以及烹饪料理的方式，通常都在这几节的经文里面。以西结书第四章第九节到第十六节："你要取小麦、大麦、豆子、红豆、小米、粗麦装在一个器皿中，用以为自己做饼，要按你侧卧的三百九十日，吃这饼。"第十节，"你所吃的要按份量吃，每日二十四克拉，按时而吃。"十一节，"你喝水也要按这样子，每日喝一心六分之一，按时而喝。"十二节，"你吃这饼像吃大麦饼一样，要用人粪在众人眼前烧烤。"十三节，"耶和华说："以色列人在我所赶他们到的各国中，也必这样吃不洁净的食物。"十四节，我说："主耶和华啊！我素来未曾被玷污。从幼年到如今，没有吃过致死的，或被野兽撕裂的，那可憎的肉，也未曾入我口。"第十五节，于是他对我说："看啊，我给你牛粪代替人粪，你要将你的饼烤在其上。"十六节，他又对我说："人子啊，我必在耶路撒冷折断他们的帐，就是断绝他们的粮，他们吃饼要按份量吃，忧虑而吃，喝水也要按这样子，惊惶而喝。"十七节，最后一节，"使他们缺粮缺水，彼此惊惶，因自己的罪孽消灭，因自己的罪孽消灭。"

　　了解经文的背景，有助于我们解开上帝话语的奥秘，以西结是一位先知——上帝的发言人，那时以色列国已经被消灭，人民被当时的世界强权巴比伦国掳到了巴比伦去。他们是亡国奴，上帝差派以西结先知，到这些亡国奴当中去，要传达上帝的讯息。在他们亡国之前，耶利米先知就不断的在警告以色人说，若他们再不悔改，再不归向神，就要亡国了。可是，他们顽梗背道，继续任意妄为，耶利米成了一位眼泪的先知。耶利米知知道，他们已经身处危险之中，不断地警告，他们还是不听，然后他亲眼见到他所预言的实现。你看这是多么心痛的事情啊！如果你告诉孩子，开车要慢一点啊，骑车要戴安全帽啊，免得危险。他每次都不听，有一天，他又是骑快车又不戴安全帽，飞出去，就这样子出了意外，最伤痛的就是你，为什么？因为你曾经警告过他，而他不听。一样的情形，上帝差派了以西结去，告诉他们说，你们应当如何行。你看哦，在这几节的经文中，有关食物的选择、搭配以及食物的运用，还有饮食的心情，食物的料理，以及错误饮食的结局，通通都很清楚的指明了。

有一次我在美国的拉斯维加斯有一个特别聚会。我每到一个地方，就会想去找全谷类食物，映入我眼前的食物，让我吓了一跳，过去没有看过一个全谷类的食物做得这么好的，能量这么高，营养这么丰富，还有最主要的，营养这么完整。正在察看是哪一家公司生产制造的，希望为它义务推广。我有这个个性，有好东西我就想要昭告天下，告诉全世界。在它包装袋上印着一节经文，就是以西结书四章九节。他说：你要取小麦、大麦、豆子、红豆、小米、粗麦在一个器皿中，用以为自己做饼。"粗麦"是小麦的一种，因为一般小麦是细麦，这个是另外一种小麦，是比较粗的一种小麦。"红豆"也可以翻成豌豆或扁豆。各位你有没有发现，它有一个特色，它全部是清一色的五谷杂粮，对不对？它清一色的就是五谷杂粮。

五谷杂粮为主食

整个健康排毒餐有一个核心，这个核心就是创世记第一章二十九节，上帝所赐给人，在伊甸园赐给人的食物，就是要以五谷杂粮为主食。现代人多数疾病的根源，都来自于不以五谷杂粮为主食，相反地，却以汉堡、炸鸡、薯条、牛排，这些精致加工的食物，甚至以白米、白面、白面包，这些精致加工过的食物做主食，身体当然要出大问题。所以第一你要选择没有加工的，是全谷类的，为你日用饮食的主食。在一餐中，至少它要占百分之五十，不可以低过百分之五十，多到六十、七十都可以。我们到农村，或是很穷的乡下去看，很奇怪，那个地方的人，一年到头没有几次肉可以吃，只有一些简单的蔬菜，而产量最大的就是五谷杂粮，他每天就是吃这一些东西，而他们身体机能却非常的好。而且你吃粗粮、杂粮，你一定要咀嚼，吃糙米，你非咬不可！而且，越咬越聪明，越咬越健康，咬一咬，说不定皱纹会减少，还有美容作用。咬的时候大量唾液产生，唾液会把食物中的致癌物质直接分解掉。你看唾液好不好？很好哇，对不对？所以，吐人家口水是最笨的。所以大卫很聪明，人家吐口水骂他，他无所谓啦！

要吃当季当地的食物

　　你看小麦、大麦、豆子、红豆、小米、粗麦，这几样食物全部都是以色列当地，而且是当季的农产物。中医认为人生病有三个主要的原因：一个叫内因，一个外因，一个叫做不内外因。什么叫做内因呢？就是说因为情绪（忧、思、悲、恐、惊）所产生的疾病。两千年前中医就讲到这个观念很了不起，圣经则在三千五百年前就讲到这个观念。情绪会影响整个人的健康状态。生病第二因就是所谓外因。外因是什么？外面气候的变化，风、暑、湿、燥、寒、火，人若不能适应这个气候的变化，就会生病。各位有没有发现，有些人遇到季节一变，就跟著生病。为什么季节一变就生病了？他的体质没有办法适应大地气候的变化。第三个不内外因，譬如说，外伤啦，意外啦，还有饮食啦，这些都算是。

　　我们现代人，为什么大部分的人（尤其是小孩子）对于季节的变化很没有适应力，季节一变化就生病。其中有一个很重要的原因，就是我们不吃当地、当季的食物。

　　我们发现上帝真的是非常慈爱，因为所有在当地所生产的食物，刚好是解决当地所特有疾病最好的药物，太了不起了。而且当季节所生产的食物，刚好就是解决在这个季节最容易发病疾病的最好药物。因为植物会纪录种植地大环境的气候、温度、湿度、太阳的照度等等。这一些讯息被这个植物纪录之后，人吃了这一些食物，自然就帮助人去适应这个季节气候的变化。因此，嗜吃进口食物的人身体一定不好，吃过季的或是提早熟的身体也不好。你问说："我怎么知道什么是当季的？"你到菜市场去看，最多摊位在卖，卖得最便宜的就对了。吃健康排毒餐有个立即的好处，就是很省钱，因为当地当季的食物，多数是最廉价的。

地瓜——适合全球人吃的的食物

　　以地居亚热带和热带气候的台湾来讲，我们应吃什么呢？糙米。一定要吃糙米，糙米是一流的米。如果住在北方、温带或寒带，吃什么？大麦、小麦、燕麦、荞麦、高粱。不管是住在南方、北方，寒带或热带，任何地方，都可以吃的一样东西，全世界都可以种的，就是地瓜（蕃薯）。地瓜（蕃薯）或叫甘薯、红薯。日本国家癌症研究中心研究，所有食物之中防癌效果最好的找出前二十名。我们最常吃的绿色花椰菜排第四名，芹菜排第七名，番茄也是前二十名，《无毒一身轻》书中所列根茎花果类多数都在前二十名。第一名是谁呢？地瓜。第二名呢？也是地瓜。

第一名是熟地瓜，第二名是生地瓜。所以你常吃地瓜一定顶呱呱，不吃地瓜慢慢就变傻瓜。这个地瓜真是好，太好太好，但你不要一个人吃，因为地瓜吃了会排气，所以你一个人吃，一排气大家都知道是你排的，所以你要怂恿大家一起吃，要放屁，大家一起放。

除了食材选择要符合当地当季盛产原则之外，食材与食材之间的搭配，更是重要。

我们再来看一下第四章第九节："你要取小麦、大麦、豆子、红豆、小米、粗麦，装在一个器皿中，用以为自己做饼……。"看这当中主食的组成，小麦、大麦、小米、粗麦属五谷类，豆子、红豆则为杂粮类。五谷类本身所含有的蛋白质，分别从百分之八到百分之十六都有，平均约百分之十。也就是说，它本身有一些蛋白质，但是不足，可用豆类来配合，因为豆类是蛋白质之王，如黄豆、黑豆和红豆的蛋白质都十分丰富。

但是，一定要记得，小麦、大麦、小米、粗麦，这四样是五谷类，豆子、红豆是杂粮则有两样。亦即，五谷与杂粮的比例，五谷类占三分之二，杂粮类占三分之一，较为理想。请大家千万记住，千万不可以等量搭配，蛋白质和淀粉**绝对绝对绝对**不可以等量搭配。这个是非常重要的关键点，一定要记住。因为蛋白质需要的是酸性的消化液，而淀粉需要的是碱性的消化液，如果你等量一起吃，消化系统容易出问题。而且务必要信守每口食物（尤其是五谷杂粮）咀嚼三十次以上的原则。因为唾液中的酵素有助于淀粉类食物的分解。

第一个原则：蛋白质跟淀粉不可以等量搭配

可是很不幸的，多数人的消化系统都不好，其中有一个很重要的原因，就是把淀粉跟蛋白质等量搭配，又不细嚼慢咽就囫囵吞下。举例：豆浆配油条。油条是淀粉，经油炸变高脂肪。然后呢，豆浆是豆类，豆类是蛋白质。还有呢，吃饭的时候配肉，饭是淀粉，肉是高蛋白质，难怪消化不良嘛！

第二个原则：蛋白质跟脂肪也不可以放在一起吃

那么第二个呢，就是蛋白质跟脂肪也不可以放在一起，要分开来，因为脂肪会延迟胃液的分泌，脂肪会减少胃液的分泌。哇，这个问题就很严重了！因为你一旦减少胃液分泌以后，蛋白质就不容易被消化，对不对？不容易被消化，那么在我们的胃里面，过了几个钟头以后，还消化不了，它可能就腐化掉、臭掉、酸掉，成为一大堆的毒素。可是现在到处都是脂肪跟蛋白质搭配的食物。例如，肉用油炒、油煎、甚至油炸。而肉是高蛋白，再加高脂肪的油，形成肠胃沉重的负担。

第三个原则：蛋白质跟糖不可以放在一起吃

第三个呢，严重的错误是什么？就是蛋白质跟糖一起料理。糖本身会在小肠里面消化吸收，而蛋白质却在胃里面消化，所以两个混在一起吃，糖就容易发酸发臭了。像我们常吃的糖醋鱼。还有呢，豆沙包，都是非常典型的高蛋白加糖的料理。尤其糟糕的是，吃炸鸡、炒排骨、牛排配可乐，身体的负担就更重了。

第四个原则：蛋白质跟蛋白质不可以放在一起吃

第四个，蛋白质跟蛋白质也不可以混在一起，尤其是动物蛋白，两种一起吃，会加重胃的负担。因为每一种蛋白质，胃都要用不同的消化液来处理，因此，一餐只吃一种动物蛋白质。目前多数人在一餐中不但吃鱼，吃鸡，吃牛，吃猪，甚至还吃兔、吃鸭、吃鹅……，你叫你的胃如何是好？

第五个原则：蛋白质跟酸性的物质不可以放在一起吃

第五个原则，第五个原则就是蛋白质跟酸性的物质不可以放在一起。因为酸性的物质会减少胃液分泌，胃液的分泌一减少，胃蛋白酶就没有办法作用。所以你吃蛋白质的时候，不可以吃酸的东西。举例：酸菜、泡菜、醋，还有酸的水果也不适合跟蛋白质配。

第六个原则：淀粉跟糖不可以放在一起吃

为什么？一如前所述，蛋白质与糖一般，淀粉和糖放在一起，糖就很容易腐化掉、坏掉、酸掉。看看我们最常吃的是什么？像面包涂甜果酱，这个甜果酱容易在你的肚子里面发酸发臭，坏掉腐败，然后就变成身体的毒素。

第七个原则：淀粉跟酸性物质不可以放在一起吃

酸性物质跟蛋白质不适合一起料理，如前述，酸性物质跟淀粉不适合相配一般，原因是一样的。因为酸性物质本身会减少胃液分泌，食物就会在整个消化的过程里面，变得很不顺畅。

第八个原则：水果要空腹吃

最后一个，切记！切记！切记！水果一定要空腹吃，水果没有空腹吃，可说是所有食物搭配中最严重的失误。水果要在饭前三十分钟以上吃，"饭后吃水果帮助消化"，这个观念需要修正了。因为水果是在小肠里面消化吸收，倘若你吃完饭菜肉后，胃已经塞满东西了，此时才吃水果，它下不去，就导致消化的问题。所以"饭后吃水果帮助消化"，这一句话加两个字就对了——"不良"。水果要单独吃，空腹吃最好。依照健康排毒餐原则吃，由于食物非常容易消化，故三个小时左右就饿了，这个时候到下一餐的时间还没到，吃水果最好。犹记在世界知名的巴马长寿村拜访时，谈及耳聪目明的百岁老人，是否也吃零食，其子孙表示，"吃水果"是他们最主要的零食。

找寻体毒大根源

形成身体里面最大毒素的根源是什么？就是高蛋白质加上高淀粉，再加高脂肪，在一餐中同时吃下这三高，如果再加上高糖份就更惨了。那你说，你讲了这么多原则，我只听懂一个"水果要单独吃"，什么蛋白质跟淀粉，什么蛋白质跟脂肪，蛋白质跟酸，蛋白质跟糖，全部都弄乱了。现在我们将它简化成三个原则。

食物要怎么搭配呢？第一，跟上帝原始的创造来学习。在上帝原始的创造里面，告诉我们一件非常重要的事情：自然界所有的植物，凡是高蛋白的一定低淀粉，凡是高淀粉的一定低蛋白、低脂肪，没有例外。你看，母奶里面的蛋白质、脂肪都低于百分之五，非常低的，而它的碳水化合物含量就非常的高。再如五谷杂粮中淀粉含量非常的高，蛋白质与脂肪就低。还有，肉类蛋白高，淀粉却低。所以要记得，淀粉、蛋白质与脂肪，其中一个高另二个就是低。

健康排毒餐的搭配，你看，脂肪建议摄取不要超过百分之二十；蛋白质宜占百分之十至十五之间；淀粉则不少于百分之五十，甚至高到百分之六十至七十都可以。然后剩下的一些就是纤维素、维生素和矿物质，这是第一个原则。可是现在最糟糕的是什么？吃饭配一大堆的肉，或是不吃饭，只吃汉堡、炸鸡、薯条、牛排，这个是很不好的。

第二个原则，就是蔬菜可以搭配所有的食物。蔬菜可以搭配蛋白质，蔬菜可以配淀粉，蔬菜可以配脂肪，蔬菜可以配所有的东西。我们已经谈过水果宜在饭前半小时以上吃，然后吃一盘生菜沙拉，我讲的沙拉，不是那个酱，那个酱很多都不健康。吃一些生菜，可以帮助我们口腔产生碱性物质，利用这个碱性的环境来消化淀粉类食物，再加上咀嚼三十下，则大功告成矣。

第三个原则，就是有什么吃什么。这是耶稣差派他七十二个门徒出去传福音的时候所交待的事项。他说："你们无论进入那一个城市，若有人摆上什么，你们就吃什么"。这就是"有什么吃什么"。当地产什么，你就吃什么。吃当地当季盛产的食物。

食物要按份量吃

我们现在再来看看，食物当怎么样吃呢？要记得，第十节到第十一节，圣经上告诉我们，"要按份量吃"。然后喝水要按这样子，这样子也是"份量"的意思。食物饮用的原则是什么？就是要按份量吃，按时而吃、按时而喝。

份量是一个比例的问题，有些人喜欢吃很多很多的蔬菜水果，但是不吃五谷杂粮，这个也是不恰当的，你吃的份量要对，然后呢？按时而吃，什么时候吃？早餐最好是六点半到七点半吃。有人说，那么早吃，吃完后，我们可不可以再回去睡；当然可以，只是你吃完不会回去睡，你吃完很可能跑厕所。

怎么喝水？什么时候喝？

"按时而喝"，什么时候喝水？最重要的三个喝水的时段：①起床后刷牙前，②下午三点，③睡前。在这三个时段中，最重要的是早上。以前我都建议大家早上喝五百毫升，后来试了一个方法，是一个日本老医师传述的。我发现非常的有效，提供给各位做参考。我将他的做法总结成两句话十二个字——**"起床后刷牙前，生饮七合好水。"**一合是一百八十毫升，七合水等于一千二百六十毫升。当然，喝不到一千二百六十毫升，喝四百毫升也可以。最重要的是①要刷牙前喝水，所以请各位晚上睡觉前刷牙，免得一早喝水时，满嘴菜渣。②要符合国家生饮标准的水，能生饮的水。③要喝好水，不好的水，愈喝问题愈多。当然，**有肾脏病、心脏病，还有肝硬化的人，请遵照医师指示来喝。**

睡觉以前喝个二百毫升水。为什么？因为睡觉的时候，随着身体自然代谢，水分蒸发，到了凌晨四点钟，为什么凌晨是危险四点钟，医学上讲的危险四点钟，心脑血管爆发最多就是在四点，为什么？因为血浓度是最高的时候，黏稠度最高的时候。你在睡觉前喝一杯水，可以帮助你血液浓度降低，血的浓度降低，这个是很好的一件事情。

怎么烹调才正确

接下来，我们再谈谈食物的料理。如果你食物选对了，搭配也对了，但烹饪的方法错了，这个食物的益处还是无法发挥。你看，大麦、小麦、小米、红豆、豆子、粗麦，好不好？好，但是如果用人的粪便去煮它，好不好？

最近刚刚有一篇报告出来，微波炉，这个是今年，就是两个月前，十月二十四号，各大报都有刊登，西班牙国家科学委员会，他们研究发现，用蒸的料理是把所有的食物保存最完整的方式，他们用了一种非常重要的抗癌的食物，绿色的花椰菜作实验，绿色的花椰菜非常好，而且它的抗氧化剂是非常高的，可是很不幸的，实验结果显示，当你用微波炉的时候，几乎都有的营养全部被破坏掉，97%的抗氧化剂，微波炉一微波都坏光了。所以，微波炉微波过的食物，这个我很早就讲过，微波炉微波过的食物里面，只剩下热量，所有的营养、能量，尤其是活性的维他命，通常都不见了！所以，你今天回家以后就把微波炉当成一个箱子来看待就可以了，不要再用它了。最好的料理方式，当推蒸、煮、烫、炖、烘，以及生食等……。

饮食的心情

各位有没有发现，现在的年轻人脾气似乎越来越暴躁？一个可能的原因是，当所吃的食物是用大火油炒的时候，人的个性很容易变得急躁。然而，现在年轻人外食的机会非常多，师傅做菜的时候，不只是锅子下面有火在烧，锅子上面也在烧。当然，人吃完东西后，里面也在烧。所以，应尽可能在家吃，在家里煮，减少在外头吃，自己煮，用炖的，用蒸的，而且一边煮一边祝福。您将拥有充满爱心的一餐！每当我在电视台或讲演会上示范健康排毒餐时，许多人都会问，为什么你做的都特别好吃？我说，因为我一边做一边祝福祷告啊！食物经过祝福祷告，真的完全不一样！完全不一样！

第十六节讲到饮食的心情，圣经说："人子啊，我必在耶路撒冷折断他们的杖，就是断绝他们的粮。他们吃饼，要按份量，忧虑而吃；喝水，也要按制子，惊惶而喝。"好可怜呢，吃东西，忧虑而吃，喝水惊惶而喝。圣经真的是太伟大了。为什么，忧虑而吃的时候，伤脾胃；惊惶而喝的时候，伤肾。你看，现代人是不是这样子，我们吃东西的时候，忧虑什么？农药、化肥、抗生素……。喝水的时候，担心水源不洁，水源被污染。现代人真的是可怜！可怜！这都是因为人离开了神。商人心中无神，就只考虑到个人利益，而不考虑到人民的健康。都知道糙米比白米健康，为什么商人要做白米？白米储存的久啊！糙米几个礼拜、几个月就长虫了。

白米只要保持干燥，两三年都不会坏掉，不会损失啊。卖不出去，可以放着慢慢卖啊。你看，白米是连虫都不吃，你还吃，真奇怪！人犯罪以后就很怪，想法逻辑都乱掉了，整个乱掉了。因为除非人回归到神的面前，否则人生价值观没有办法重建，人的生命会一团乱。再如，明明苹果皮是整个苹果最营养的部分，可是我们偏偏不吃皮。为什么不吃皮？因为有农药，因为有打蜡。不对！应该是我要吃皮，请不要打蜡！这样才对。你看，人离了神以后，逻辑整个乱掉了。可怜啊！真的可怜！吃东西忧虑，喝水惊惶，你说怎么办？

饮食错误的结局

再来，圣经第十七节告诉我们，错误的饮食所导致的后果。"使他们缺粮缺水，彼此惊惶，因自己的罪孽消灭。"那么在现代中文译本里面，把"惊惶"翻成"绝望"，那么在新译本里面，他说："因为自己的罪孽而消灭"、"因自己的罪孽衰弱而死"衰弱而死。我觉得新译本翻的还是非常非常贴切，比较容易懂。因为自己的罪孽衰弱，你看，死的原因是什么？因为罪而死？但是，工具是什么？缺粮缺水而死。现代人，缺粮缺水不是说没有粮食可以吃，没有水可以喝，而是没有好粮可以吃，没有好水可以喝，命就送掉了嘛。在末后的时代，这个情形会越来越严重，人因缺好粮好水，然后人就慢慢死掉。阿摩司书里告诉我们，"人饥饿非因无饼，干渴非因无水，乃因不听耶和华神的话。"（八章十一节）人背逆了神，到最后就是死。

最后我想谈谈，魔鬼的诡计是什么？魔鬼的诡计是什么？保罗在哥林多书里面讲，他说，他很清楚地知道魔鬼的诡计，然后他又说，要攻破敌人坚固的堡垒，把人的心意夺回，使他归顺基督。可是各位你知道，今时代魔鬼的诡计是什么？其实他在每一个时代都有不同的策略使人远离神，这个时代，他有一个策略，就是从人基本的生理欲望来着手，来攻击你。我每次想到耶稣告诉西门的话说，"西门，西门，撒旦想要得着你们，好筛你们，像筛麦子一样。"我看到这话的时候，心里面就一阵的震惊。因为撒旦每天都在等，每天都在想要得着我们。各位你知道，我们每日生活最大的使命是什么？是跟人抢灵魂？不对！是跟魔鬼在抢灵魂。当有人要去算命的时候，我就说，你就是把你自己的命交给算命仙背后那个灵去主使。这不是吓他，是真的。但是，当我们把他引起上帝面前的时候，是把他生命的主权交给上帝来主管。

人有四大基本的生理欲望。这四大基本欲望是仇敌魔鬼攻击这个时代人最好的方法，为什么？因为它是最基本的。你非得有不可。第一，饮食的欲望，就是吃的欲望，每个人都有吃、喝的欲望。第二个是什么？排泄的欲望。有吃就有排嘛。你如果有进没有出，排不出来，很容易就百病丛生，便秘是通往文明病最快速的一条道路。第三，睡眠的欲望。睡不好觉，很多病都会跟着发生，免疫系统、记忆力、逻辑推理、情绪，全部都受影响。最后一个，性的欲望。人类有这四大基本欲望，饮食、排泄、睡眠和性。

所以，你看，魔鬼如果要攻击一个非常有恩赐的传道人，或是前途似锦的年轻人，你看他会从哪里攻击？他先从女性着手。用女人去迷惑他，让他坠落，让他沉沦。其实这方法是很容易防守的，下一个才是可怕的方法，就是它让他透过饮食的错误，再讲一次，他透过这些饮食的错误导致他排泄的问题，导致他睡眠的问题。让人逐渐地整个人都崩溃掉。魔鬼在这个时代里的策略，一定是先把真正爱神的人，真正对社会有贡献的人，透过错误的饮食，造成整个身体的问题，他就不能有所作为了。

各位亲爱的朋友，如果您是对社会、对国家、对民族、对家庭、对社区，有贡献或梦想的人，顾惜您的身体吧，毕竟没有健康，一切枉然，有了健康，才有成功的本钱。祝福您！

健康排毒餐常见问题

Q&A

① Q：排毒餐中的"一份"份量是多少？

　A：排毒餐中所指的一份，会因为每个人的食量而有所不同。建议一份以五十公克或六十公克为基准，再视需要增减之。

② Q：排毒餐中的根茎花果类蔬菜，除了书上所示，还有哪些？

　A：根类食材　如：胡萝卜、白萝卜、芜菁、辣根、根恭菜、牛蒡、菊薯、豆薯。

　　　茎类食材　如：蒟蒻、芋、笋、嫩茎莴苣、球茎甘蓝、榨菜、山葵、马铃薯、山药、莲藕、芦笋、百合、荸荠、姜、洋葱。

　　　花类食材　如：花椰菜、青花菜、金针花、韭菜花、昙花。

　　　果类食材　如：西红柿、甜椒、辣椒、茄子、枸杞、黄秋葵、甜玉米、菱角、莲子、破布子、小黄瓜与其它瓜类。

③ Q：吃排毒餐觉得手脚冰冷，怎么办？

　A：手脚冰冷乃是因为身体的循环、新陈代谢不佳所致。

　　　在吃的部分，可以透过性温的食材，例如：姜、葱、洋葱，来协助改善。在日常生活部分则可以藉由泡澡来纾缓改善。

④ Q：吃地瓜会一直放屁，有什么方式解决？

　A：因为地瓜本身含有气化酶，因此当它进入消化系统消化时，便会产生气体；若身体肠道系统此时又呈酸性，则产气量将更多，甚至会有胀气现象发生。唯有让身体的肠道系统维持一定的弱碱性，这样放屁、胀气的状况才能随之舒缓改善。

⑤ Q：吃排毒餐分泌物变多？

　A：这是典型的排毒反应，恭喜您，请继续加油。

⑥ Q：排毒期间重症患者为什么不可以吃芽菜类、豆类与叶菜类？

　A：自行孵育的黄豆芽和绿豆芽可以食用，市场上所售的芽菜类则须特别谨慎，因为潜藏含有漂白剂与除草剂的可能性极高，苜蓿芽则不建议吃。豆类则是大多数豆类含大量植物油和蛋白质一般人适量的吃是无妨，但癌症病人常吃，多吃会吃进过量油脂和蛋白质，而过量油脂和蛋白质会使身体慢性中毒（例如肥胖症和癌症）。叶菜类不宜生食的原因是因为叶菜类的农药残留机会较根茎类大，且叶菜类容易长寄虫。

❼ Q：南瓜、黄豆、菇类是很好的抗癌食物，为什么吃排毒餐不能吃？

A：南瓜、菇类在中医的观点上是较容易"发"的食物（所谓"发"意指容易引起身体过敏反应），而黄豆则是临床上的研究显示不适合肿瘤病人食用，故建议在食用排毒餐的当下，避免食用这三种食物。

❽ Q：不吃鱼肉蛋奶的话，要怎么摄取足够蛋白质？

A：吃排毒餐可以由藻类、豆荚类、坚果类、杂粮类来摄取蛋白质。

❾ Q：排毒反应有哪些？怎么知道是否为排毒反应？

A：可能产生的排毒反应列举有：头痛、虚弱、感到不舒服、皮肤敏感、大便缓慢、拉肚子、多尿、疲倦、不想动、神经紧张、易怒、消极及忧郁、发烧或其它类似感冒的症状。有的宿疾，被药物压制没有真正痊愈的会发出来。如高血压患者，血压可能暂时更高，有糖尿病者血糖可能更高（不用担心，这是好现象），不需理会，过几天自然会恢复正常。无论如何，大多数人会发觉这些反应是可以忍受的，而且你应该很高兴，因为这套健康排毒餐对你特别有效。排毒反应所持续的时间三天至两个星期不等，视个人体质而异。

❿ Q：排毒期间如何缓解排毒之不适症状？

A：在排毒反应时，要多休息、多睡觉、多喝好水或多吃植物综合酵素，症状就会减轻。

⓫ Q：吃排毒餐期间是否可以吃中药？

A：吃排毒餐期间可以吃中药，不会有冲突。而且，常会有相乘效果，可放心使用。

⓬ Q：吃排毒餐体重是不是会一直下降？如果本身就很瘦，不想体重减轻怎么办？

A：吃排毒餐的初期，体重会下降，因为排毒餐中的食材本身纤维含量高，会刺激肠道蠕动，增加排便，加上低油低盐低糖，所以体重会下降。但排毒餐会帮助体质的调整，因此体重不会一直下降。一般来说，瘦到比标准体重再瘦一点点后，就会再回到标准体重。

⓭ Q：身体虚冷可以吃排毒餐吗？

A：身体虚冷可以吃排毒餐，食用期间可以熬煮姜汤服用，或者在烹调过程中佐以添加青葱、蒜、洋葱等食材。

⑭ Q：吃排毒餐是否一定要配合植物综合酵素和植物能量素（昆布粉）？

A：吃排毒餐期间如能配合植物综合酵素和昆布粉，则排毒的效果将会更完全、更显着。

⑮ Q：书上说慢性病和癌症患者所吃的东西必须由专业人员测试过，哪里可以有这样的专业人员？

A：各地都有已陆续经过训练的工作人员和志(义)工。

⑯ Q：化疗、放疗或电疗期间可以吃排毒餐吗？需要注意什么？

A：化疗、放疗或电疗期间可以吃排毒餐，但须注意食材的来源是否有污染，生食部分的蔬果建议买自然农耕的食物，再以解毒机解毒过后才食用。

⑰ Q：是否只能喝昆布汤？

A：汤的部分可以利用海藻类、蔬菜来熬汤，其中可以添加昆布，但亦需要注意食材的多样化，避免偏食状况产生。

⑱ Q：排毒餐是否一点调味品都不能加？

A：食用排毒餐初期可先从低油低盐低糖的调味方式，循序渐进的让味蕾苏醒，进而能够不添加任何调味品，让味蕾真正感受食物的味道，并能减轻身体各脏器的负担。若用调味料，建议以竹盐取代白盐，以冷压橄榄油代替其它油类。

⑲ Q：除了吃糙米，还可以添加哪些谷类？

A：糙米可搭配以下食材一起煮食。

谷类：胚芽米、小米、薏仁、野米、糯米（红、白、黑）。

麦类：大麦、小麦、荞麦、印加麦、黑麦（裸麦）。

杂粮：高粱、玉米、苋米、芡实、珍珠米、洋薏仁、莲子、绿豆、红豆。

干豆类：扁豆、米豆、黑眼豆、菜豆（黑、红）。

鲜豆类：四季豆、长豆、毛豆、皇帝豆、甜豆、豌豆、肉豆、豆荚。

发酵豆：纳豆。

⑳ Q：排毒餐是否一定要在书上所写的时间内吃完？

A：排毒餐如能在书上所说的时间内吃完，效果最佳；如作息无法配合，则亦要按时定量。无论如何，逾时吃总比没吃好。

㉑ Q：上班族要怎么吃排毒餐？

A：上班族吃排毒餐可将一果二蔬搅打成蔬果汁饮用，至于地瓜和糙米的部分，则可于睡前煮好，早上再做成手卷或寿司进食之。

㉒ Q：夜间工作者要怎么吃排毒餐？需要补充什么？

A：夜间工作者吃排毒餐同书上所述即可，额外需补充维生素B群和植物综合酵素。但身体经络运行皆有其一定的规律，故长远地为身体健康着想，最好避免夜间工作。

㉓ Q：早上一定要喝七合好水（一千二百六十毫升的好水）吗？喝不完怎么办？

A：起床后刷牙前喝水能有助于身体排毒，当然早上要一口气喝完七合水是有点困难，因此初期可先由五百毫升开始，再陆续增加即可。若您早餐是将一果二蔬打成果汁，则一早的好水五百至七百毫升.足够矣。

㉔ Q：排毒餐要吃多久，才会有效？癌症才会有改善？

A：吃排毒餐其实是一种饮食方法、生活方式，从饮食开始净化，进而净化我们的身体，癌症患者由于身体酸碱值长期处于酸性，故如欲透过排毒餐来净化身体，提升脏器健康，则至少要持续食用四至六个月来改善。我再说，健康排毒餐是一种生活，是一种从饮食开始生活模式。

㉕ Q：排毒餐是不是只要吃二十一天就可以？

A：吃二十一天排毒餐是对于现在身体没有疾病的人而言；对于慢性病患者或肿瘤患者，则至少需要四个月的时间，而且三餐都吃，并配合十四天强力排毒，还要力行健康每日七件事。

㉖ Q：什么是好水？好水哪里买？

A：四百年前明朝李时珍所编《本草纲目》所述"雪水"，即是我心目中的好水。唯今世上长寿村多数都在半山腰或各地，以致于经常可得天上来的好水。一般人可依书中所列需求，挑选优良的净水系统使用。

㉗ Q：酵素是不是每个人都需要补充？一次要吃多少？

A：酵素是帮助身体生化反应进行的催化剂，存在于生菜与蔬果当中。除非您每天皆能够摄食足够量的生菜与蔬果，否则建议您能额外补充之。就没有疾病的人而言，可于三餐饭前补充之；对于有慢性病或肿瘤的患者，建议搭配排毒餐食用，补充方式如《无毒一身轻》书上所述即可。

㉘ Q：酵素是不是就是酵母？

A：酵素（Enzyme）不是酵母（Yeast），两者是不一样的。身体所有的活动与反应几乎都需要酵素参与，才能顺利进行，酵素可以维持身体正常功能、消化食物、修复组织……等。酵母含有丰富的维生素B群与植物性蛋白质，可改善容易疲劳的现象，对于常有嘴角破皮困扰的人，也可发挥不错的改善效果。

㉙ Q：吃昆布是不是可以代替植物能量素（昆布粉）？

A：昆布粉是经由德国高科技生物技术从数种藻类中萃取出来的矿物质补充剂，有别于一般的昆布，昆布粉可补充身体必需的七种矿物质，快速调整酸性体质为碱性体质。当然吃昆布虽对身体有益，但仍无法取代昆布粉。

㉚ Q：肾脏病人不能吃藻类，那可以吃昆布粉吗？

A：一般而言，肾脏病人需注意钾的摄取，昆布粉本身是矿物质的补充剂，异于一般的海藻昆布食品，所以肾脏病人可以食用昆布粉，无须担心。

㉛ Q：住在中国内地，蔬果选择性少，要如何吃排毒餐？

A：健康排毒餐，是一种健康饮食与生活模式，故无论您在何方，均可以过书中所介绍的生活方式。

㉜ Q：小朋友要怎么吃排毒餐？

A：小朋友吃排毒餐比大朋友更重要，更有帮助，而且影响一生。

㉝ Q：婴儿不喝牛奶，要喝什么？

A：婴儿最好喝母奶，如不喝母奶则可以喝糙米浆、小米、豆奶或羊奶。两岁以上小朋友，则更不应该喝牛奶，牙齿已长齐，应正常均衡摄取取食物。

㉞ Q：吃排毒餐期间感觉身体比较虚弱？

A：吃排毒餐期间并非身体比较虚弱，乃是身体因为毒素减少而感到轻松。

㉟ Q：吃排毒餐很容易饿，肚子饿可以吃什么？

A：健康排毒餐消化快，不增加身体负担，故您容易感觉肚子饿，这是正常现象，饿时可以水果、坚果、地瓜来消除饥饿感。

㊱ Q：怎么知道身体是酸性还是碱性？

A：可以用一般药房所售pH值试纸测唾液即可知。

㊲ Q：是不是所有的东西都要连皮吃？

A：一般来说是的，但也要特别注意，龙眼、荔枝等，它们的外层是壳而非皮。

Introduction

What is a healthy, detoxifying diet?

Many people believe that if you never get sick, you must be in good health; however, it is exactly this type of misapprehension that frequently leads unknowingly to the gradual deterioration of healthy bodies. And the primary causes of this lapse into ill health are improper nutritional habits and lifestyle.

The fact is modern people must keep themselves in good condition under intense, competitive pressure. In a frantic search for equilibrium they develop an endlessly expanding appetite for new foods, and over a long period of time become exposed to all kinds of high-fat, high-cholesterol, high-sodium, low-fiber, low-carbohydrate, chemically-enriched substances. This will eventually cause the body's immune system to become weak and imbalanced, and one will inevitably fall prey to all kinds of chronic illness and disease. At this point, our highly-developed medical technology induces us into the trap of resorting to pharmaceutical preparations, meanwhile causing us to overlook the erroneous dietary habits and poor lifestyle which underlie most health issues.

Therefore, the concept of a healthy, detoxifying diet involves allowing the body to take in the nutrients it needs, while eliminating those substances which are burdensome or actively harmful to physical well-being. What this means is that only when we have cleared our bodies of toxins can we begin to enjoy a state of perfect wellness, and naturally avoid the threat of disease.

Recommendations for a healthy diet

◆How to eat a healthy breakfast

Breakfast should consist of one part fruit, two parts vegetables, one part sweet potato, and one part brown rice. Procedural guidelines:

1. Utilize the following principles when choosing fruits: be sure that they are locally grown, in season, and picked at peak production times. Any fruits that are imported or are out-of-season and that have been kept under refrigeration are unsuitable for consumption.
2. Vegetables should also be chosen in accordance with the above principles. They can be divided into four major groups: root, stem, flower and fruit.
3. When selecting sweet potatoes, bear in mind that the yellow-fleshed kinds are the most nutritional, and remember to eat sweet potatoes along with their skin. Those suffering from chronic illnesses may increase the quantity of sweet potato to two parts per meal.
4. When preparing brown rice you can add in small red beans, purple rice varieties, Job's tears (a kind of wild grass seed), soybeans or any other type of grain.
5. If sweet potatoes are not grown in your locale, regular varieties of potato may be substituted.

◆Lunch and dinner meal tips

Lunch and dinner menus should consist of 60-65% whole-grain cereals, 25-30% vegetables, 10-15% legumes and seaweed, and 5-10% soup broth. Procedural guidelines:

1. In food preparation one should steam, boil, scald or stew - of which steaming is by far the recommended method.
2. Proportionally, the whole-grain part of the menu should include 70% staples like wheat and rice, along with 30% coarser food grains.
3. Eat 1/2 to 3/4 of all vegetables raw in order to allow your body to absorb the optimal quantity of enzymes.
4. Leafy and sprouted vegetables are excellent for the health, but they are relatively unsatisfactory for the diet of those who are in the process of recuperating from illness.
5. Those suffering from cancer, high uric acid levels or kidney disease should not eat the full portion of proteins from legumes, etc.
6. In soups, you may use liberal amounts of seaweed or laver: the broth should be boiled.
7. Eat fruit as a between-meal snack, but remember not to eat two or more types of melon at the same time: this might cause diarrhea.
8. Every day, drink at least 3,000 cc of cold water.

Twelve dietary taboos

When putting a detoxifying diet plan into effect, why must one choose foods so carefully? This is because the assimilation of certain kinds of unsuitable food and drink may indeed aid in detoxification, but can also introduce other toxins into the body. In the following list of food taboos, you will see foods which are likely to cause secondary harm to the body.

1. Fish, shrimp, crabs and other seafood: Due to the fact that the world's bodies of water are becoming ever more polluted, the living things populating these waters have in turn absorbed many pollutants, especially large quantities of heavy metals which are harmful to the kidneys.
2. Meat:Besides causing the human body to become acidic, meats have also been injected with many antibiotics and hormones designed to fatten animals quickly for human

consumption. Such pharmaceutical preparations linger on in meats and are harmful when eaten.
3. Eggs:Eggs have high levels of concentrated protein that is difficult for the body to digest and absorb. They also contain complex hormones which can cause allergic reactions.
4. Milk:After undergoing Pasteurization, the calcium contained in cow's milk will become non-organic: in this form it cannot fulfill the body's calcium requirements, and may also increase the incidence rate of gall or kidney stones, or of calculus formation. Moreover, once milk has been broken down in the digestive tract, a strong acid resembling "ammonia" is produced. Ironically, in order to reestablish a proper acid-base equilibrium, the alkaline calcium contained in the bones is dissolved and leeched out, thus leading to a greater calcium deficiency.
5. Oils:Foods that have been prepared using oil, whether they are sauted or deep-fried, will take from four to twelve hours to digest -- this is a huge burden for the body. Additionally, the fats contained in oil can cause hardening of the arteries, make blood vessels lose their elasticity, lead to the build-up of fatty deposits, and create dangerous obstructions to blood circulation.
6. Salt:By consuming heavily salted food you are taking in large quantities of sodium. As the body's store of sodium increases, its corresponding store of potassium will decrease and a dangerously high state of acidity will ensue: this might cause cells to become cancerous.
7. Sugar:When refined sugar enters the body, it triggers the release of calcium and vitamin B. Furthermore, sugar absorption leads to thickening of the blood: this will cause a decrease in vitality and a greater feeling of fatigue.
8. Monosodium glutamate:Monosodium glutamate is a commonly utilized seasoning that stimulates the taste buds, making foods seem tastier. However, once it has been heated it is difficult to eliminate from the body, and it can influence the central nervous system and optical nerves. Eaten over a long period of time, it will cause dryness of the mouth and tongue, headaches, inability to concentrate, fatigue and hair loss.
9. Soy sauce:There is a large amount of sodium in this product, which might have an unhealthy influence on the blood pressure.
10. All refined and processed foods:Refined and processed foods have neither nutritional nor energizing properties: this is due to the fact that during the refining process, a considerable amount of nutritional elements are lost.
11. Caffeinated foods and beverages:Because caffeine stimulates the nervous system it can boost energy, make the heart beat faster, elevate blood pressure and make one feel full of vitality. Caffeine also has pain-relieving effects and can be addictive, so it is a potential health hazard.
12. Alcoholic foods and beverages; chilled or frozen products:Alcohol is profoundly harmful to the body; it can cause headaches, damage the liver, have deleterious effects on the central nervous system, increase the risk of cancer and heighten the incidence rate of coronary disease. Consuming chilled or frozen products may easily damage the kidneys -- women in particular should avoid this type of food and drink.

The ten main principles for making healthy dietary choices

1. Emphasize whole-grain foods

Unprocessed wheat, rice and other coarser grains contain an abundance of nutrients and dietary fiber. This fiber is useful for preventing constipation, alleviating diarrhea and warding off cancer of the colon and large intestine - none of these advantages are provided by refined or processed foods. Moreover, whole-grain foods are beneficial for the spleen, and cause the stomach's digestive and assimilative functions to improve. Cereals should be selected carefully for suitability; they should be locally-grown, hence different types of grain will be appropriate in different locales. For example, cereals grown south of the Yangtze River (also Southeast Asia) include brown rice, red rice, millet, Job's tears[1] and so on; among North American grains there are wheat, barley, oats, buckwheat, etc.

2. Seed-bearing vegetables

Vegetables contain generous amounts of alpha-carotene, folic acid, vitamins A and E, as well as fiber. If one eats a sufficient quantity of vegetables daily, this will fulfill all of the body's nutritional requirements and keep one in peak condition. This will also help the body fight infection and become disease-resistant. Vegetables are classified according to which part is generally eaten: there are leafy green, cruciferous, seed, pod, fruit and gourd, rhizome, corm, tuber, mushroom and seaweed, nuts and dried bean varieties. By utilizing them in different pairings and groupings, they will supply the body with all of its nutritional requirements.

3. Fruits with pits

Fresh fruits contain a generous amount of vitamins and minerals, especially vitamins A and C; they also provide fiber, natural sugars and water. Fruit is highly nutritional and quite tasty. This type of food is easily digested and assimilated by the body, especially when put through a blender along with the peel and drunk as fruit juice -- in which case the entire digestion process will only take one half hour to complete. Another thing to keep in mind is that only fruits with seeds or pits are truly energizing. Do not select the "convenient" newer varieties that have been genetically altered, such as seedless grapes, watermelon, etc. - eating them can be harmful for the body.

4. Locally-grown produce

Generally speaking, 'locally-grown' implies produce that has been grown on the same latitude or within the same climatic zone. Different parts of the world are dissimilar, so foods taken by people living in different locales are not the same. In fact, plants native to certain areas also function as medicaments for curing local diseases. Therefore, people living in a tropical climate should not eat foods imported from polar or temperate climatic zones, and so on.

5. Peak-season produce

All agricultural produce is planted, grown and harvested at specific times and seasons; therefore, we should consider these agricultural laws and rhythms when selecting foods for our own consumption, for in so doing we fulfill our own natural rhythms, as well. Foods grown during a certain season also serve as medicinal plants which can cure the illnesses most readily caught at that time. This is because crops register temperature, seasonal variations, humidity, angle of sunlight, cosmic rays and soil qualities. Having recorded all of this information, produce is then consumed by people and naturally aids their bodies to adjust to these climatic and seasonal changes. Therefore, those who always eat imported, out-of-season or pre-ripened fruits and vegetables will not be in the best of health.

As to judging what counts as peak-season produce, just go to the market and look for those fruits and vegetables that are the most plentiful and also the most inexpensive. But still keep in mind that what you select should be locally grown.

6. Ripe produce

Every type of plant has its own growth period, but merchants nowadays want produce picked unnaturally early; they also utilize lots of chemical fertilizers, pesticides, hormones, and so on. Such chemical compounds enter our bodies along with the foods we consume, profoundly influencing our physical well-being.

7. Total utilization of produce

Every part of fruits and vegetables has its own nutritional value, so eating all parts together will yield the best health benefits. Be sure that you include every part of fruits and vegetables in your meals; do not throw areas like the peel or leaves away just because their texture seems odd or their flavor is not so pleasant. If your eating habits are like this, even though your diet might include many kinds of produce, your health will never improve as much as you would like.

8. Heating in water as the best food preparation method

Cooking in hot water -- i.e. boiling, poaching, steaming, stewing or scalding -- is the best way to prepare foods. In October, 2003, a report was issued by the Spanish Science Commission stating that according to their research, boiling was the ideal cooking method, since it preserves the nutritional contents of food in their entirety.

On the other hand, the cooking method most harmful to the body is deep-frying, which transforms any ingredients into high-fat foods. When fats are consumed in excess, the blood vessels are apt to become clogged with fat, leading to an increased likelihood of coronary disease. Eating too much high-fat food will cause obesity and throw the metabolism into a state of disequilibrium; in addition, it will invite disease, increasing the liver's burden as this organ breaks down the body's wastes.

9. Recommended proportions of raw foods at mealtimes

At every meal, it is best to keep 50% or more of all fruits and vegetables for raw consumption. Due to the fact that vitamins and enzymes are easily destroyed or washed away during the cooking process, cooked foods are less nutritious and the digestion might suffer as a result. As soon as you resume eating raw foods, bodily functions will begin to operate efficiently, the aging process will be slowed down, and you will be brimming with vitality.

10. Fasting

By fasting in a healthy and reasonable way, overworked digestive organs will be allowed to rest, toxins can be quickly eliminated from the system, and the constitution will be tuned up and readjusted. You may fast from one to seven days, beginning with a one-day fast and gradually building up your capacity. During a fast nothing should be eaten, and only good-quality water should be taken. Accompany this regimen by maintaining slow and even breathing, easing up on heavy work, and keeping the intestines well-irrigated: in this way, physical health and well-being will be naturally and effortlessly enhanced.

1 Job's tears:This grain is actually a kind of wild grass seed. It is grown for table use in parts of China, and may even be higher in protein than most other cereals. These seeds are also used as jewelry beads.

Getting Prepared for this Detoxification Program

All food planning and preparation should be centered around single portions. For those who are unwell due to recent surgery, whose digestion is poor, or for children, the recommended quantities of water or food ingredients may be decreased or diluted according to individual judgment. Afterwards, thickness and water content can gradually be increased.

Those who are temporarily unable to cope with a full detoxification regime may build up slowly; for example, one can start with the recommended breakfast, and then successively add on other meals.

For those who have trouble adjusting to the full dietary plan and its stipulation to avoid all seasonings, natural seasonings or seasoned health-food preparations, health-food anti-carcinogenic soups, and so on, may be used as flavor enhancers.

Healthy do-it-yourself anti-carcinogenic soup

Ingredients:
A - Kelp
B - Chinese black mushrooms, white turnip, turnip greens, large tomatoes, corn, carrots, burdock root, soy bean sprouts
C - Fresh ginger
D - Water
Proportions - A : B : C = 4 : 2 : 1
Preparation:
1. Assemble all ingredients according to the above proportions and individual requirements. Wash thoroughly, and then dice everything along with outer peel and put in a pot.
2. Pour water into the pot: the proper quantity should be 4-5 times the volume of the dry ingredients. Bring to a rolling boil over high heat.
3. Turn heat down to low and continue to stew the ingredients for two hours, then strain out the diced vegetables: the fluid contents can be used as cooking stock or soup broth.
4. Ideally one should drink this vegetable broth right away, as soon as it is done. For those who would prefer to make it in large quantities, wait until the stock has cooled, then either put it in a keep-fresh container or an ice-box container and store it in the freezer.

Healthy Do-it-Yourself Seasoning

Ingredients: Black sesame seeds, white sesame seeds, lecithin, brewer's yeast, pine nuts
Proportions: Use equal amounts of every ingredient
Preparation:
1. First, grind up the black and white sesame seeds along with the pine nuts.
2. Mix all ingredients evenly together, then store in an airtight container.
3. During food preparation, use in appropriate quantities as needed.

Healthy Do-it-Yourself Salad Dressing

[The author's thanks go to Mrs. Zhang, the pastor's wife at Hong Kong's 611 Spiritual Energy Hall, who kindly provided this recipe.]
Ingredients: 1 tsp. honey, 1 lemon, 1 tbsp. olive oil
Preparation:
1. First, squeeze the lemon and extract its juice.
2. Put all ingredients in a large bowl, and mix thoroughly with an egg-beater or blender until it becomes glossy, sticky and dense.
3. Pour into a keep-fresh container: the dressing may be stored in the refrigerator for about one week.
4. For those who would like to create different flavors, try mashing other kinds of fresh fruit and adding this to the mixture.

Recommended Seasoning Ingredients

Natural seasonings include: lemon, kelp, Chinese black mushrooms, basil, onion, ginger, garlic, chili pepper, corn
Health-food products: raisins, bamboo salt, rice vinegar, brown sugar, honey, maple sugar, natt[1], miso, rice wine, himamatsutake mushroom[2]

Multi-Grain Brown Rice Medley

Ingredients: Brown rice - 70%, Multi-grain mixture (Lotus seeds, Job's tears, Chinese wolfberry, millet, small red beans, red jujube) - 30%
Items to keep in mind during food preparation and at mealtimes:
1. Before cooking, soak the brown rice in water for 4 hours; the multi-grain mixture should be soaked for one hour. Steep these ingredients in good-quality water - do not use tap water.
2. A pinch of bamboo salt, a small quantity of oil or prepared charcoal sections may be boiled in the pot prior to the insertion of the main ingredients. This will enhance the quality of the rice, mitigate its coarseness and astringency, and make it keep longer.
3. After meals, do not eat pastry or drink additional beverages: doing this would impede the digestion and render detoxification ineffective.

4. During hot summer weather, for children, or for those with hot constitutions, use one type of grain only; for example, use either brown rice or semi-polished rice[3] as an accompaniment for sweet potatoes.
5. During cold winter weather, or for those with weak, chilly constitutions, a wider variety of starches may be selected to accompany meals.
6. For those who live in tropical or polar climatic zones, hulled rice, millet, oats or buckwheat may be added to supplement the brown rice.
7. Eating wheat and grains together will provide more gluten, which can enhance physical stamina; however, this mixture tends to make the body acidic, so it is unwise to eat this combination over a long period of time.
8. Those suffering from excess stomach acid or who constantly feel hungry can correct these conditions by selecting alkaline foods like brown rice or natto to accompany meals.
9. White rice is suitable for alkaline body types. To correct cases of diarrhea, boiled rice congee will yield excellent results.

If you absolutely cannot do without cooking oil, please be sure to utilize cold-pressed olive oil.
Conversion Table for Cooking Measurements:
1 cup = 240 cc. = 16 tbsp.   1 tbsp. = 15 cc. = 3 tsp.   1 tsp. = 5 cc.   1/2 tsp. = 2.5 cc.
1/4 tsp. = 1.25 cc.
For those in a normal state of health who find that eating more raw foods for lunch and dinner leaves them feeling still hungry, 3-5 types of cooked vegetables may be added: they should be boiled or fried in water; these foods can also be poached, steamed, scalded, simmered, or stewed in soy sauce.

1 Natto is a traditional Japanese food made from fermented soy beans. It is covered with a sticky paste, and has a distinctive odor. The Japanese eat natto with rice. It is rich in nutrients, such as saponin (a cancer controller), proteins, oligosaccharide, food fibre, and vitamins B1, K2 and E.
2 Himamatsutake [also known as Royal Sun Agaricus, or Agaricus Blazei Murrill] is an edible mushroom with medicinal properties. It is known as the number one Japanese nutritional supplement, for it contains a wealth of enzymes, amino acids, vitamins and minerals. It has been found effective in the treatment of lung cancer, and prevents oncogenesis, tumors and tumor metastasis.
3 Semi-polished rice retains 75% of its outer wrapper of bran, whereas so-called brown rice has 80% of its outer skin. White rice retains only 70% of this outer casing.

Dr. Lin's Twenty-One Health Reminders

1. A good way to get rid of lingering agricultural chemicals

If you wish to eat raw vegetables in peace of mind, first deal with the problem of lingering agricultural chemicals. Besides carefully choosing fresh vegetables that have been grown without chemical fertilizers or pesticides, there are three other means of avoiding chemically-treated foods:
1. The simplest way is to grow your own vegetables.
2. Find a farmer who can grow your food for you.
3. Make use of the 03 Ozone, namely the OZONE Vegetable Detoxifier. When selecting this kind of device, be sure that it will dispense from 200 to 250 mg. of ozone per/hour: be especially careful not to exceed 300 mg, which would have a detrimental effect on the health. This device must be made in accordance with the German manufacturing code, for Germany has the world's highest standards.

2. Be careful about food additives

Due to the rapid development of food chemistry and food processing technology, modern life is now full of all kinds of processed foodstuffs; one can see snack foods, instant food packets, fast foods, etc., everywhere, all of which are packed with large quantities of food additives. These so-called food additives serve the purpose of adding coloration, seasoning, preservatives, aroma enhancers, quality stabilizers and anti-oxidizers, and also have a wide range of other uses in the processes of manufacture, packaging, shipping, storage and so on. All of this adds to or touches upon a food product's price and quality.

Besides food additives such as sugar, salt, wine, vinegar, and so on, that count as natural ingredients, many others are synthetic chemical substances. That is to say, food additives are only designed to extend a product's period of freshness or make the color, aroma and flavor more appealing. None of this enjoys any health benefits; furthermore, food additives influence a person's health and can be dangerous cancer-inducing agents. Therefore, even though there are legal standards governing food additives, if one wants to prevent chemical toxins from entering the body, the appropriate preventive measure is total avoidance.

3. Instructions for drinking good-quality water

It goes without saying that replenishing the body's supply of water is important for sound health. Besides drinking a daily requirement of 3,000 cc, there are three periods within the course of a day during which one should drink some water: after getting up in the morning, at approximately 3 p.m. in the afternoon, and in the evening between 7 and 9 p.m. During the summer months of July and October, the body's water requirements will increase substantially.

Taking 1,260 cc of cold water immediately after getting up in the morning will yield excellent results. Those suffering from kidney ailments, coronary disease or cirrhosis of the liver should drink water in accordance with their physician's instructions. Moreover, there is a medical saying that "4 a.m. is a deadly time", because strokes most often occur during the pre-dawn hour of 4 o'clock in the morning. At this time, the blood's density and viscosity levels are at their highest: if one drinks 200 cc of water before going to bed, this can help to reduce blood density.

In addition, whether or not one's drinking water is of a good quality is also important, for water not only quenches thirst but also provides the body with necessary minerals and trace elements. Drinking water should answer to a number of criteria. It should retain its original mineral content while being free of carbonation, extraneous substances and heavy metals. Water should be slightly alkaline, with an alkalinity level of 7.4; it should be in accordance with fresh drinking water standards; it should contain oxygen; its molecular structure should be regular and have a high density; and electric-powered water filters should not be utilized in its processing.

4. The all-important sweet potato

Do not underestimate the importance of the sweet potato! Among all detoxifying foods, it is the most important - that means, you must eat sweet potatoes.

That is because the sweet potato is not only high in fiber and low in fat, but also has an incredibly rich supply of vitamins, minerals and amino acids: just about every nutrient required by the human body is to be found in the sweet potato. Cooked sweet potatoes appear as number one on the list of the top forty anti-carcinogenic foods as set forth by the Japanese Cancer Research Center, and raw sweet potatoes are listed as number two, which demonstrates how mightily the sweet potato contributes to human health. Something else to be aware of is that yellow-fleshed sweet potatoes provide more energy than the red varieties.

Sweet potatoes may either be baked or boiled: they should be baked at temperatures lower than 15℃ and boiled at 15℃ and above. And be sure not to forget to eat sweet potatoes with their skins.

5. The best time to eat a detoxifying breakfast

What time should one eat breakfast for the best detoxification results? It is best to take breakfast between 6:30 and 7:30 in the morning; more precisel, those suffering from chronic diseases should eat breakfast between 6:30 and 7 a.m., whereas for those whose intention is only to stay fit, eating between 6 and 7:30 a.m. is best. Why is this? It has to do with the operating times of our internal organs. God created the marvelous human body so that each of its organs comes into play at a different time; each organ looks after its own set of functions, but still operates in cooperation with other organs. The morning hours of 5-7 a.m. correspond to the large intestinal meridian[1]: during this time period, intestinal peristalsis operates most intensely.

Therefore, once proper eating and drinking habits have been established, right after eating a detoxifying breakfast one will have a healthy bowel movement, eradicating any previous eliminatory problems.

6. The body's reactions to detoxification

Several days after beginning a detoxifying diet, some people may feel unwell as an apparent side-effect. This is actually a reaction caused by the body functions' having taken a turn for the better: an "improvement reaction" [known by doctors as the Jarisch-Herxheimer reaction - or 'Herx' reaction for brevity.] Once the body has absorbed detoxifying foods it can begin to assimilate all kinds of nutrients, and as soon as the body has taken in these balance-inducing elements, the cells become enlivened and begin clearing the system of wastes. Chinese medicine refers to this as the "feeling worse while getting better reaction".

Generally speaking, the more serious the disease, the more intense will be the Herxheimer reaction. It may occur at different times within the course of treatment, and will last for varying periods of time; the exact nature of the reaction will also vary. Whenever this uncomfortable change for the better starts to take place, keep on with your dietary regime - on no account give up!

Some common recuperative reactions are:
Headache, dizziness, heightened body temperature, joint pains, nausea, breathing difficulty, pimples, diarrhea, weakness, increased urination, lethargy, nervousness, irritability, depression

7. When eating, chew slowly and swallow carefully for enhanced brain power

At every meal, be sure to chew each mouthful of food 30 times - do not wolf down your food. The longer you chew, the healthier you will become: you will feel more youthful, and your dental health will also benefit. Try this little experiment: place your hands on your temples, and then make chewing movements. You will find that your temples move, as well. This is because when chewing, there is also activity around your brain, enlivening this organ, enhancing brain development in children and warding off senility in elderly people.

Furthermore, biting into and chewing food encourages the production of saliva, which not only contains digestive enzymes that help the stomach to assimilate foods but also possesses strong antiseptic properties. Saliva can help to eradicate the cancer-inducing agents that foods may contain.

Careful chewing also aids in the reduction of draining mental pressure because during the process of chewing food, the enormous feelings of tension experienced by modern people are released, leaving one feeling cheerful and content.

8. If you consume too little dietary fiber, watch out for intestinal cancer

Eating too many highly-refined processed foods will lead to a heavy deficiency of nutritional fiber, causing digestive system imbalance.

What is known as dietary fiber is a substance that is stored in plants and cannot be broken down by digestive tract enzymes: it has neither caloric nor nutritional elements. This fiber stimulates intestinal peristalsis; hence, as food being digested travels through contracted intestinal pathways, more cholesterol, fats, cancer-inducing agents and other harmful substances can be extracted. This greatly reduces the rate of incidence of intestinal, rectal and colon cancer.

Moreover, by assimilating enough fiber the stomach will take a longer time to discharge its contents, giving one an increased feeling of satiety and promoting weight control. This effect will also reduce the absorption of cholesterol and triglyceroids, and will also cut down on tooth decay.

9. Always eat fruits that are in season

In Chinese medicine, all of the ills of the human body are relegated to three causes: internal and external causes, as well as a type that is neither internal nor external. Internal causes have to do with moods: worries, thoughts, sorrow, fear and shock; such moods will influence the entire body's state of illness. External causes have to do with variations in weather conditions: wind, summer heat, humidity, dryness, cold, and heat; as soon as the body becomes unable to adjust to changing weather conditions, illness ensues. The third cause of human ailments has to do with unexpected problems, such as suffering an injury or eating and drinking harmful substances. For the most part, people get sick very easily from external causes, and one important factor leading to this kind of illness is eating out-of-season foods.

All fruit and vegetable produce is grown and harvested at different times; however, with the help of agricultural technology, modern people can now savor any kind of produce at any time. Foods nevertheless grow in accordance with fixed rules and will vary qualitatively with seasonal changes; hence, people should follow the rhythm of nature in their eating habits.

10. When eating fruits and vegetables, do not remove the skin

When preparing fruits and vegetables such as radishes, Chinese yam, burdock root, pumpkin, potatoes, muskmelon, pears, and so on, many people routinely remove the outer skin or peel. Perhaps they do not know that the outer skin is actually the most nutritious part. For the most part the inner flesh is acidic, whereas the peel is alkaline. This means that every part of a vegetable or fruit has its own special nutritional value: whether it is the peel, the flesh or pulp, the stalk, stems, roots or leaves, one should eat everything in order to establish acid-base equilibrium and bring the fullest healing effects into play.
Picture captions:
Oranges - The white-colored part of an orange peel is beneficial for the respiratory system.
Lemons - The pectin contained in lemon peel can lower cholesterol.
Bananas - Banana peel is beneficial for the heart. To prepare bananas, first wash them and then slice them across into thin circles, leaving a tiny ring of peel on each slice. In this way, they are easily consumed along with their peel.
Celery - Celery leaves contain heterozooid, which protects the health.

11. Milk is only for cows

Since childhood, the idea that milk is highly nutritious has been instilled in our minds. Milk is both a protein and calcium source, hence supermarket shelves are congested with any and every type of dairy product; however, contained in milk and other dairy products is a large quantity of assorted proteins which are not only significant causes of food allergies, but that also cause the stomach to secrete additional amounts of stomach acid and enzymes, making ulcers in the digestive system flare up more intensely. Besides this, there are other ailments like chronic rhinitis, swollen lymph glands, chronic ear inflammation (otitis), etc., that will show enormous improvement if one simply stops consuming dairy products.

Furthermore, the idea that milk and dairy products can compensate for the body's lost calcium is erroneous; in fact, the more protein is absorbed by the system, the more calcium will be allowed to drain out of bone matter. This just goes to show that if one wishes to maintain a state of calcium equilibrium in the body and keep the bones strong and healthy, one ought to cut down on calcium consumption rather than taking a greater amount of calcium supplements.

12. Eating sugar will make you age faster

Sugar has an enticing sweetness that is irresistible for many people, but if one eats an excessive amount of it over a long period of time, healthy body fluids of a weakly alkaline nature will be influenced by acidic sugar, thus becoming either weakly acidic or neutral. Due to this chemical change the body's cells will age at a faster rate; the hair will also be affected, and will whiten or turn a lack-luster shade.

Moreover, after sugar has been absorbed into the system, insulin secretion will be stimulated and the sugar will be transformed into fat. Such changes will have a deleterious effect on the normal appetite; it will prevent the absorption of vitamins, minerals and other nutritional elements, and may easily lead to unwanted weight gain.

Even more serious results of excessive sugar consumption are a heightened incidence rate of gallstones, uterine tumors and mammary gland cancer, as well as dissipation of the body's store of calcium leading to osteoporosis. By stimulating the stomach's secretion of fluids, sugar intake can cause this organ's mucous membranes to become damaged, causing gastritis and stomach ulcers.

13. Say good-bye to stomach pain and feel great!

For modern people, the pace of life is fast, work pressure is enormous and dietary habits are abnormal -- all of which has made stomach-ache one of the most common health annoyances. Viewed from a Chinese medical perspective, anything that obstructs the flow of qi in the spleen and stomach will cause stomach-ache symptoms.

As soon as a detoxification plan is under way and fresh, healthy food and drink has been restored to one's diet, the stomach and intestinal tract will be purified, so that peristalsis can once again function normally and symptoms of nausea, bloating and constipation will disappear. Additionally, normal digestive absorption will resume, allowing the system to derive a full range of nutritional elements - especially vitamins A and C -- from foods; the finest result of this process is that mucous membranes lining the walls of the stomach will be repaired and resume their original functioning.

Besides altering your diet, try to find ways of eliminating stress from your life: let the mind and body relax, and follow natural patterns in the alternation of work and recuperation. In this way, stomach-aches will be cured once and for all.

14. Staying healthy by eating cereal staples and other multi-grain foods

According to traditional Chinese medicine, eating the five basic cereal foods will nourish the "true qi"[2] of the five major internal organs.[3] Chinese medical classics stress that "Of the ten-thousand things born under heaven, the five cereal crops are the finest". This means that the five main cereals and other courser grains serve to nourish the spleen: once the spleen is healthy, the stomach will also be healthy and the entire body will thrive.

This is due to the fact that besides providing starches, unrefined multi-grain foods also contain an abundant supply of vitamins, minerals and all-important, health-promoting dietary fiber. This fiber can absorb toxins, bile and other cancer-inducing substances, and then cause their speedy elimination, thus dramatically decreasing the incidence rate of intestinal cancer as well as absorbing oils, fats and cholesterol. Fiber definitely promotes good health.

The starches contained in cereals are "resistant starches" that are widely stored in carbohydrates. Eating this kind of starch will not result in unwanted weight gain; on the contrary, since the small intestine has a hard time breaking it down and digesting it, the stomach will feel full for a longer time and the growth of beneficial intestinal bacteria will be stimulated, maintaining intestinal acidity. This process accelerates the breaking down and elimination of toxins; it also aids in controlling body weight.

15. Getting to know the body's natural clock

The human body operates according to its own natural laws and time patterns: if you adhere to the operational laws of this physiological clock, it will greatly aid physical maintenance and recuperation. There are three periods of time that one should pay special attention to:
1. Between 5 and 7 o'clock in the morning is when the large intestinal meridian discharges its wastes: this is the most opportune time for ridding the body of toxins.
2. From 9 to 11 p.m. is when the Triple-burner meridian's[4] immunological functions can recuperate; at this time, the body is beginning to enter a resting state.
3. Between 11 p.m. and the early morning hour of 3 a.m. the liver and gall bladder meridians can restore themselves. This crucial time period, when the liver recuperates and new blood is created, must absolutely be spent in sleep.

Those of a weak constitution or suffering from illness should grab this golden opportunity for health improvement and become habituated to going to sleep at 9 p.m.

16. Getting used to a meatless diet

Many people have a hard time overcoming their desire to eat meat, but here are a few ways of gradually changing one's dietary habits:
1. Reduce your meat consumption to one meal per day, and only eat one kind of meat at this time. Later on, it will be possible to extend the time lapse between meals that include

meat.

2. If you absolutely must have meat, restrict your intake to fish only.
3. Fish should only be consumed once or twice a week.
4. Be sure to have dinner before 6 p.m. every evening! Meals taken after 6 o'clock are burdensome for the digestive system and cause great damage to the body.
5. When cooking meat, it should be either boiled or steamed.
6. Restrict your meat consumption to 15% of your total dietary consumption.
7. Only eat meats at a temperature of 15_ C or below: at higher temperatures, meats can be damaging to the constitution.
8. Only eat meat at the very end of a meal.

17. Kelp - Straight from the ocean's energy storehouse to you!

Kelp [known as kombu in Japanese] is a richly nutritious plant that grows in the ocean: it is one of Asia's secret longevity elixirs. It contains quite a number of minerals that are highly important to the body, such as calcium, iron, manganese, copper, magnesium, potassium, silicium, etc.; additionally, kelp has a large amount of iodine, protein and other mineral substances, as well as vitamins A, B and C. All of these can be easily assimilated by the human body.

By eating kelp one can regulate cellular oxidation, boost the metabolism and effectively expel radiation from the system. This sea vegetable is also useful for maintaining the blood at its optimal state of weak alkalinity: it transforms acidic constitutions into alkaline ones. Moreover, because it contains a significant amount of dietary fiber it will expand as soon as it enters the intestinal tract, encouraging beneficial bacteria to go to work on sediments lingering in the large intestine and in this way contributing to better health.

It is true that nowadays the ocean is heavily polluted, which in turn has influenced the quality of seaweed. If one is uncertain regarding the dietary safety of kelp, it is better to purchase the active kelp powders that are sold commercially.

18. Enzymes are crucial for metabolic normality

In order for the body to operate normally countless metabolic reactions must constantly occur, and in order to maintain these reactions enzymes come into play. Enzymes help to regulate the physical constitution, promote cellular metabolism, protect and repair damaged body parts, and accelerate the elimination of wastes.

At times when due to increasing age, stress, excessive pressure in daily living, illness or imprudent dietary habits our bodies become deficient in enzymes, the metabolism will suffer: we will feel tired and lack strength, and will also suffer from weak digestion, flatulence, poor appetite, imbalanced internal secretions, unwanted weight gain and other undesirable symptoms.

The best way to regularize the body's supply of enzymes is to eat more fresh vegetables and fruits. Besides their usefulness in boosting our store of carbohydrates, vitamins and minerals, these foods' most important function is to ensure a sufficient supply of enzymes: particularly rich in enzymes are pineapples, avocadoes, bananas, mangoes and sprouts. If you feel that your dietary supply of enzymes is insufficient, it is also possible to choose commercially sold synthetic enzyme supplements.

19. Getting rid of excess weight

We are all aware of the fact that when our body weight exceeds normal standards we will suffer from more chronic illnesses and even run an increased risk of developing cancer. And of course, there are many who spend their entire life struggling with weight-loss diets.

In fact, if you want to get rid of excess weight, your very first step should be to allow your metabolism to return to normal functioning: this is because as soon as the metabolism is functioning regularly it will be next to impossible to put on weight. Furthermore, once you start eating healthy, detoxifying meals it will not only be unnecessary to suffer from hunger and cut down on dietary intake, but by utilizing the many enzymes and nutrients contained in raw foods the body and its metabolic functions will once again operate normally, stepping up the removal of toxins and wastes. On the average, one can lose one or two pounds a month in this way, and in the process of losing weight one will also become healthier and better-looking.

20. Get enough sleep for better health and enhanced well-being

Sleep is fundamental for good health: if one gets insufficient sleep, it is a good idea to start catching up. Moreover, insufficient sleep will heavily influence the functioning of the body's organs and immunological system, decreasing the ability to work and study efficiently; this might even lead to personality changes.

If you wish to get sufficient sleep and experience better-quality sleep as well, here are seven points to observe:
1. Go to sleep at the same time every night - before 11 p.m. is best.
2. Arrange for a comfortable sleeping environment with proper lighting, warmth and humidity; also, choose bedding made of natural materials.
3. Utilize abdominal breathing: breathe in through the nostrils and out through the mouth.

4. Do not eat for two hours before going to sleep.
5. Keep yourself in a happy frame of mind.
6. Get used to sleeping in the nude: this will promote muscle extension and cause the blood circulation to be free and unimpeded.
7. Before going to sleep, soak for ten to twenty minutes in a hot bath. You can add coarse salt or prepared slices of charcoal[5] to your bath water for even better results.

21. If you suffer from bad moods, you will never be in good health

Moods have an enormous influence on a person's health, and medical research has already proven that indulging in a good belly laugh on a regular basis will boost the immunological system. Those who are constantly over-critical of others and scold people tend to have weaker immune systems: this leads naturally to a state of physical discomfort. One should try to stay in a good mood at all times and places, constantly practicing happiness, prayer and thankfulness. There is also a trick known as the "good cheer method" which will make you get happier with every chuckle, ensuring the most natural kind of well-being.

This method consists of three steps:
1. Thinking of something that makes you happy, laugh three times out loud: Ha! Ha! Ha!
2. Laughing three times "Ha! Ha! Ha!", accompany this by stamping on the ground with both feet three times: Dong, dong, dong!
3. Laughing "Ha! Ha! Ha!" and stamping "Dong, dong, dong!", now start clapping: Clap! Clap! Clap!

1 According to Chinese traditional medicine, the body's internal organs are governed by acupuncture channels [meridians], each of which becomes most active at specific hours of the day or night.
2 'True qi': Chinese medicine differentiates qi into a wide range subcategories. This type of qi circulates in the meridians and nourishes the internal organs.
3 The ancient Chinese classics are not unanimous in identifying the Five Grains, hence it can be inferred that they are simply staple grains like rice, wheat, corn, millet, and so on. Since different locales and climatic zones will not support the same crops, there is as not definition for this term.
As for the Five Organs, these consist of five Yin organs - the heart, liver, spleen, lungs and kidneys, which store the body's building materials, as well as the five Yang organs - the large and small intestines, the gall bladder, stomach and bladder that control bodily functions.
4 The Triple-burner meridian runs from the left eye to the left fingertip. In Chinese medicine, the actual Triple-burner is a set of "organs" in the trunk corresponding to the area above the diaphragm, the area below the belly button, and the space between these two.
5 This charcoal is made of halved bamboo sections, and is used widely in Asia to purify water.

21 Day-by-Day Detoxification Diet Plan

DAY I Breakfast

◆Vegetable Salad
Ingredients:Guava 200 g. Red cabbage 30 g. Corn kernels 1 tbsp.
Preparation:
1. Wash the guava, and then chop it into small chunks. Set it aside, ready to use.
2. Take the red cabbage and pull it apart leaf-by-leaf: wash thoroughly. Chop it into small pieces.
3. Bring a pot of water to a boil and drop in the corn kernels; boil until they are done, then scoop them out and let them cool off.
4. Finally, put all of the ingredients on a plate and serve.
If you decide to blend these ingredients in a blender, you can also add in a suitable amount of lemon juice, honey, white sesame seeds, B-complex brewer's yeast, lecithin and pine nuts (or cashews), as well as synthetic vegetable enzymes, whole-grain flour, source calcium (made of kelp powder), plant seed fiber, and so on. With these additions, the effects will be even better.

◆Sesame Sweet Potato Balls
Ingredients:Black sesame 3 tbsp. Sweet potatoes 60 g.
Preparation:
1. Pour roasted black sesame seeds onto a plate, ready for use.
2. Put the sweet potatoes in a rice cooker and steam until totally tender and done.
3. Remove the sweet potatoes from the rice cooker, then place in a large bowl and allow them to cool. Once they have cooled off, use a large soup spoon to mash them into a paste.
4. Wash your hands, and then take up a suitable amount of mashed sweet potato: knead this into a ball in the palm of your hands.
5. Roll the sweet potato balls in the plate of sesame seeds: be sure that each ball is entirely covered with seeds. Serve.
If you have purchased raw sesame seeds, first pour them into a baking pan and roast them at a low temperature. They will now be ready to use.

◆Brown Rice and Job's Tears Medley
Ingredients:Job's tears 1 cup Brown rice 3 cups Filtered water 6 cups
Preparation:
1. Pour the Job's tears and brown rice into the inner pot of your rice cooker; pour in hot

water and let the grain soak for 30 minutes.

2. Place the inner pot in the rice cooker; pour 1 cup of water into the outer pot. Cook until the on-off button pops up, and then let it simmer for another 10 minutes. Serve.

DAY 2 Lunch
◆Three-Mushroom Soup with Bread
Ingredients:
Dried Chinese black mushrooms 5 stalks
Enoki mushrooms [Winter mushrooms, Flammulina velutipes (Fr.) Sing] 30 g.
Beech mushrooms [Hypsizygus marmoreus (Peck) Bigelow] 30 g.
Mixed-grain bread 2 slices
Healthy Anti-Carcinogenic Soup Stock or filtered water 250 cc.
Manioc starch 1 tsp.
White sesame seeds 1 tsp.
Ginger threads just a few
Preparation:
1. Soak the dried mushrooms until they are soft, and then chop them into thin strips. Set aside, ready to use.
2. Wash the enoki and beech mushrooms, and set them aside, too.
3. Drop the ginger threads into the soup stock and boil. Now, drop in the black, enoki and beech mushrooms.
4. Mix the manioc starch in water: blend evenly. When the soup stock has once again come to a boil, pour in the starch mixture and whisk it into a sticky paste.
5. Pour the thickened soup into a bowl - it's ready to go. Now, put the bread on top and sprinkle on the white sesame seeds. Serve.

◆Vegetable Sticks
Ingredients:Small cucumbers 1 cuke Carrots 80 g. Daikon turnips 50 g.
Plum juice 1 tbsp.
Preparation:
1. Wash the cucumber, carrots and daikon: chop into long slices.
2. Soak the daikon strips in plum juice for 10 minutes (this will lighten their astringent taste), and then stir in the other ingredients. Serve.
If you still find the daikon too pungent, you can soak it in water for 5 minutes to make its taste a bit more bland.

◆Cold Kelp Roots with Dressing
Ingredients:Kelp roots 50 g. Garlic 2 heads
Preparation:
1. Grind the garlic into a paste and set it aside.
2. Wash the kelp roots thoroughly, and then parboil in vigorously boiling water. Remove from the water, and let them dry. Now, stir the garlic paste into the kelp; mix evenly and serve.
For a change of flavor, you can add in some sesame seeds, sesame oil, ginger paste, lettuce fronds or miso.

Day 1 Dinner
◆Brown Rice with Soy Beans
Ingredients:Soy beans 1 cup Brown rice 3 cups
Preparation:
1. The night before you make this dish, soak the soy beans in filtered water, or else soak them in good water for 6 hours on the same day.
2. Soak the brown rice in water for 4 hours before cooking.
3. Drain the water from the rice and beans, and then pour them into the inner pot of a rice cooker. Pour in 6 cups of good water.
4. Place the inner pot in your rice cooker: in the outer pot, add 1 cup of water. Cook until the on-off button pops up, and then simmer for another 10 minutes. Serve.

◆Ashitaba Leaf and Bean Curd Soup
Ingredients:Ashitaba leaves (a plant belonging to the celery family) 50 g.
Silken tofu 1 piece Carrots 30 g. Bamboo salt a pinch
Healthy Anti-Carcinogenic Soup Stock, or filtered water 300 cc.
Preparation:
1. After washing the ashitaba leaves, chop them into approximately 5-cm.-long sections. Set these aside, ready to use.
2. Cut the soft tofu into approximately 3-cm.-long pieces; set aside.
3. Chop the carrots into thin slices and set these aside.
4. In a pot, bring the soup stock to a boil. Drop in the carrots and tofu; when the water returns to a boil, drop in the ashitaba leaves and bamboo salt. Wait until the mixture returns to a boil, and then turn off the heat.

◆Laver and Bitter Melon Rolls
Ingredients:Bitter melon 100 g. Western cabbage 30 g. Nori strips 2 strips
Preparation:
1. Cut open the bitter melon and wash it. Chop it into thin sections, and then parboil for 1 minute. Now, let it soak in plum juice for 30 minutes to alleviate its acidity.

2. Wash the cabbage, and then chop it into fine strips. Set it aside.
3. Spread the nori sheets out on a table-top: drop on the shredded cabbage and bitter melon slices. With your hands, roll everything up together. Serve.

DAY 2 Breakfast
◆Vegetable Juice
Ingredients:Apples 200 g. Baby cucumbers 60 g. Carrots 50 g. Filtered water 300 cc.
Preparation:
1. Chop the apples, cucumbers and carrots into small pieces, and then drop everything into a juice blender.
2. Add the water to the juice blender: blend until smooth. Serve.
1. For a taste change, you can also add in a suitable amount of lemon juice, honey, black or white sesame seeds, B-complex brewer's yeast, lecithin, pine nuts (or cashews), as well as synthetic plant enzymes, whole-grain flour, source calcium, plant seed fiber, and so on.
2. One half hour after drinking this fruit and vegetable juice, have a bowl of sweet potato rice. Especially for those with gastric problems and poor digestion, symptoms of flatulence may be felt if the two dishes are eaten in close succession.

◆Brown Rice, Sweet Potato and Wolfberry Balls
Ingredients:Sweet potatoes 60 g. Wolfberries 2 tbsp. Brown rice 2 cups
Preparation:
1. Put the brown rice into the inner pot of your rice cooker, wash it in clear water, and then add 3 cups of good water.
2. Wash the sweet potato until its outer peel is clean, and then chop it into small chunks (about 1 cm.); stir this into the brown rice.
3. After putting the inner pot into the rice cooker, pour 1/2 cup of water into the outer pot; boil for about 20 minutes, until fully cooked.
4. When it has cooled off a bit, blend the wolfberries evenly into the rice mixture with a rice ladle. Scoop out a suitable amount of this mixture and form it into rice balls - you will need to use a bit of pressure to squeeze it into the desired shape. It is now ready to serve.

Day 2 Lunch
◆Baked Purple Rice Rolls
Ingredients:Purple rice 2 cups Wolfberries 2 tbsp.
Preparation:
1. Put the purple rice and wolfberries into the inside pot of a rice cooker. Wash in clear water, and then add 3 cups of good water.
2. Put the inner pot into the rice cooker: cook for 20 minutes, until the rice is done.
3. Wait until the rice has cooled off a bit, and then scoop out a suitable amount with a rice ladle. Use either your hands or a rice-ball mold to knead the rice into triangular rolls.
4. Drop the rice rolls into a frying pan and cook over low heat until the rolls have become slightly hard on the outside.
5. Flip the rice balls over and cook until the surface has become slightly dry and hard on both sides. Serve.

◆Chinese Yam and Kelp Soup
Ingredients:Chinese yam 30 g. Kelp 30 3. Scallion 1 stalk
Healthy Anti-carcinogenic Soup Stock, or good water 250 cc.
Ginger threads 10 g. Bamboo salt a pinch
Preparation:
1. Chop the Chinese yam into long slices and soak the kelp. Set aside, ready to use.
2. Wash the scallions, and then mince finely. Set these aside.
3. Pour the soup stock into a pot; add the kelp and ginger threads, and then bring the ingredients to a vigorous boil. Drop in the Chinese yam and bamboo salt: let the water return to a boil, then turn off the heat.
4. Remove from the pot and pour into a bowl. Sprinkle on the minced scallion and serve.

◆Three-Color Salad
Ingredients:Pumpkin 60 g. Cauliflower 60 g. Garden pea kernels 1 tbsp.
Miso 1 tsp. Sesame sauce 1 tsp.
Preparation:
1. Chop the pumpkin into approximately 5-cm.-long chunks.
2. Wash the cauliflower thoroughly, and then cut into short florets. Set aside, ready to go.
3. Bring a pot of water to a rolling boil. Drop in the pumpkin and cauliflower; boil until they are done. Now, add the peas and boil for another minute. Ladle out of the pot and let the mixture cool.
4. Put all of the ingredients into a bowl: stir in the miso and sesame sauce. Serve.

Day 2 Dinner
◆Millet Pancakes
Ingredients:Millet 1 tbsp. Corn kernels 50 g. Whole-wheat flour 150 g.
Good water 50 cc.
Preparation:
1. Pre-soak the millet in good water for 30 minutes, or soak in hot water for 10 minutes.
2. Either mince or grind up the corn kernels, and then mix it in with the millet, flour and

good water. Knead this into dough.

3. Knead the dough into a ball, and then flatten it out with a rolling pin to form a thin piece of dough.

4. Over low heat, preheat a frying pan, and then lay the pancake dough out along the bottom of the pan. Cook until the surface has turned a golden-brown color. Serve right away.

◆Chinese Mushroom Shish Kebab

Ingredients:
Fresh black Chinese mushrooms 7 stalks
Garlic 2 heads
Mashed ginger 1/2 tsp.
Soy sauce 1/2 tsp.
Preparation:
1. Wash the black mushrooms thoroughly, and then remove their lower stems. Skewer them one-by-one through the center on bamboo skewers.
2. Put the shish kebab into the oven and cook at 250o F. for about 5 minutes.
3. Remove the outer skin of the garlic heads, and then grind them into a paste in a grinder. Now, blend this in with the ginger paste and soy sauce to make a sauce.
4. Take the shish-kebab out of the oven. Baste with sauce before serving.

◆High-Fiber Assorted Veggie Salad

Ingredients:
Shredded kelp 50 g.
Tiny bamboo shoots 50 g.
Corn kernels 1 tbsp.
Black vinegar 1 tsp.
Soy sauce 1 tsp.
Sesame oil 1/2 tsp.
Preparation:
1. Blend together the black vinegar, soy sauce and sesame oil to make a sauce.
2. Bring a pot of water to a rolling boil. Individually, drop in the shredded kelp, bamboo shoots and corn kernels: boil each ingredient separately until it is done.
3. Ladle the ingredients from the pot and let them cool. Put in a bowl; finally, scatter on the corn kernels as a garnish, and sprinkle on some sauce. Serve.

◆Russian Soup

Ingredients:
Western cabbage 50 g.
Stringbeans 10 pods
Large tomatoes 80 g.
Western onions 50 g.
Carrots 30 g.
Healthy Anti-Carcinogenic Soup Base, or filtered water 1,000 cc.
Bamboo salt according to taste
Preparation:
1. Pluck the leaves one-by-one from the cabbage and wash them. Wash the stringbeans, and then cut them into halves.
2. After washing the tomatoes, slice them into 4 sections: set aside for later use. Chop the onions and carrots into about 1-cm.-long cubes.
3. Pour the soup stock into a pot and bring it to a boil; add in the tomato and boil. Now, put in the carrots and onions and boil everything for another 15 minutes.
4. Put the cabbage and string beans into the pot and boil for about 15 minutes. Finally, add the bamboo salt and serve.

Day 3 Breakfast

◆Bananas

Ingredients:
Banana 1 piece of fruit
Preparation:
1. Remove the banana skin and eat the fruit as is.
1. To enhance the flavor, you can add a pinch of cinnamon to your banana.
2. Bananas are best eaten when small black dots have appeared on the peel.

◆Sweet Potato Pancakes

Ingredients:
Sweet potatoes 60 g.
Sweet potato flour 150 g.
Bamboo salt 1/2 tsp.
reparation:
1. After washing the sweet potato skins thoroughly, steam the potatoes in a rice cooker until soft and well-done.
2. Remove the sweet potatoes from the rice cooker and place them in a large bowl. After peeling them, use a large soup spoon to mash them into a paste.

3. Add the sweet potato flour and bamboo salt to the bowl: blend evenly to form dough.
4. Now, separate the dough into parts: knead into round balls of about 5 cm. in diameter. Use a rolling pin to flatten the dough into pancake shapes.
5. Over low heat, preheat a non-stick frying pan. Place the pancakes in the pan and cook them until the surface has turned golden-brown. Remove from the pan and serve.

◆Brown Rice and Vegetable Congee

Ingredients:Brown rice 1/2 cup Tomatoes 60 g. Small cucumbers 50 g.
Healthy Anti-Carcinogenic Soup Base, or filtered water 500 cc.
Preparation:
1. After washing the tomatoes and cucumbers, chop them into approximately 1-cm.-long cubes.
2. Put the soup stock and brown rice in a pot, cook until the rice is soft and done, and then turn off the heat.
3. Pour the tomato and cucumber cubes into the pot: stir them evenly into the rice congee. Serve.
You may also add some nuts or walnuts (about 5), or else boil 50 g. of potato cubes along with the brown rice.

Day 3 Lunch

◆Mixed-Grain Steamed Buns

Ingredients:Pine Nuts 1 tbsp. Black sesame seeds 1 tbsp. Wolfberries 1 tbsp.
Millet 1 tbsp. Whole-wheat flour 150 g. All-purpose flour 150 g. Yeast 4 g.
Brown sugar 1/2 tsp. Baking powder 3 g. Filtered water 150 cc.
Preparation:
1. Put the whole-wheat flour, all-purpose flour, and baking powder in a bowl. Slowly, stir in yeast mixed with good water: knead the mixture into dough as you are adding in the yeast.
2. Soak the millet in hot water for 10 minutes, and then pour it into the large bowl along with the pine nuts, black sesame seeds, wolfberries and brown sugar. Mix these ingredients evenly into the dough.
3. Place the dough in a dark, cool spot and let it rise for 20 minutes.
4. Form the dough into round balls; steam these in a rice cooker for 30 minutes. Serve.

◆Mixed Veggies

Ingredients:
Water bamboo [Zizania latifolia Turcz] 1 bunch
Enoki mushrooms (Winter mushrooms) 20 g.
Wood ear mushrooms [Auricularia auricular judae] 20 g.
Hot pepper 1 pod Cilantro 1 stalk Black vinegar 1 tsp. Soy sauce 1 tsp.
Preparation:
1. Wash and parboil the water bamboo and wood ear mushrooms, and then chop them into thin slivers along with the hot peppers. Set aside, ready to use.
2. After washing the cilantro, chop it into about 1-cm.-long sections.
3. Bring a pot of water to a rolling boil: drop in the enoki mushrooms and parboil until they are soft and done. Ladle them out of the pot and set them aside.
4. Take a large bowl: pour in all of the ingredients and mix evenly. Serve.

◆Soya Sprout Soup

Ingredients:Soya sprouts 50 g. Green garlic 1 head
Healthy Anti-Carcinogenic Soup Stock, or good water 1,000 cc. Bamboo salt a pinch
Preparation:
1. After washing the green garlic thoroughly, dice it finely.
2. Wash the soya sprouts, and then drop them into a pot of boiling soup stock; boil for about 15 minutes until done, then turn off the heat.
3. Remove the soup from the pot and pour it into a bowl. Garnish with minced garlic and bamboo salt. Serve.

Day 3 Dinner

◆Black-and-White Rice

Ingredients:Job's tears 1 cup Gingko 9 nuts Purple rice 1 cup Brown rice 1 cup
Preparation:
1. Soak the Job's tears in good water for 2 hours, soak the brown rice in good water for 4 hours, and soak the gingko in hot water until they are slightly softened.
2. Put all of the ingredients into the inner pot of your rice cooker and add 5 cups of good water.
3. Place the inner pot inside the rice cooker. Into the outer pot, add half a cup of water: cook for about 20 minutes. Serve.

◆Tomato and Nori Salad

Ingredients:Large tomatoes 200 g. Nori 2 sheets Pine nuts 1 tbsp.
Preparation:
1. After washing the tomatoes, cut them into 4 sections and put them on a plate.
2. With a scissor, cut the nori into thin strips. Sprinkle these on the tomato sections.
3. Finally, garnish the tomatoes with pine nuts and serve.

If you feel that the results are too bland, you can add some plums as a garnish.

◆Plain and Simple Vegetable Soup

Ingredients:Baby corn 4 ears Stringbeans 5 pods Carrots 30 g.
Healthy Anti-Carcinogenic Soup Base 250 cc.

Preparation:

1. Wash the baby corn and stringbeans, chop them into halves and set them aside.
2. After washing the carrots, cut them into thin slices; set aside.
3. Bring the soup stock to a boil in a pot. First, drop in the carrots and cook them until they are slightly softened; now, drop in the corn and stringbeans.
4. Bring the pot to a boil once again, and then add some bamboo salt before removing it from the pot. Serve.

Day 4 Breakfast

◆Healthy Vegetable Juice

Ingredients:Grapes 60 g. Western celery 60 g. Chinese yam 40 g. Filtered water 300 cc.

Preparation:

1. Wash the ingredients in good water: if you additionally use a vegetable detoxifier to purify them, that's even better.
2. Chop the ingredients into small chunks, and drop them into a juice blender along with some filtered water. Blend them well.

You can also add some lemon juice, honey, black or white sesame seeds, B-complex brewer's yeast, lecithin, pine nuts (or cashews), as well as synthetic plant enzymes, whole-grain flour, source calcium, plant seed fiber, and so on. Season to taste.

◆Sweet Potato and Veggie Salad

Ingredients:Sweet potatoes 100 g. Walnuts 1 tbsp. Sweet red pepper 20 g.
Western celery 30 g.

Preparation:

1. Cut the sweet potato into 3-cm.-long chunks; chop the sweet red pepper into thin slivers.
2. Bring a pot of water to a boil, and then drop in the sweet potato chunks and boil until well-done and soft. Ladle them from the pot and set aside.
3. After washing the celery, chop the middle part into about 20-cm. sections. Now, chop them into 3-cm.-long pieces.
4. Spread the sweet potato chunks, sweet red pepper, walnuts and celery out along the bottom of a platter. Sprinkle on some plum juice and serve.

◆Brown Rice

Ingredients:Brown rice 2 cups
Healthy Anti-Carcinogenic Soup Stock 2 cups

Preparation:

1. Soak the brown rice in good water for 4 hours; strain the water from the rice.
2. Put the brown rice and soup stock into the inner pot of a rice cooker. Place this pot in the rice cooker, then add 1/2 cup of good water to the outer pot and cook for about 20 minutes. Serve.

Day 4 Lunch

◆Nutritious Veggie-Covered Rice

Ingredients:Western celery 1 stalk Western mushrooms 3 stalks Corn kernels 1 tbsp.
Pumpkin 50 g. Brown rice 1 cup Healthy Anti-Carcinogenic Soup Stock 2 cups
Bamboo salt a pinch

Preparation:

1. Put the brown rice into the inner pot of a rice cooker: rinse it off a bit in clear water, and then pour in 11/2 cups of good water.
2. Place the inner pot in the rice cooker, and add 1/2 cup of good water to the outer pot. Cook for around 20 minutes; pour it into a bowl and set it aside, ready to use.
3. Wash the celery and chop it into 3-cm.-long sections. Set it aside.
4. After washing the mushrooms, cut them in half. Chop the pumpkin into approximately 3-cm.-long chunks.
5. Heat up a frying pan, and then pour in the soup stock, celery, mushrooms, corn kernels, pumpkin and bamboo salt.
6. Wait until all of the ingredients are soft and done: remove from the pot and scatter over the rice. Serve.

◆Chinese Long Bean Veggie Rolls

Ingredients:Chinese long beans 50 g. Lettuce 30 g. Sesame sauce according to taste

Preparation:

1. Chop the long beans into about 10-cm.-long sections. Bring a pot of water to a rolling boil; drop in the long beans and boil until done. Set aside.
2. Spread out the lettuce leaves: drop 3 pieces of long bean and a bit of sesame sauce onto each leaf, and then roll up the lettuce leaves to form veggie rolls.
3. Continue according to step #2 and finish rolling up all of the ingredients. Serve.

◆Chinese Mushroom and Kelp Soup

Ingredients:Dried Chinese black mushrooms 30 g. Kelp sprouts 30 g.
Healthy Anti-Carcinogenic Soup Stock 500 cc. Shredded ginger 10 g.Bamboo salt a pinch

Preparation:

1. Soak the mushrooms in water until they are soft; set them aside.
2. the soup base in a pot. Add in the Chinese mushrooms, kelp sprouts, shredded ginger and bamboo salt: boil for about 10 minutes, then turn off the heat and remove them from the pot.

Day 4 Dinner

◆Millet Rice Dish

Ingredients:Millet 1 cup Brown rice 1 cup

Preparation:

1. Pour the brown rice and millet into the inner pot of a rice cooker and rinse them off a bit. Now, pour in 3 cups of water.
2. Replace the inner pot in the rice cooker, and add one half cup of water to the outer pot. Cook for about 20 minutes. Serve.

◆Salad

Ingredients:Shredded kelp 30 g. Large cucumber 60 g. Western onions 30 g.
Hot red peppers one half Sesame oil 1/2 tsp. Black vinegar 1 tsp. Soy sauce 1 tsp.

Preparation:

1. Wash the cucumber, onions and pepper; slice them into thin slivers. Set aside.
2. Parboil the shredded kelp in hot water, then let it drip-dry.
3. Place all of the ingredients into a large bowl, mix evenly and serve.

◆Bean Curd and Mustard Greens Soup

Ingredients:Tofu 1 cake Mustard greens 50 g. Carrots 30 g.
Healthy Anti-Carcinogenic Soup Stock 250 cc. Bamboo salt a pinch

Preparation:

1. Wash the mustard greens, and then slice them into approximately 3-cm. pieces. Set them aside.
2. Chop the tofu into small chunks; shred the carrots. Set aside.
3. Bring a small pot of soup stock to a boil. Toss in the carrots and cook until they are soft. Successively drop in the tofu and mustard greens.
4. Once the pot has returned to a boil, add in the salt. Now, turn off the heat.

Day 5 Breakfast

◆Vegetable Juice

Ingredients:Red grapes 15 fruits Western celery 30 g. Carrots 50 g. Good water 200 cc.

Preparation:

1. Wash the celery and carrots, and then chop them into small pieces.
2. Place all of the ingredients in a juice blender, and blend until smooth and even. Serve.

The body is unable to absorb plant fiber, so you can strain this out of the fruit and veggie juice, or else squeeze the juice from these ingredients and drink.

◆Sweet Potato and Jujube Brown Rice Rolls

Ingredients:Sweet potatoes 60 g. Red jujubes 2 tbsp. Brown rice 1 cup

Preparation:

1. Wash the sweet potatoes, chop them into 1-cm.-long chunks, and then set them aside.
2. Put the brown rice and jujubes into the inner pot of a rice cooker; after rinsing them in clear water, add in the sweet potato and 2 cups of good water.
3. Put the inner pot into the rice cooker and steam for 45 minutes. Remove from the cooker and let it cool.
4. Scoop out a suitable amount of rice with a rice ladle: in your hands, knead this into bite-sized rice balls.
5. Each person can eat a different quantity of rice balls, so make enough to satisfy everyone.

Day 5 Lunch

◆Noodles in Cool Broth

Ingredients:
Ashitaba noodles 80 g.
Kelp sprouts 30 g.
White sesame seeds 1 tbsp.
Healthy Anti-Carcinogenic Soup Stock 300 cc.
Miso 1 tsp.

Preparation:

1. Pour the soup stock into a bowl.
2. Bring a pot of water to a rolling boil, and then drop the ashitaba noodles evenly into the water. Cook at a low boil for 6 minutes, then drop in the kelp sprouts.
3. After the water returns to a boil, turn off the heat. Ladle the noodles and kelp out of the pot and put them in the bowl. Add miso and scatter on some sesame seeds. Serve.

◆Garlic Paste and Boiled Amaranth

Ingredients:
Amaranth 50 g.
Garlic 2 heads
Sesame oil 1/2 tsp.
Bamboo salt a pinch

Mashed ginger 10 g.

Preparation:

1. Wash the amaranth, drop into a pot of boiling water and parboil.
2. Ladle out the amaranth and let it dry, then chop it into sections of about 7 cm.
3. Peel the garlic, and then dice it into small cubes. Mix this evenly with the sesame oil, bamboo salt and mashed ginger. Serve.

◆Spiced Greens

Ingredients:

Winter savory [Satureja montana] 30 g.

Young soybeans 30 g.

Hot red pepper 1 pod

Cold-pressed olive oil 5 drops

Preparation:

1. Wash the winter savory and chop it into 1-cm.-long pieces. Set it aside, ready to use.
2. Bring a pot of water to a rolling boil: drop in the young soybeans, and then add the winter savory and boil for 1 minute. Ladle this out and let it dry.
3. Chop up the pepper into small cubes. Mix it with the winter savory, soybeans and olive oil: serve.

Day 5 Dinner

◆Purple Rice Rolls

Purple rice 2 cups

Zongzi wrappers (Reed or bamboo leaves used as wrappers for triangular rice dumplings) 2 sheets

Preparation:

1. Wash the zongzi wrappers and clip each one into several 10-cm.-long strips.
2. In the inner pot of a rice cooker wash the purple rice, and then add 3 cups of good water. Steam until it is done.
3. When the rice has cooled off a bit, scoop out a suitable amount with a rice ladle and put it on a zongzi leaf. Roll the wrapper around the rice to form a triangular rice roll.
4. Make as many rice rolls as your family requires.

◆Cold Daikon Slivers with Sauce

Ingredients:

White turnip (daikon) 50 g.

Orange 1 fruit

Preparation:

1. Put the orange into a vegetable peeler and remove its peel. Set it aside.
2. Slice the peeled orange into sections, then squeeze out the juice.
3. Wash the daikon, and then chop it into slivers.
4. Put the daikon, orange peel and orange juice into a large bowl. Mix evenly and serve.

◆Braised Assorted Veggies

Ingredients:Cassava starch 10 g. Ginger 20 g.

Healthy Anti-Carcinogenic Soup Stock, or good water 80 cc. Kelp roots 30 g.

Sweet yellow pepper one half Sweet red pepper one half

Preparation:

1. Wash the sweet red and yellow pepper, and then chop into small slivers. Set them aside.
2. Mash the ginger into a paste with a ginger grinder. Set it aside.
3. Bring the soup stock to a boil. First, drop in the kelp roots and bring again to a boil; before removing this from the pot, add in the sweet pepper. Finally, add water to the cassava starch and whisk it into the mixture. Serve.

◆Tomato and Corn Soup

Ingredients:Large tomato 1 fruit Corn 1 ear Green soya kernels 1 tbsp.

Healthy Anti-Carcinogenic Soup Stock 1,000 cc.

Preparation:

1. Wash the tomato, and then slice it into thin sections.
2. Shuck the ear of corn: chop the ear into slices.
3. Bring a pot of soup stock to a boil. Drop in the tomato and corn; when the soup has returned to a boil, drop in the green soya kernels. Turn off the stove.
When you shuck the corn, do not throw away the corn silk - boil this along with the other ingredients.

Day 6 Breakfast

◆Nutritious Veggie Juice

Ingredients:Carrots 60 g. Western celery 60 g. Apples 100 g. Good water 200 cc.

Preparation:

1. Wash all of the ingredients in good water: if you purify the apples in a fruit and vegetable detoxifier, that's even better.
2. Chop the ingredients into small chunks. Drop these into a juice blender along with some good water and blend into fruit juice.
You can also add in a suitable amount of lemon juice, honey, black or white sesame seeds, B-complex brewer's yeast, lecithin, pine nuts (or cashews), as well as synthetic plant enzymes, whole-grain flour, source calcium, plant seed fiber, and so on.

◆Thick Sweet Potato Soup

Ingredients:Bamboo salt a pinch Ginger 3 slices

Sweet potatoes 2 spuds Healthy Anti-Carcinogenic Soup Stock, or good water 500 cc.

Preparation:

1. Chop one sweet potato into chunks; along with 500 cc. of soup stock, put it into a juice blender and blend until smooth.
2. Wash the other sweet potato and chop it into thin slivers. Set it aside.
3. Put the soup stock and sweet potato water into a pot and boil: add in the shredded sweet potato, bamboo salt and ginger. Boil over low heat for about 10 minutes. Serve.

◆Veggie and Rice Sandwich

Ingredients:Roundhead lettuce (iceberg) 50 g. Tomato 1 fruit Brown rice 2 cups

Preparation:

1. Put the brown rice in a rice cooker. Into the inner pot pour 3 cups of good water; in the outer pot, add 1 cup of good water. Boil until the on-off button pops up.
2. Slice the tomato and shred the lettuce. Set them aside.
3. Preheat a frying pan at a low heat setting. With a rice ladle, scoop out a suitable amount of cooked brown rice, separate it into 2 parts, and cook each separately.
4. Place one sheet of rice onto a platter. Take 2 tomato slices along with enough lettuce, and put these on top of the rice. Do likewise to the other sheet of cooked rice. Serve.

Day 6 Lunch

◆Health-Food Noodles with Dry Dressing

Ingredients:Black sesame seeds 1 tsp. Miso 1 tsp. Spaghetti squash 1 gourd

Health-boosting noodles 80 g.(These noodles are made with chrysanthemum flour and other health-promoting ingredients: see Dr. Luke's website)

Preparation:

1. Drop the noodles evenly into a pot of water that has been preheated to a rolling boil. After cooking over slow heat for 6 minutes, ladle them out. Set aside.
2. Remove the skin from the spaghetti squash and then chop it into small chunks. Put this in a pot of boiling water, cook until done, and then ladle from the pot.
3. In a large bowl, pour the noodles, squash, black sesame seeds and miso. Mix evenly and serve.

◆Salad

Ingredients:Pineapple 50 g. Garden pea pods 30 g. Cilantro 1 stalk

Hot red pepper 1 pod Plum juice 1 tsp. Plum vinegar 1 tsp.

Preparation:

1. Remove the pineapple skin and wash the hot pepper: chop them into approximately 1-cm.-long chunks. Set them aside.
2. Wash the pea pods and parboil them in water that has been heated to a rolling boil. Ladle them from the pot and let them dry; chop them into small sections and set them aside.
3. After washing the cilantro, chop it into small pieces. Set it aside.
4. Put all of the ingredients in a large bowl: mix well and serve.

◆Okra Soup

Ingredients:Okra 50 g. Kelp braids 30 g. Carrots 30 g. Bamboo salt a pinch

Healthy Anti-Carcinogenic Soup Stock, or good water 500 cc.

Preparation:

1. Wash the okra, and then slice slant-wise in half. Set aside.
2. Wash the carrots, slice them thinly, and set them aside.
3. In a pot, bring the soup stock to a boil. Drop in the kelp braids and carrots and bring to a boil again. Before removing from the pot, drop in the okra and bamboo salt. Turn off the heat.

Day 6 Dinner

◆Brown Rice Cake

Ingredients:Purple rice 1 cup Pine nuts 1/2 cup Raw peanuts 1/2 cup

White sticky rice 1/2 cup Cold-pressed olive oil 1 tsp. Bamboo salt a pinch

Preparation:

1. Wash the purple rice and sticky rice; soak them in good water for 1 hour.
2.Evenly mix in the pine nuts and peanuts, adding 2 cups of good water. Separately, pour into small bowls.
3. Put the small bowls into a rice cooker: in the outer pot, add 1 cup of good water. Steam until the button pops up.
4. Take out the already prepared rice cake and sprinkle on the olive oil and bamboo salt: mix evenly, form into a ball and serve.

◆Vegetables Braised in Good Water

Ingredients:Cabbage sprouts 50 g. Cauliflower 100 g. Cold-pressed olive oil 1 tbsp.

Bamboo salt a pinch

Preparation:

1. Wash the cabbage sprouts and cauliflower, and then chop into small pieces.
2. Preheat a non-stick frying pan over medium heat: add the cauliflower along with 1/2 cup

of water.

3. Now, drop in the cabbage sprouts, cover the pot and stew for about 3 minutes; turn off the heat. Before removing from the pot, mix in the olive oil and bamboo salt. Serve.

◆Two-Color Root Vegetable Soup

Ingredients:Carrots 50 g. Daikon turnip 50 g. Asparagus 50 g. Miso 2 tsp.
Healthy Anti-Carcinogenic Soup Stock, or good water 1,000 cc.
Preparation:

1. Chop the carrots and daikon into slices, and cut the asparagus into small pieces. Set them aside.
2. Bring a pot of soup base to a boil; now, drop in the carrots and daikon.
3. Wait until the mixture boils again, and then add the asparagus and miso. Stir everything together evenly, and then turn off the heat.

Day 7 Breakfast

◆Veggie Salad

Ingredients:Lettuce 120 g. Sweet red pepper 50 g. Corn kernels 50 g.
Preparation:

1. Pull the lettuce apart leaf-by-leaf and wash thoroughly. Now, tear the leaves into small strips and place them on a plate.
2. Wash the sweet red pepper, and then chop it into thin slivers: place it on the plate.
3. Parboil the corn kernels: scatter them on top of the other ingredients. Serve.

◆Avocado and Sweet Potato Soup

Ingredients:Raw avocado 60 g. Sweet potato 60 g. Bamboo salt a pinch
Healthy Anti-Carcinogenic Soup Stock, or good water 300 cc.
Ingredients:

1. Chop the raw avocado and sweet potato into small cubes. Set them aside.
2. Bring the soup stock to a boil in a pot, and then drop in the avocado and sweet potato. Once the pot boils again, add in the bamboo salt. Now you can turn off the heat.

If you have bought ripe avocados, you don't have to boil them; add them to the mixture just before removing it from the pot. Serve.

◆Healthy Steamed Buns

Ingredients:Cashews 1 cup Raisins 1/2 cup All-purpose flour 200 g.
Whole-wheat flour 100 g. Yeast powder 5 g. Baking powder 3 g. Good water 180 cc.
Preparation:

1. Crush the cashews into small, thin bits.
2. In a large mixing bowl, put the whole-wheat flour, all-purpose flour, baking powder and yeast. Add good water, and then mix the ingredients and knead them.
3. Drop the cashews and raisins into the mixing bowl: knead evenly to form dough.
4. Cover the bowl with a damp piece of cloth: set it aside for approximately 20 minutes, until the dough rises.
5. Knead the dough again, then form it into a long, narrow loaf. Cut into small sections; place this in a rice cooker and steam for about 15 minutes. Serve.

Day 7 Lunch

◆Job's Tears Rice Cooked in Healthy Soup Stock

Ingredients:Lettuce 30 g. Chinese black mushrooms 5 stalks Nori 2 sheets
Job's tears 1/2 cup Brown rice 1 cup
Healthy Anti-Carcinogenic Soup Stock, or good water 2,000 cc.
Preparation:

1. Wash the lettuce, chop it into thin strips: set it aside. Shred the nori sheets and set them aside.
2. Wash the black mushrooms and soak them until they have softened; mince finely.
3. In a pot, pour the soup stock, mushrooms, Job's tears and brown rice. Cook over high heat until the mixture comes to a boil, and then turn the heat to low and simmer for 40 minutes.
4. After removing the mixture from the pot and ladling it into bowls, garnish with lettuce and nori. Serve.

◆Cold Coral Greens with Sauce

Ingredients:Coral grass [Glehnia ittoralis Fr. Schmidt et Miq.] 10 g.
Soy beans 1 tbsp. Mint 2 leaves Good water 200 cc. Miso just a dab
Preparation:

1. First, soak the coral grass in warm water until it softens, and then chop it into strips. Set aside.
2. Wash the mint leaves, mince them, and set them aside.
3. Presoak the soy beans in good water for 4 hours. After boiling them over high heat, scoop out the bean skins that have floated to the surface. Now, cook over medium heat until soft: mash them into a paste.
4. Mix the coral grass, soya paste and mint together evenly. Serve.

◆Bitter Gourd and Pineapple Soup

Ingredients:Bitter gourd (balsam pear) 50 g.

Pineapple 50 g. Healthy Anti-Carcinogenic Soup Stock, or good water 250 cc.
Preparation:

1. Remove the pineapple skin, and chop the fruit into slivers along with the bitter gourd. Chop the pineapple skin into large pieces. Set aside.
2. Boil the soup stock in a pot. First, add in the pineapple skin and boil for 10 minutes; afterwards, drop in the bitter gourd and pineapple and bring the mixture to a boil again. Now you can turn off the heat.
3. Remove the pineapple skin: ladle the remaining mixture into bowls and serve.

Day 7 Dinner

◆Potato Pizza

Ingredients:Green pepper 30 g. Egyptian beans (a type of fava bean) 1 tbsp.
Cherry tomatoes 50 g. Potatoes 250 g. Cassava starch 1 tbsp.
Preparation:

1. Boil the Egyptian beans in rapidly rolling water, and then let them dry. Set aside.
2. Bring a pot of water to a boiling boil: drop in the potatoes and boil until they are thoroughly done. Ladle them out and chill.
3. Mash the potatoes with a large soup spoon; after mixing in the cassava starch, use a rolling pin to flatten the mixture out into round, thin pizza dough.
4. With a fork, prick the dough lightly: cover the entire round with fork-marks.
5. Cut the tomatoes into sections, chop the peppers into small cubes, and mix these with the Egyptian beans. Cover the dough with this mixture.
6. Place the dough in the oven and bake at 450o F. for 15 minutes. When the surface has turned golden-brown, it is ready to serve.

◆Raw Veggie Rolls

Ingredients:White-fleshed Chinese yam 50 g. Lettuce 50 g. Plum juice 1 tsp.
Plum vinegar 1 tsp.
Preparation:

1. Peel the Chinese yam, slice it into fine slivers, and then soak it in good water for 10 minutes. Now, add the plum juice and plum vinegar: let this soak for an hour in order to lessen the astringency.
2. Wash the lettuce leaf-by-leaf. Set aside.
3. Place one lettuce leaf on the counter-top, and then put 2 Chinese yam strips in the middle. Cover this with another lettuce leaf: roll this up.
4. Continue making veggie rolls until all of the ingredients have been used. Serve.

◆Vegetable Soup

Ingredients:Purple cabbage 50 g. Western mushrooms 5 stalks Rosemary a pinch
Celery 30 g. Healthy Anti-Carcinogenic Soup Stock, or good water 500 cc.
Bamboo salt a pinch
Preparation:

1. Wash the red cabbage and celery, chop them and set them aside.
2. Wash the mushrooms and chop them into halves. Set aside.
3. Bring a pot of soup stock to a boil; add in the cabbage, celery and mushrooms. Once the mixture has returned to a boil, turn off the heat.
4. Before removing from the pot, add in the rosemary and salt while everything is still hot. Serve.

Day 8 Breakfast

◆Plum-Flavored Tomatoes

Ingredients:Tomatoes 50 g.
Preparation:

Wash the tomatoes: after they have dried, add in the plums. Mix, put into a bowl, and serve.

◆Sweet Potato and Ginger Soup

Ingredients:Sweet potatoes 120 g. Tender ginger 30 g. Good water 500 cc.
Cinnamon powder 1 tsp.
Preparation:

1. Chop the sweet potato into chunks and mince the ginger. Set aside.
2. Bring a pot of good water to a boil: drop in the sweet potato and ginger and cook until the mixture returns to a boil. Remove from the pot, sprinkle on the cinnamon and serve.

◆Vegetable and Brown Rice Sushi Rolls

Ingredients:Small cucumbers 60 g. Burdock root 50 g. Millet 1/2 cup
Plum juice 2 tbsp. Cooked brown rice 1 cup Nori sushi wrapper 1 sheet
Preparation:

1. Cut the cucumbers lengthwise into strips, roll the strips in a bit of bamboo salt, and then wash off the salt in good water.
2. Brush the burdock roots to remove dirt adhering to the surface. Slice into fine sections with a thin knife, and them put the burdock into the salty rinse water from step #1 and parboil for 1 minute. Ladle from the pot, and let it soak in the plum juice for 30 minutes to

lessen the astringency.

3. Take the nori sheet and spread it out on a bamboo sushi-rolling mat. With a rice ladle, scoop up some brown rice and lay it out evenly atop the nori.
4. Take 2 strips of cucumber and 2 pieces of burdock root. Lay these out over the nori and rice: space them so that they are located at 2/5, 4/5 and 5/5 intervals across the nori base.
5. Very slowly, roll up the bamboo mat, rolling up the nori sheet with its contents.

Burdock root contains a lot of fiber, and it is difficult to digest for those who suffer from intestinal disorders. If this is the case, the root can be chopped in a juice blender or boiled before eating. You can also boil it without removing the skin - by drinking the broth, your body can absorb its mineral contents.

Day 8 Lunch
◆Oat and Mung Bean Cake
Ingredients:Oat flour 1 cup Mung bean kernels 1/2 cup Pumpkin seeds 1 tbsp. Sunflower seeds 1 tbsp. High-gluten flour 1/2 cup All-purpose flour 1 cup Good water 200 cc.
Preparation:
1. Put the mung beans and some good water together in a juice blender and mix until smooth.
2. Mix together the whole-wheat flour, oat flour, pumpkin seeds and sunflower seeds. Slowly add in the mung bean and water mixture: mix into dough.
3. Knead the dough into a round cake with a diameter of about 5 cm.; place this in a pan, and then put it in a rice cooker. With 1 cup of good water, steam the dough until the on-off switch pops up. Serve.
◆Cold Shredded Burdock Root with Sauce
Ingredients:Burdock root 50 g. White sesame seeds 1 tbsp.
Preparation:
1. Shred the burdock root and let it steep in hot water.
2. Mix evenly with sesame seeds and serve.
◆Red and Green Salad
Ingredients:Large tomato 1 piece of fruit Bean sprouts 30 g. Peanut flour 1 tbsp. Plum juice 1 tsp.
Preparation:
1. Wash the bean sprouts and let them dry off: place in a bowl.
2. After washing the tomato, cut it into quarters and place it in the bowl.
3. Finally, scatter on the peanut flour and plum juice. Serve.
◆Fresh from the Ocean
Ingredients:Kelp 30 g. Daikon turnip 30 g. Bamboo shoots 30 g. Healthy Anti-Carcinogenic Soup Stock, or good water 500 cc. Sliced ginger 3 slices Bamboo salt a pinch
Preparation:
1. Soak the kelp until it softens, cut it into strips, and set it aside.
2. Wash the daikon and bamboo shoots, and then chop them into thin slices. Set aside.
3. Bring a pot of soup stock to a boil, and then drop in all of the ingredients. Over low heat, cook at a rolling boil for about 10 minutes. Turn off the heat and serve.

Day 8 Dinner
◆Raw Veggies with Mashed Potato and Corn
Ingredients:Soy beans 30 g. Corn 50 g. Potatoes 120 g. Lettuce 30 g. Miso 1 tsp. Black pepper powder 1/2 tsp.
Preparation:
1. Bring a pot of water to a rolling boil, and then drop in the potatoes and cook until they are well-done. Ladle them from the pot and allow them to cool off.
2. Put the soy beans and corn into the same pot of boiling water; boil for 1 minute. Ladle them out and let them cool.
3. Peel the potatoes and mash them with a large soup spoon: now, mix in the soy beans, corn, miso and black pepper. Stir until evenly mixed.
4. Wash the lettuce and shred it. Spread the lettuce out over a platter, and then put the mashed potato mixture on top. Serve.
◆Deep-Green Silver Thread Rolls
Ingredients:Raw Romaine lettuce 100 g. Bean sprouts 50 g. Rice vinegar 1 tsp. Soy sauce 1 tsp. Sesame oil 1/2 tsp.
Preparation:
1. After washing the bean sprouts, cook them in rapidly boiling water until done; ladle from the pot and allow them to dry.
2. Mix the bean sprouts evenly with the rice vinegar, soy sauce and sesame oil.
3. Pull apart the Romaine lettuce leaf-by-leaf and wash it. Set it aside.
4. Place one lettuce leaf on a plate, and put a suitable quantity of bean sprouts in the center. Roll up the leaf. Serve.
◆Health Protection Soup
Ingredients:Rehmannia (dried rhizome of a Chinese medicinal herb) 30 g. Baby corn 50 g. Kelp sprouts 30 g. Black vinegar 1 tsp.

Healthy Anti-Carcinogenic Soup Stock, or good water 1,000 cc. Bamboo salt a pinch
Preparation:
1. Cut the baby corn in half, and set aside.
2. Bring a pot of soup base to a boil, drop in all of the ingredients, and bring again to a boil. Let the ingredients cook over low heat for 20 minutes. Serve.

Day 9 Breakfast
◆Vegetable Salad
Ingredients:Asparagus 30 g. Pumpkin 30 g. Apple vinegar 1 tsp. Plum juice 1 tsp.
Preparation:
1. After washing the asparagus, chop it into approximately 7-cm.-long sections. Set it aside.
2. Wash the pumpkin and chop into bite-sized chunks: set aside.
3. Bring a pot of water to a rolling boil, toss in the ingredients, and boil for 1 minute; ladle from the pot and allow to dry. Now, stir in the apple vinegar and plum juice evenly. Serve.
◆Sweet Potato Shortcake
Ingredients:
Sweet potatoes 120 g.
Sweet potato flour 100 g.
Bamboo salt a pinch
Preparation:
1. After steaming the sweet potatoes until they are done, remove the peel. While they are still warm, mash them: set them aside.
2. Add the sweet potato flour and bamboo salt to the mashed sweet potatoes, mix evenly and form into dough.
3. Knead the dough into a long, narrow loaf; divide into several sections. With a rolling pin, flatten to a suitable thickness.
4. Preheat a frying pan at a medium heat setting. Drop on the thick slices of dough and fry until both sides have turned golden-brown. Serve.
◆Brown Rice Congee with Fruit and Almonds
Ingredients:
Almonds 30 g.
Job's tears 1/2 cup
Kiwi fruit 1 piece of fruit
BPreparation:
1. Cut the kiwi fruit into small cubes, and set it aside.
2. Put the almonds into an airtight bag, and use a knife handle or meat-pestle to smash them into small bits.
3. Bring a pot of soup stock to a boil, and then pour in the brown rice and Job's tears. Cook over low heat until the mixture has become porridge.
4. Turn off the heat: drop in the almond and kiwi, blend in evenly, and serve.
If you are in the mood for a new taste effect, just stir a different kind of fruit into the congee.

Day 9 Lunch
◆Black Rice Zongzi
Ingredients:
Purple rice 2 cups
Taro 1 root
Cashews 1 tbsp.
Cilantro 1 stalk
Healthy and Zesty Seasoning Powder 2 tsp.
Zongzi wrappers (made of reeds or bamboo leaves) 2 sheets
Cotton thread 1 string
Preparation:
1. Wash the purple rice, and then soak it in water for 1 hour. Set it aside.
2. Steam the taro until it is done, peel it and mash it. Now, mix in the cashews.
3. Knead the taro paste into a long strip, slice it and set it aside.
4. Take 2 sheets of zongzi wrapper: fold into a triangular cone shape. Fill with 2 tbsp. of purple rice, then drop on some taro paste, and finally cover it with 1 spoonful of purple rice.
5. Wrap the upper edge of the zongzi leaf underneath to cover the filling; wrap the cotton thread around the zongzi three times, and then fasten it with a slip-knot. Now, steam in a rice cooker.
6. Wash the cilantro and chop it into small pieces. Mix this with some Healthy and Zesty Seasoning Powder for use as a dip.
Use the above proportions to make more zongzi, if you wish. Uneaten zongzi can be stored in a refrigerator, or placed iummediately in a freezer. When you want to eat them, simply take them out and heat them. Serve.
◆Salad
Ingredients:
Baby corn 30 g.
Corn kernels 1 tbsp.

Small cucumbers 1 cuke
Preparation:
1. Slice the cucumber lengthwise; cut the baby corn ears in half.
2. Bring a pot of water to a rolling boil: drop in the corn kernels and baby corn, and boil for 2 minutes. Ladle out and let them dry.
You can also substitute okra for the baby corn.

◆Dumpling Soup
Ingredients:Bean curd 1 cake Laver 10 g. Basil 10 g. Vegetarian soup stock 1,000 cc.
Miso 1 tsp. Sweet potato flour 1 tsp.
Preparation:
1. Put the tofu in a flour bag (or a piece of cheesecloth) and squeeze out all of its moisture: stop when no more water comes out.
2. Take the tofu and mix it in with the miso and sweet potato flour. Now, knead this bean paste into small balls: in batches, drop them in a pot of boiling water.
3. Finally, add in the laver. When the water returns to a boil, turn off the heat. Add in the basil while the mixture is still hot. Serve.

Day 9 Dinner
◆Steamed Buns with Red Beans
Ingredients:Whole-wheat flour 100 g. All-purpose flour 200 g. Yeast powder 3 g.
Baking powder 2 g. Good water 150 cc. Red beans 10 g. Warm water 1 cup
Preparation:
1. Soak the red beans in good water for 2 hours, and then heat them until they are soft. Place them in a juice blender and blend until smooth.
2. Into a large mixing bowl, pour the whole-wheat flour, all-purpose flour, yeast and red bean water (from step #1): knead this evenly to form dough.
3. Cover the bowl with a wet piece of cloth and let the dough set for about an hour, until it rises.
4. Knead the dough again, and then roll it into a thin loaf. Cut this into thin slices and place these in a rice cooker: steam for approximately 15 minutes. Serve.
Use the same proportions to make a larger batch of buns: the unused dough can be refridgerated or stored in the freezer. Just take this out, steam it, and serve. Generally speaking, frozen dough will keep for 30 days, while refridgerated dough is good for 3 days.

◆Three-Pepper Salad
Ingredients:Green peppers 30 g. Sweet red peppers 30 g. Sweet yellow peppers 30 g.
Walnuts 10 g. Plum juice 1 tsp. Plum vinegar 1 tsp.
Preparation:
1. Wash the green, red and yellow peppers, and then dice them into thin slivers; place on a platter.
2. Finally, add a garnish of walnuts; sprinkle on the plum juice and plum vinegar. Serve.

◆Winter Mushroom and Veiled Lady Mushroom Soup
Ingredients:Winter mushrooms 6 stalks
Veiled lady mushrooms [Dictyophora indusiata (Vent. Ex Pers) Fisch] 10 g.
Healthy Anti-Carcinogenic Soup Stock, or good water 1,000 cc.
Preparation:
1. First, soak the two kinds of mushroom in good water: when they are thoroughly soaked, chop the veiled lady mushrooms into small pieces. Set aside.
2. Bring a pot of soup base to a boil. Drop in the mushrooms, cook over low heat for 20 minutes, and then turn off the heat.

Day 10 Breakfast
◆Western Pears
Ingredients:Western pear 1 piece of fruit
Preparation:
Wash the pear and serve.

◆Veggie Salad
Ingredients:Broccoli 50 g. Daikon turnip 30 g.
Preparation:
1. Wash the broccoli and chop it into small pieces. Bring a pot of water to a rolling boil, drop in the broccoli and parboil. Ladle this out and allow it to dry; place on a plate.
2. Pare the daikon and shred it: put it on the plate and sprinkle on the plum sauce. Serve.

◆Brown Rice with Sweet Potato
Ingredients:Sweet potatoes 60 g. Brown rice 2 cups
Preparation:
1. Wash the sweet potatoes, chop thinly, and set them aside.
2. Put the brown rice into the inner pot of a rice cooker and rinse it in good water. Add 3 cups of good water, and drop in the sweet potato.
3. Place the inner pot in the rice cooker and cook the ingredients for about 20 minutes. Serve.

Day 10 Lunch
◆Rice with Braised Tomatoes

Ingredients:Brown rice 2 cups Large tomatoes 60 g. Daikon turnip 40 g.
Baby corn 3 ears Manioc flour 1 tsp.
Preparation:
1. Pour 3 cups of good water in with the brown rice, place in a rice cooker and steam.
2. Wash the daikon and tomatoes, and then chop them into small cubes.
3. Wash the baby corn, cut into roughly 1-cm.-long sections, and set aside.
4. Preheat a frying pan: add in the tomato, daikon, baby corn, plus 1/2 cup of good water. Cover the pot and let the ingredients stew.
5. Add 2 spoonfuls of good water to the manioc flour, blend well, and then whisk it into the pan. Remove the pan from the stovetop.
6. Put the cooked rice in a bowl, and sprinkle on the braised vegetables. Serve.

◆Inlaid Mushrooms
Ingredients:Garden pea kernels 200 g. Mung beans 100 g. Black pepper powder 1/2 tsp.
Water horseshoe (a Guangzhou specialty vegetable) 5 pods Kelp 10 g.
Chinese black mushrooms 10 stalks Manioc flour 20 g.Bamboo salt a pinch
Preparation:
1. Soak the black mushrooms and set them aside.
2. Cook the peas and mung beans until they are done; use a knife handle to flatten them to a paste.
3. Smash the water horseshoe into small bits. Add in the bean paste, manioc flour, bamboo salt and black pepper: blend everything evenly to form a filling.
4. Shred the kelp, and stir this into the filling mixture.
5. Put a bit of manioc flour into the center of each mushroom, and then insert a suitable portion of filling, until it is slightly convex. Place on a pan.
6. Put this pan in a rice cooker and cook for approximately 12 minutes. Serve.

◆Cauliflower Soup with Wood Ear Mushrooms
Ingredients:Cauliflower 50 g. Wood-ear mushrooms 30 g. Carrots 30 g.
Healthy Anti-Carcinogenic Soup Stock, or good water 500 cc.
Preparation:
1. Wash the cauliflower and then chop it into small chunks. Set it aside.
2. Slice the wood-ear mushrooms and carrots into small pieces. Set this aside.
3. Bring a pot of soup stock to a boil, and drop in the carrots, cauliflower and mushrooms in order. When the soup boils again, turn off the heat.

Day 10 Dinner
◆Salad
Ingredients:Pumpkin 30 g. Soft bean curd 1 cake Sweet red pepper 30 g.
Preparation:
1. Remove the tofu from the package and put it on a plate.
2. Chop the pumpkin and red pepper into small cubes: mix together and scatter over the tofu. Finally, sprinkle on some plum juice and serve.

◆Japanese-Style Brown Rice with Chinese Yam
Ingredients:Brown rice 2 cups Chinese yam 100 g. Soy sauce 1 tsp.
Preparation:
1. In the inner pot of a rice cooker, pour in the brown rice and rinse it in good water. Now, add in 3 cups of good water.
2. Place the inner pot in the rice cooker and pour 1 cup of good water into the outer pot. Cook until the on-off button pops up.
3. Ladle out the rice and put it in a bowl. Grind the Chinese yam into a paste, and then mix it with some soy sauce. Use this as a topping for the rice.

◆Three-Color Silk Thread
Ingredients: Kelp tendrils 30 g. Celery 30 g. Mung bean sprouts 30 g. Garlic 2 heads
Ginger paste 1 tsp. Sesame oil 1/2 cup
Preparation:
1. Parboil the kelp tendrils in water that has come to a rolling boil. Ladle it out and allow it to dry, and then chop into sections. Set aside.
2. Wash the mung sprouts, let them dry, and set them aside.
3. Wash the celery, and then chop it: set it aside.
4. Mash the garlic in a grinder.
5. Mix all of the ingredients together. Serve.

◆Qi-Enhancing Wax Gourd Soup
Ingredients:Wolfberries 1 tbsp. Wax gourd 100 g.
Dang'gui [Angelica sinensis (Oliv.) Diehls] 10 g.
Healthy Anti-Carcinogenic Soup Stock, or good water 500 cc.
1. Chop the wax gourd into chunks: do not remove the outer skin. Set it aside.
2. Pour the soup stock into a pot and bring it to a boil. Add the dang-gui and wax gourd, and stew them over low heat until the gourd is fully done. Before turning off the heat, drop in the wolfberries. Serve.

Day 11 Breakfas

◆Vegetable Juice
Ingredients:Grapes 15 g. Red dragon Chinese yam 50 g. Carrots 30 g.Good water 300 cc.
Preparation:
1. Chop the Chinese yam and carrots into small bits.
2. Put all of the ingredients into a blender: mix until smooth. Serve.
1. You can also add in a suitable amount of lemon juice, honey, black or white sesame seeds, B-complex brewer's yeast, lecithin, pine nuts (or cashews), as well as synthetic plant enzymes, whole-grain flour, source calcium, plant seed fiber, and so on - with these additions, the mixture will be even more effective.
2. Those with cold, weak physical constitutions may add a slice of ginger, a pinch of cinnamon, some hot water, or Healthy and Zesty Seasoning Powder to their juice. This will not only correct their health problem, but will also give them an increased feeling of satiety.
◆Sweet Potato Pancakes
Ingredients:Whole-wheat flour 150 g. Sweet potatoes 100 g. Black sesame seeds 1 tbsp.
Preparation:
1. After steaming the sweet potato until it is done, peel it and mash it into a paste.
2. Mix all of the ingredients together in a large bowl; knead this to form dough.
3. Knead the dough and form it into a long loaf: slice this into a number of sections. Use a rolling pin to flatten each piece into a round sheet.
4. Preheat the oven to 400o F. Bake the pancakes for 15 minutes: serve.
◆Brown Rice and Nori Triangular Rice Balls
Ingredients:Nori 2 sheets Brown rice 2 cups
Preparation:
1. Put the brown rice in a rice cooker, add in 3 cups of water, and cook until it is done.
2. Cut square nori sheets into 4 sections: set these aside.
3. Remove the brown rice and allow it to cool. With a rice ladle, scoop out a suitable amount; with your hands, mold it into a triangular shape.
4. Wrap the rice in a sheet of nori, and it is ready to serve.
5. Make enough of the rice balls to satisfy the appetite of each family member.
Day 11 Lunch
◆Western Onion Bagels
Ingredients:Western onion 1/2 bulb Yeast powder 1/2 tsp. Warm water 1/4 cup Whole wheat flour 2 cups, or 250 g. Young soy bean kernels 1 cup
Preparation:
1. Mix the yeast with some warm water (approximately 100o F.); wait until it begins to ferment and expand.
2. In a large bowl, mix the yeast water and flour together until they form dough - it should have a shiny, smooth surface.
3. Place a piece of wet cloth over the bowl, and let it set for an hour.
4. Mince the onions, and then mix them evenly into the dough. Separate the dough into quarters; once again, cover with a wet cloth and let the dough set for 5 minutes.
5. Now, knead the dough into long loaves that are about 25 cm. in length: join the two ends together to form a ring.
6. Bring a pot of water to a rolling boil: turn down the heat setting to low, and parboil the dough rings. Ladle them out and let them dry.
7. Place the bagels on a piece of paper; when they are dry, put them into the oven and bake at 400 o F. for 15 minutes. Serve.
8. Boil the young soy beans, and then ladle them out of the pot. Mash them with a soup spoon to form a paste. This paste can be spread onto the sliced bagels.
Utilize the proportions given in the recipe to make larger batches of bagels. You can store uneaten bagels in the refrigerator, or put those without soy bean spread in the freezer. When you want to serve them, take them out and spray them with a little water, and then toast them briefly in the oven. Generally speaking, bagels will keep at room temperature for about 3 days; in the freezer, they will last for 60 days.
◆Salad
Ingredients:Iceberg lettuce 80 g. Tomatoes 100 g. Corn kernels 30 g.
Preparation:
1. Pull apart the lettuce and wash each leaf. Chop into small pieces and put them on a platter.
2. Wash the tomatoes, chop them, and then put them on top of the lettuce.
3. Parboil the corn, then remove it from the pot, let it dry, and use it as a salad garnish. Serve.
◆Zesty Soup
Ingredients:Elephant-foot rolls 6 rolls Chinese black mushrooms 6 stalksBamboo shoots 50 g.
Healthy Anti-Carcinogenic Soup Stock, or good water 800 cc.
Preparation:
1. Soak the black mushrooms in hot water. On top of each mushroom, lightly carve a cross with a knife.
2. Peel the bamboo shoots and then chop them into pieces; set them aside.
3. Bring a pot of soup stock to a boil, and then drop in the black mushrooms and bamboo shoots. Cook for about 20 minutes over low heat.
4. Finally, drop in the elephant-foot rolls. When the water returns to a boil, turn off the heat and serve.

Day 11 Dinner
◆Thai-Style Cold Noodles
Ingredients:Green algae noodles 80 g. Sesame seeds 1 tbsp. Lemon 1/2 fruit Cilantro 1 stalk Garlic 2 heads
Preparation:
1. Bring a pot of water to a rolling boil, and then drop in the noodles evenly. Boil them for about 6 minutes; turn off the heat and ladle them out of the pot. Put the noodles in a bowl.
2. Wash the cilantro, dice it, and set it aside.
3. Use a grinder to grind the garlic into a paste: set this aside.
4. Slice and squeeze the lemon. Mix the lemon juice with the cilantro and garlic paste: use this sauce to coat the noodles.
5. Before serving, blend everything together evenly. It's ready.
◆Cold Veggies with Sauce
Ingredients:Soya sprouts 50 g. Kelp sprouts 30 g. Soy beans 30 g.
Healthy and Zesty Seasoning Powder 1 tbsp.
Preparation:
1. Wash the soya sprouts, allow them to dry, and then put them on a plate.
2. In a pot of boiling water, cook the soya and kelp sprouts until they are soft and done; remove from the pot and let them dry. Put them on the plate.
3. Finally, scatter on some seasoning powder and serve.
◆Appetizing Soup
Ingredients:Small cabbage 2 heads Tender ginger 20 g. White pepper powder 1 tsp.
Healthy Anti-Carcinogenic Soup Stock, or good water 1,000 cc.
Preparation:
1. Wash the cabbage, chop it into small sections, and set it aside.
2. Shred the ginger: set it aside.
3. Bring a pot of soup stock to a boil, and then drop in the cabbage and ginger. When the water has returned to a boil, turn off the heat.
4. Before removing the mixture from the pot, stir in the white pepper. Serve.
Day 12 Breakfast
◆Fruit and Veggie Salad
Ingredients:Orange 1piece of fruit Sweet red pepper 1/2 pod Cabbage 50 g.
Preparation:
1. Peel the orange, cut it into sections, and set it aside.
2. Wash the red pepper and cabbage: slice them into fine slivers.
3. Put all of the ingredients together in a bowl and serve.
The vegetables can be purified in a vegetable detoxifier before use.
◆Brown Rice with Sweet Potato and Lotus Seeds
Ingredients:Sweet potato 1 spud Fresh lotus seeds 100 g. Brown rice 1 cup
Preparation:
1. Cut the sweet potato into small chunks; set it aside.
2. Put the brown rice into the inner pot of a rice cooker; mix in the sweet potato, lotus seeds, plus 2 cups of good water.
3. Place the inner pot inside the rice cooker. In the outer pot, pour 1 cup of good water: cook until the on-off button pops up. Serve.
If you are using dried lotus seeds, you must first soak them in good water for 1 hour.
Day 12 Lunch
◆High-Fiber Rice
Ingredients:Brown rice 2 cups Pine nuts 1/2 cup Pumpkin seeds 1/2 cup
Preparation:
1. Rinse off the brown rice in the inner pot of your rice cooker, and then add in 3 cups of good water.
2. Place the inner pot inside the rice cooker; cook for about 20 minutes until the on-off button pops up.
3. Open the rice cooker: while the rice is still warm, mix in the pine nuts and pumpkin seeds. Serve.
◆Salad
Ingredients:Golden tomatoes 10 pieces of fruit Purple cabbage 50 g. Asparagus 30 g.
Apple vinegar 1 tbsp. Plum juice 1 tbsp.
Preparation:
1. Wash the purple cabbage, shred it, and then let it soak for 10 minutes in apple vinegar and plum juice to tone down its pungent flavor.
2. Wash the asparagus and cut it in half lengthwise. Parboil in rapidly boiling water for 1 minute, ladle from the pot, and put it on a plate.
3. Finally, wash the tomatoes, allow them to dry, and put them on the plate. Serve.
◆Zesty Soup
Ingredients:Kelp braid 50 g. Braided bean curd skin 50 g. Scallions 20 g.
Healthy Anti-Carcinogenic Soup Stock, or good water 500 cc. Bamboo salt a pinch
Preparation:

1. Bring the soup stock to boil in a pot, and then drop in the kelp and bean curd braid along with the bamboo salt. When the soup stock boils again, turn off the heat.
2. Wash the scallions, dice them finely, and scatter them over the soup. Serve.

Day 12 Dinner
◆Vegetarian Stuffed Buns
Ingredients:Bamboo shoots 50 g. Cabbage 50 g. Chinese black mushrooms 15 stalks
Garlic 3 heads Whole-wheat flour 300 g. Yeast powder 5 g.
Preparation:
1. In a grinder, mash the garlic into a paste.
2. Slice the bamboo shoots, cabbage and mushrooms finely; add in the garlic paste and mix evenly to make the filling.
3. Stir the yeast powder into some warm water and blend it well. Let this sit for 20-30 minutes: wait until there are signs of fermentation and expansion.
4. In a large mixing bowl, pour the whole-wheat flour and yeast mixture. Knead this by hand until it forms dough with a sleek, shiny surface. If the dough is too dry to form the proper consistency, you can add in a suitable amount of water.
5. Cover the bowl of dough with a wet cloth and let this sit for about an hour. Wait until the dough rises.
6. Knead the dough again, and then shape it into a long loaf with a diameter of approximately 3 cm. Chop this into small sections: roll out each one with a rolling pin to form the bun wrappers.
7. With a soup spoon, scoop out some filling and place it in the center of the wrapper. With your fingers, wrap up the filling and seal the dough edges.
8. Put the finished buns in a rice cooker, steam for about 12 minutes, and serve.
You can make a bigger batch of buns according to the above proportions. The uneaten buns can be stored in the refrigerator, or placed in sealed bags or containers and put in the freezer. Remove them from the fridge before you need them, and steam them. Serve. In general, they will keep for 30 days in the freezer.

◆Cold Seaweed Rolls with Dressing
Ingredients:Small cucumbers 80 g. Nori 1 sheet White sesame seeds 1 tsp. Iceberg lettuce 60 g.
Preparation:
1. Separate the lettuce leaf-by-leaf, wash it, and tear each leaf by hand into halves, starting from the bottom of the leaf. Place on a plate.
2. Chop the cucumber into thin slivers, and place on top of the lettuce.
3. Dice the seaweed finely: along with the sesame seeds, use it to garnish the lettuce.
4. Form into rolls.

◆Black Bean Soup
Ingredients:Black beans 30 g. Red jujubes 30 g.
Veiled lady mushrooms [Dictyophora indusiata (Vent. Ex Pers) Fisch] 10 g.
Healthy Anti-Carcinogenic Soup Stock, or good water 1,000 cc.
Preparation:
1. Soak the mushrooms and jujubes in water until they expand, and then chop the mushrooms into sections.
2. Pour the soup base into a pot; add in the black beans, mushrooms and jujubes. Boil over low heat for about 20 minutes, until the black beans have become soft and well-done. Serve.

Day 13 Breakfast
◆Oranges
Ingredients:Oranges 250 g.
Preparation:
Wash the oranges, cut them into sections, and serve.
Remember to eat them along with the white inner peel.

◆Sweet Potato and Red Jujube Soup
Ingredients:Sweet potatoes 60 g. Red jujubes 30 g. Good water 600 cc.
Preparation:
1. Soak the jujubes in water for an hour, and set them aside.
2. Chop the sweet potatoes into small cubes: set them aside.
3. Pour some good water into a pot and bring it to a boil. Add the jujubes, and boil them at a medium heat setting. Now, add in the sweet potato and continue boiling for another 20 minutes. Serve.

◆Rice and Nori Sandwich Roll

Ingredients:Large cucumbers 50 g. Chinese yam 50 g. Brown rice 2 cups
Millet 1/2 cup Apple juice 2 tbsp. Bamboo salt a pinch
Preparation:
1. Chop the cucumber and Chinese yam, and then soak them in a mixture of bamboo salt and apple juice for 20 minutes.
2. Put the brown rice and millet into the inner pot of a rice cooker; add in 3 cups of good water, place in the rice cooker, and cook until done.
3. Open the nori sheet. Use a rice ladle to scoop out a suitable amount of cooked rice: spread

this evenly over the nori.
4. Cover 1/2 of the surface with the chopped cucumber and Chinese yam, and then use the other half of the sheet to cover the sandwich. Serve.

Day 13 Lunch
◆Potatoes with Gravy
Ingredients:Potatoes 60 g. Western mushrooms 10 stalks Green pepper 50 g. Sweet potato flour 1 tsp.
Preparation:
1. In water that has reached a rolling boil, cook the potatoes until they are tender and done. Slice them and put them on a plate.
2. Chop the mushrooms and pepper into small sections, and set them aside.
3. Preheat a nonstick frying pan over low heat; drop in the mushrooms, pepper and a small amount of good water. Stir-fry evenly.
4. Dissolve the sweet potato flour in good water, pour this into the frying pan and whisk. Remove the mixture from the pan, and use it as a gravy to coat the potatoes

◆Salad
Ingredients:Spinach 50 g. Apples 60 g. Walnuts 30 g. Nori 1 sheet Sesame seeds 1 tsp.
Miso 1 tsp. Apple vinegar 2 tsp.
Preparation:
1. Chop the spinach and parboil in rapidly boiling water for 1 minute. Ladle out and place on a platter.
2. Cut the apple into sections: along with the crushed walnuts and sesame seeds, put on top of the spinach.
3. Finally, tear the nori sheet into small pieces and scatter over the spinach. Add the miso and apple vinegar as a sauce. Serve.

◆Mexican Refried Beans Soup
Ingredients:Pinto beans 100 g. Western celery 50 g. Carrots 50 g. Tomatoes 50 g.
Healthy Anti-Carcinogenic Soup Stock, or good water 500 cc.
Bamboo salt a pinch Black pepper powder a pinch
Preparation:
1. Presoak the pinto beans in good water for an hour, and then pour out the water and set aside.
2. Chop the celery, carrots and tomatoes into small cubes.
3. Bring a pot of water to a rolling boil. Toss in the beans and cook over low heat for 30 minutes. Now, ladle them out and mash them into a paste.
4. Bring a pot of soup base to a boil. Drop in the celery, carrots and tomatoes: bring the pot to a boil once again. Now, add in the mashed beans, bamboo salt and black pepper; continue cooking for another 10 minutes. Serve.

Day 13 Dinner
◆Veggie Rice
Ingredients:Pak-choi 80 g. Scallion 1 stalk Brown rice 1 cup Millet 1 cup
Vegetarain soup stock 3 cups
Preparation:
1. Mince the scallion and pak-choi: set them aside.
2. Preheat a nonstick frying pan. Add in the scallion and pak-choi, and lightly stir-fry. Ladle this from the pan.
3. Soak the brown rice and millet in water for 1/2 hour, and then drain the water. Add the soup stock, scallion and pak-choi: mix evenly.
Put the mixture in a rice cooker; in the outer pot, add 1 cup of water. Cook until the on-off switch pops up. Serve.

◆Double Gourd Inlaid Bean Curd
Ingredients:Large cucumber 30 g. Bitter gourd 30 g. Young soy beans 1 tbsp.Bamboo salt a pinch
Bean curd 1 cake Carrots 30 g. Sweet potato flour 1 tbsp. Black pepper powder a pinch
Preparation:
1. Chop the carrots into small cubes.
2. Mash the tofu thoroughly in a large bowl; add in the green soy beans, carrots, sweet potato flour, black pepper and bamboo salt. Mix evenly to make a filling.
3. Cut the cucumber and bitter gourd into about 2-cm.-long pieces: scoop out the middle of each piece, and add enough filling to create a slightly convex surface. Place them on a plate.
4. Put the plate into a rice cooker and steam until done. Serve.

◆Flavorful Laver Soup
Ingredients:King oyster mushrooms [Pleurotus eryngii (DC. Ex Fr.)] 50 g. Laver 20 g.
Healthy Anti-Carcinogenic Soup Stock, or good water 350 cc. Miso 1 tsp.
Preparation:
1. Slice the mushrooms lengthwise into thin pieces.
2. Bring a pot of soup base to a boil, and then drop in the mushrooms, laver and miso. When the mixture has returned to a boil, turn off the heat. Serve.

Day 14 Breakfast
◆Fruit and Veggie Salad

Ingredients:Papaya 250 g. Green pepper 30 g. Daikon turnip 30 g. Passionfruit juice 1 tbsp.
Preparation:
1. Cut the pepper across to form rings, remove the seeds, and wash. Once they have dried, place them on a plate.
2. Remove the seeds and skin of the papaya, cut it into chunks, and put it on the plate.
3. Finally, chop the daikon into slivers: scatter these over the plateful of salad. Drizzle on some passionfruit juice and serve.
If you would rather blend the above ingredients into juice, you can also add in a suitable amount of lemon juice, honey, black or white sesame seeds, B-complex brewer's yeast, lecithin, pine nuts (or cashews), as well as synthetic plant enzymes, whole-grain flour, source calcium, plant seed fiber, and so on. With these additions, you will experience even better effects.

◆Crispy Green Honey Cake
Ingredients:Ashitaba 200 g. Honey 200 g. Sweet potato flour 2 tbsp.
Preparation:
1. Along with 1 cup of good water, put the ashitaba leaves in a juice blender and blend until smooth.
2. Put the ashitaba juice, honey and sweet potato flour in a large bowl and mix evenly; with a rolling pin, flatten this out into a thick sheet.
3. Put the flattened sheet on a plate, place it in a steamer pot, and cook at high heat for about 20 minutes.
4. Let the mixture cool off a bit, and then take it out of the pot, slice it, and serve.

◆Sweet Potato and Brown Rice Congee
Ingredients:Sweet potatoes 60 g. Brown rice 2 cups Good water 1,500 cc.
Preparation:
1. Dice the sweet potato finely, and set it aside.
2. Put the brown rice and good water in a pot: simmer over low heat for 30 minutes, and then add in the sweet potato. Continue to cook the mixture for 20 minutes. Serve.

Day 14 Lunch
◆Cakes with Cashew and Semi-Refined Rice
Ingredients:Potato 1 spud Cashews 50 g. Coarse semi-refined rice flour 250 g.
Preparation:
1. Drop the potato into rapidly boiling water and cook until thoroughly done. Ladle ot out and peel it; mash it into a paste.
2. Crush the cashews into small grains, and then mix evenly with the rice flour.
3. Keep stirring as you slowly pour in the water and mashed potato. Form this mixture into dough, and then use a rolling pin to flatten it out into a pancake.
4. Preheat a nonstick frying pan to low heat, put in the pancake, and cook until it has turned golden-brown on both sides.

◆Nori and Hundred-Leaf Tofu Rolls
Ingredients:Nori 1 sheet Hundred-leaf bean curd 1 cake
Malabar spinach [Basella rubra] 50 g. Miso 1 tsp. Rice vinegar 2 tsp. White sesame seeds 1 tsp.
Preparation:
1. Clip the nori into 3-cm.-wide by 10-cm.-long strips.
2. Chop the tofu into 1-cm.-thick by 5-cm.-wide thin slices.
3. Wash the Malabar spinach, and then parboil it in rapidly boiling water. Chop it into about 7-cm.-long pieces.
4. Spread the nori out flat on a counter-top, and drop on 1 slice of tofu. Then, add some Malabar spinach, and finally roll the nori and tofu up.
5. Make a sauce using miso, rice vinegar and white sesame seeds. Pour this onto the rolls before serving.

◆High-Fiber Salad
Ingredients:Soya sprouts 50 g. Salad bamboo shoots 50 g. Carrots 50 g. Cashews 10 nuts
Sesame seeds 1 tsp. Miso 1 tbsp.
Preparation:
1. Wash the bean sprouts, and then allow them to dry. Place them on a plate.
2. Chop the bamboo shoots and carrots finely, and them put them on the plate.
3. Crush the cashews, and then mix them with the sesame seeds and miso to make a dressing. Add this to the salad and serve.
For salad bamboo shoots, you can use store-bought cooked bamboo shoots that have been vacuum-packed, or else you can use local, seasonal produce - any type of fresh bamboo shoot will do as a substitute.

◆Wax Gourd and Shredded Ginger Soup
Ingredients:Chinese wax gourd 150 g. Ginger 100 g.
Healthy Anti-Carcinogenic Soup Stock, or good water 350 cc. Sesame oil just a dab
Preparation:
1. Chop the wax gourd into pieces, shred the ginger, and set it aside.
2. Bring a pot of soup stock to a boil, and then drop in the wax gourd and ginger. Cook for about 10 minutes over low heat, until the wax gourd is stewed to rags. Turn off the heat; before removing from the pot, add a few drops of sesame oil.

Day 14 Dinner

◆Nutritious Noodles
Ingredients:Red chrysanthemum noodles (made with a patent health-food flour) 80 g.
Spinach 50 g. Baby corn 6 ears Kelp braids 30 g. Sweet peas 30 g. Bamboo salt a pinch
Healthy Anti-Carcinogenic Soup Stock, or good water 500 cc. Sesame oil a few drops
Preparation:
1. Bring a pot of water to a boil: drop in the noodles and cook in rapidly boiling water. Now, turn the heat down to low and continue cooking for about 6 more minutes. Ladle the noodles from the pot, and place them in a bowl.
2. Cut the baby corn in half, chop up the spinach, and set them aside.
3. Take another clean pot, and use it to boil the soup stock. Drop in the kelp braids and baby corn: when the water boils again, add the spinach, sweet peas and bamboo salt.
4. Let the water return to a boil, and then turn off the heat and pour the soup into the bowl. Add a few drops of sesame oil and serve.

◆Strange Green Tracks Salad
Ingredients:Small cucumbers 100 g. Iceberg lettuce 50 g. Alfalfa sprouts a small quantity
Quinary powder ("Five Treasures" powder: a patent Chinese medicinal preparation) 1 tbsp.
Tomato 1 fruit
Preparation:
1. Chop up the cucumbers and cut the tomato into sections: put them on a plate.
2. Pull the lettuce apart and wash it leaf-by-leaf; chop it into small slices, and put it on the plate.
3. Finally, scatter the alfalfa sprouts on top of the salad, sprinkle on some Quinary powder, and serve.
Leafy and sprouted vegetables should be eaten in the summertime, by those with hot, dry constitutions, or else by those who are in normal, healthy physical condition.

Day 15 Breakfast
◆Fruit and Veggie Juice
Ingredients:Celery 60 g. Grapefruit juice 150 g. Plum juice 1 tbsp. Good water 200 cc.
Preparation:
1. Wash and dice the celery: set it aside.
2. Put all of the ingredients into a juice blender, and mix them until smooth. Serve.
1. You can also add in a suitable amount of lemon juice, honey, black or white sesame seeds, B-complex brewer's yeast, lecithin, pine nuts (or cashews), as well as synthetic plant enzymes, whole-grain flour, source calcium, plant seed fiber, and so on. This will lend even better results.
2. If you have been drinking vegetable juice for a long time and begin to feel weak and in poor physical condition, experiencing numerous bowel movements with soft and loose stools, this means that the detoxifying diet has gone on too long. Take a temporary respite from high-fiber foods, squeeze your vegetables into juice, and supplement this with vegetable proteins and oils.

◆Sweet Potato Balls
Ingredients:Sweet potatoes 120 g. Sweet potato flour 100 g.
Preparation:
1. Put the sweet potato in a rice cooker and steam until they are thoroughly done.
2. Remove from the rice cooker, peel and mash into paste. Now, add in the sweet potato starch.
3. Knead the mixture into a loaf that is approximately 2 cm. in diameter. Cut this into slices that are 2 cm. apart.
4. Bring a pot of water to a rolling boil, and drop in the sweet potato rounds. Boil them until they float to the surface, and then ladle them from the pot.

◆Rice Mixed with Baby Cucumbers
Ingredients:Small cucumbers 3 cukes Brown rice 2 cups Bamboo salt a pinch
Olive oil a few drops
Preparation:
1. Put the brown rice in the inner pot of a rice cooker, rinse it off, and then add 3 cups of good water.
2. Place the inner pot in the rice cooker, and add 1 cup of good water to the outer pot. Cook until the on-off button pops up.
3. Wash the cukes, chop them into thin slices, and add them to the rice along with the bamboo salt and olive oil. Mix well and serve.

Day 15 Lunch
◆Soup-Covered Noodles
Ingredients:Ashitaba noodles 80 g. Wood-ear mushrooms 10 g. Garden pea pods 50 g.
Carrots 30 g. Vegetarian soup stock 1,000 cc.
Preparation:
1. Bring a pot of water to a rolling boil, drop in the ashitaba noodles and boil them. Turn the heat down to low, and continue cooking for about 6 minutes.
2. Remove the noodles from the pot with a noodle ladle, and then rinse them off in cold water to cool them off. Let them dry, and then put them in a bowl.
3. Chop the mushrooms and carrots into slivers, and set them aside.
4. Take another clean pot: use it to boil the soup stock. Add in the carrots, and wait until the soup boils again. Now, drop in the mushrooms and pea pods: cook for 1 minute, and then

turn off the heat.

5. Pour the soup directly onto the noodles and serve.

◆Salad

Ingredients:Western celery 50 g. Corn 1 ear Sweet red pepper 50 g.

Preparation:

1. Chop the corn into sections and parboil; ladle from the pot and allow to dry, and then put on a plate.
2. Slice the celery slant-wise into sections and chop the red pepper into chunks; put them on the plate, and serve.

◆Thick Pumpkin Soup

Ingredients:Pumpkin 150 g. Laver 50 g. Bamboo salt a pinch

Healthy Anti-Carcinogenic Soup Stock, or good water 500 cc.

Preparation:

1. Chop the pumpkin into chunks, and put it in a juice blender along with 500 cc. of soup base. Blend until smooth.
2. Put the pumpkin juice, along with the remaining soup stock, in a pot: bring to a leaping boil.
3. Toss the laver and bamboo salt into the pot; boil until the laver expands and opens up. Serve.

Day 15 Dinner

◆Chinese Yam Cupcakes

Ingredients:Chinese yam 200 g. Brown rice flour 200 g. Sticky rice powder 200 g.

Mashed ginger 20 g. Healthy Anti-Carcinogenic Soup Stock, or good water 1,000 cc.

Bamboo salt a pinch

Preparation:

1. Chop the Chinese yam into about 1-cm.-long cubes: set this aside.
2. Mix the brown rice and sticky rice flours into the soup stock: blend evenly to form a thick rice solution. Pour this into a pot and cook over low heat until the mixture becomes dense and sticky.
3. Drop in the Chinese yam, mashed ginger and bamboo salt: mix together evenly.
4. Pour into a bowl to 4/5 full, and then put in a rice cooker and steam for approximately 30 minutes. Serve.

◆Braised Bean Curd

Ingredients:Silken tofu 1 cake String beans 30 g. Carrots 30 g.

Dried Chinese mushrooms 5 stalks Healthy Anti-Carcinogenic Soup Stock, or good water 100 cc.

Preparation:

1. Soak the Chinese mushrooms until they open, and then chop them into cubes. Set them aside.
2. Chop the soft tofu into small pieces; chop the string beans and carrots into cubes. Set them aside.
3. Preheat a frying pan at a low heat setting. Pour in all of the ingredients, lightly stir-fry, and then remove from the pan and serve.

◆Four Celestial Beasts Soup with Job's Tears

Ingredients:Job's tears 1 cup Chinese yam 25 g. Lotus seeds 50 g. Gorgon fruit 25 g.

China root (a fungus found on fir-tree roots) 25 g. Good water 1,500 cc.

Preparation:

1. Put all of the ingredients in a pot and boil at high heat in rapidly boiling water.
2. Turn down the heat to low, and let the mixture simmer for about an hour. Turn off the heat.

Day 16 Breakfast

◆Fruit and Veggie Salad

Ingredients:Pineapple 60 g. String beans 30 g. Cherry tomatoes 6 pieces of fruit

reparation:

1. Wash the tomatoes, slice them in half, and put on a plate.
2. Peel the pineapple and chop into small chunks.
3. Bring a pot of good water to a boil: add in a pinch of bamboo salt. Parboil the string beans in rapidly boiling water, and then ladle them out; let them dry and chop them. Serve.

◆Mashed Sweet Potato with Wolfberries

Ingredients:Sweet potatoes 2 spuds Wolfberries 2 tbsp.

Preparation:

1. Wash the sweet potatoes, and then peel them. Put them in a pan along with the wolfberries: steam them until they are soft and well-done.
2. Take out the pan, and mash the sweet potatoes into a paste. Blend in the wolfberries evenly.
3. With a soup spoon, ladle out a suitable amount of sweet potato and place it in the palm of your hand. Form the mashed potato into a round cake and serve.

◆Brown Rice

Ingredients:Brown rice 2 cups Healthy Anti-Carcinogenic Soup Stock, or good water 4 cups

Preparation:

Wash the brown rice, and then add it to the soup stock. Steam this mixture for about 30 minutes until it is done. Serve.

Day 16 Lunch

◆Whole-Wheat Pot-Stickers

Ingredients:Dried Chinese black mushrooms 50 g. Cabbage 1/2 head Wolfberries 20 g.

Pine nuts 20 g. Scallions 50 g. Tender ginger 30 g. Whole-wheat flour 300 g. Olive oil 1 tsp.

Preparation:

1. Soak the mushrooms until they open up, chop into small cubes, and set aside.
2. Shred the cabbage, scallions and ginger. Wrap them in gauze and wring out the juice. Add in the wolfberries and pine nuts, mixing evenly to make the dumpling filling.
3. Mix a suitable amount of boiling water in with the flour. Once this is evenly blended in, add in a sufficient quantity of cold water: knead this into dough.
4. Use plastic wrap to cover the dough: wait for about 15 minutes, and then knead the mixture into a loaf that is approximately 3 cm. in diameter.
5. Cut the loaf of dough into slices spaced 2 cm. apart. Use a rolling pin to flatten out each slice into a round dumpling wrapper.
6. Drop 1 spoonful of filling onto the center of each wrapper, and then seal the dumplings by squeezing together the ends of the dough.
7. Pour some oil into the bottom of a nonstick frying pan, heat up the pan, and then set the dumplings in rows along the bottom of the pan. Adding 5 tsp. of water, cover the pot and cook for about 10 minutes over low heat, until the dumplings turn golden-brown on the surface. Serve.

This recipe can be extended by using the proportions given above. Just put the extra dumplings in a sealed plastic bag or container and store them in the freezer. Take them out as needed, fry and serve.

◆Bitter Gourd Salad with Plum Sauce

Ingredients:Bitter gourd 50 g. Purple cabbage 50 g. Plum sauce 2 spoonfuls

Preparation:

1. Wash the bitter gourd and red cabbage, shred them, and put them on a plate.
2. Before serving, drizzle on some plum sauce. Your salad is ready.

If the bitter gourd is too bitter for your taste, simply remove the inner white section of the gourd, or else lightly parboil before serving.

◆Red Lotus Soup

Ingredients:Red jujubes 50 g. Wood-ear mushrooms 30 g. Lotus seeds 50 g.

Healthy Anti-Carcinogenic Soup Stock, or good water 1,500 cc.

Preparation:

1. Slice the mushrooms into sections and set them aside.
2. Bring a pot of soup stock to a boil, and then drop in all of the ingredients. When the soup boils again, turn down the heat to low and simmer for about 40 minutes.

Day 16 Dinner

◆Turnip Cake

Ingredients:White turnips 300 g. Brown rice flour 300 g. Sticky rice flour 300 g.

Chinese toon (Chinese cedar), [Toona sinensis (A. Juss.) Roem; Cerella sinensis] 20 g.

Healthy Anti-Carcinogenic Soup Stock, or good water 300 cc.

Preparation:

1. Shred the turnip, dice the Chinese toon into tiny bits: set them aside.
2. Preheat a nonstick frying pan. Saute the shredded turnip, and then cover the pan and let them simmer until they are soft and done.
3. Mix the whole-wheat flour and sticky rice flour into the soup stock: pour into a pot, and then add in the Chinese toon. Stir until a thick, sticky sauce is formed.
4. Pour the rice sauce into a large bowl. Put this in a steamer and steam at a high heat setting for about 40 minutes.
5. Put the steamed turnip cake onto a plate: refridgerate. Now, slice and serve.

◆Clear Yellow Salad

Ingredients:Young soy beans 30 g. Sweet yellow pepper 50 g. Asparagus 30 g.

Orange 1 piece of fruit Bamboo salt a pinch

Preparation:

1. Chop the asparagus into sections, and parboil along with the young soy beans in a pot of water with bamboo salt. When they are done, ladle out of the pot and let them dry: put them on a plate.
2. Wash the yellow pepper, and then chop it into fine slivers. Put on the plate.
3. Cut the orange in half, squeeze out the juice, and sprinkle it over the salad. Serve.

◆Kelp and Zucchini Soup

Ingredients:Kelp threads 30 g. Zucchini 50 g. Cilantro 20 g. Miso 1 tsp.

Healthy Anti-Carcinogenic Soup Stock, or good water 1,000 cc.

Preparation:

1. Wash the zucchini, slice it finely, and set it aside.
2. Bring a pot of soup stock to a boil, and then drop in the kelp threads, zucchini and miso. When the mixture returns to a boil, turn off the heat.
3. Wash the cilantro thoroughly, mince it, and scatter it over the soup as a garnish. Serve.

Day 17 Breakfast

◆Good Complexion Fruit and Veggie Juice

Ingredients:Tomatoes 100 g. Chinese yam 30 g. Carrots 30 g. Good water 250 cc. Plum juice 1 tsp.

Preparation:

1. Chop the tomatoes, Chinese yam and carrots into chunks: set them aside.
2. Put all of the ingredients into a juice blender, mix until smooth, and serve.

1. You can also add in a suitable amount of lemon juice, honey, black or white sesame seeds, B-complex brewer's yeast, lecithin, pine nuts (or cashews), as well as synthetic plant enzymes, whole-grain flour, source calcium, plant seed fiber, and so on. With such additions, the health benefits will be even better.

2. If you are prone to flatulence, you can blend the fruits and vegetables in separate batches, drinking them 20 minutes apart. In any case, pineapple can be blended in with the vegetable juice: it will alleviate symptoms of flatulence and relieve constipation. You can also add some bamboo salt to the fruit and vegetable juice.

◆Sweet Potao Rolls

Ingredients:Whole wheat spring roll wrappers 1 sheet Sweet potatoes 100 g. Sesame paste add according to taste

Preparation:

1. Wash the sweet potatoes, steam them until they are fully cooked, and then mash them into a paste.
2. Lay out the moistened spring roll wrapper on a counter-top, spread on some sesame sauce, and put the sweet potato paste onto the section of the wrapper nearest you.
3. Roll up the wrapper and serve.

◆Job's Tears and Brown Rice Balls

Ingredients:Brown rice 1 cup Job's tears 1 cup
Quinary powder ("Five Treasures": a Chinese medical tonic which can be drunk as a tea or added to foods) 2 tbsp.

Preparation:

1. Presoak the brown rice in good water for 4 hours, and soak the Job's tears in good water for 2 hours. Afterwards, put them into the inner pot of a rice cooker and add 3 cups of good water.
2. Place the inner pot inside the rice cooker; into the outer pot, pour 1 cup of good water. Steam until done.
3. Let the rice mixture cool, and then mix in the Five Treasures powder.
4. With a soup spoon, scoop out a sufficient quantity of rice, put it in the palm of your hand and knead it into a ball. It's done.
5. Keep on repeating step #4, making enough rice balls to suit your family.

Day 17 Lunch

◆Lumpy Wheat Dumplings

Ingredients:Napa cabbage 30 g. Kelp shoots 30 g. Pumpkin 30 g. Day lilies 30 g. Whole wheat flour 200 g. Healthy Anti-Carcinogenic Soup Stock, or good water 1,000 cc.

Preparation:

1. Add a suitable amount of warm water to the whole wheat flour, mix and knead into dough.
2. Wash the napa cabbage, and then shred it. Chop the pumpkin into chunks. Set them aside.
3. Bring a pot of soup stock to a boil over high heat.
4. Pinch up a small ball of dough between two fingers, and then flatten it slightly; toss it into the soup. Repeat this step until all of the dough has been used up.
5. Wait until the soup boils again: drop in the napa cabbage, kelp sprouts, pumpkin and day lilies.
6. Turn off the heat after the pot has returned to a boil.

◆Perfect Match Salad

Ingredients:String beans 50 g. Carrots 50 g. Miso 1 tsp. Sesame seeds 1 tsp.

Preparation:

1. Slice the string beans slant-wise, chop the carrots, and cook them in rapidly boiling water for 14 minutes. Ladle them from the pot, allow them to dry, and then put them on a plate.
2. Mix some good water into the miso and sesame seeds to make a dressing. Sprinkle this over the salad and serve.

Day 17 Dinner

◆Lotus Seed and Red Bean Rice

Ingredients:Fresh lotus seeds 50 g. Red beans 1/2 cup Brown rice 2 cups

Preparation:

1. Presoak the red beans in good water for 2 hours, and soak the brown rice in good water for 4 hours.
2. Put all of the ingredients into the inner pot of a ricer cooker, add in 4 cups of good water, and cook until the on-off button pops up. Serve.

If you have purchased dried lotus seeds, presoak them in good water for 2 hours.

◆Dazzling Salad

Ingredients:Green peppers 50 g. Yellow tomatoes 50 g.

Preparation:

1. Chop the green peppers across, remove the seeds, and wash them. After that, continue cutting them cross-wise to make pepper rings. Put these on a plate.
2. Wash the yellow tomatoes, let them dry, and then put them on the plate. Serve.

◆Red Phoenix Vegetable Soup

Ingredients:Red phoenix greens (Gynura) 50 g. Kelp 30 g. Garlic 1 bulb
Healthy Anti-Carcinogenic Soup Stock, or good water 350 cc. Bamboo salt a pinch

Preparation:

1. Wash the red phoenix greens thoroughly, chop them, and set them aside.
2. Peel the garlic, chop it, and set it aside.
3. Bring a pot of soup stock to a boil: toss in the kelp.
4. When the pot boils again, add in the gynura greens, garlic and bamboo salt. Wait until the stock boils once again, and then turn off the heat.

Day 18 Breakfast

◆Fruit and Veggie Salad

Ingredients:Pears 80 g. Sweet red peppers 50 g. Broccoli 50 g.

Preparation:

1. Cut the pear into sections and slice the peppers into thin strips: put them on a plate.
2. Wash the broccoli thoroughly, chop it into small chunks, and parboil in rapidly boiling water. Ladle this from the pot and let it dry: put it on the plate.

If you decide to put the above ingredients into a blender and drink them as juice, you can also add in a suitable amount of lemon juice, honey, black or white sesame seeds, B-complex brewer's yeast, lecithin, pine nuts (or cashews), as well as synthetic plant enzymes, whole-grain flour, source calcium, plant seed fiber, and so on. This will enhance the nutritional effects.

◆Sweet Potato and Ginger Soup

Ingredients:Sweet potatoes 100 g. Tender ginger 30 g. Good water 600 cc.

Preparation:

1. Chop the sweet potatoes into gear-hob shapes, and shred the ginger.
2. Put the chopped ingredients into a pot of boiling water, simmer over low heat for 20 minutes, and serve.

◆High-Fiber Cone-Shaped Dumplings

Ingredients:Corn flour 100 g. Brown rice flour 100 g. Sesame powder 30 g. Walnuts 50 g.

Preparation:

1. Crush the walnuts finely and set them aside.
2. Put all of the ingredients into a large mixing bowl, add in a suitable amount of warm water (about 100o F.), and knead into dough.
3. Separate the dough into roughly egg-sized rolls, knead them into rounded cone-shaped loaves, and put them on a plate.
4. Put the plate into a steaming basket, steam for about 30 minutes, and serve.

1. Use the same recipe proportions to make a bigger batch of rolls: the uneaten ones can be refrigerated, or put into sealed wrappers or containers and placed in the freezer. Just take them out and steam them again before serving.

2. If you prefer sweeter rolls, you can add brown sugar to the dough.

Day 18 Lunch

◆Chinese Yam and Mixed-Grain Rice

Ingredients:Chinese yam 70 g. Job's tears 1 cup Brown rice 1 cup

Preparation:

1. Presoak the Job's tears in good water for 2 hours, and soak the brown rice in good water for 4 hours.
2. Chop the Chinese yam into short strips and set it aside.
3. Put all of the ingredients into the inner pot of a rice cooker along with 3 cups of good water. Put the pot into the rice cooker; into the outer pot, pour 1 cup of good water. Steam until the on-off switch pops up. Serve.

◆Salad

Ingredients:Soya sprouts 50 g. Corn kernels 30 g. Pumpkin seeds 20 g.
Lemon 50 g. Honey 1 tbsp.

Preparation:

1. Wash the soya sprouts and let them dry off: put them on a plate.
2. Parboil the corn kernels in rapidly boiling water; ladle them out, let them dry, and drop them onto the soya sprouts.
3. Squeeze the lemon, and sprinkle the juice along with the honey onto the salad. Serve.
4. Finally, scatter on the pumpkin seeds as a garnish.

◆Zesty Soup

Ingredients:Kelp sprouts 30 g. Garden peas 30 g. Beech mushrooms 30 g.
Healthy Anti-Carcinogenic Soup Stock, or good water 350 cc.

Preparation:

Bring a pot of soup stock to a boil, and then drop in all of the ingredients. When the soup boils again, turn off the heat.

Day 18 Dinner

◆Fragrant Bean Soup

Ingredients:Soy beans 1/4 cup Brown rice 1 cup

Preparation:
1. Presoak the soy beans for 4 hours.
2. Rinse off the brown rice a bit, and then, along with the the soy beans, put them in the inner pot of a rice cooker. Add 4 cups of good water.
3. Put the inner pot into the rice cooker, pour 1 cup of good water into the outer pot, and cook until done.

◆Crispy Celery Salad
Ingredients:Western celery 50 g. Baby bamboo shoots 50 g. Cashews 30 g.
Rice vinegar 1 tsp. Soy sauce 1 tsp. Sesame oil 1/2 tsp.
Preparation:
1. Bring a pot of water to a rolling boil, parboil the baby bamboo shoots, and then ladle them from the pot and let them dry.
2. Wash the celery, chop it, and then put it on a plate.
3. Put the bamboo shoots and cashews directly onto the plate.
4. Make a dressing by mixing the rice vinegar, soy sauce and sesame oil together. Sprinkle this on the salad and serve.

◆Tomato and Bean Curd Soup
Ingredients:Tomatoes 80 g. Silken tofu 1 cake Laver 50 g.
Preparation:
1. Chop the tomatoes and tofu into chunks: set them aside.
2. Bring a pot of soup stock to a boil, and then drop in the tomato, tofu and laver. When the water has boiled again, turn off the heat.

Day 19 Breakfast
◆Apples
Ingredients:Apple 1 piece of fruit
Preparation:
Wash the apple, chop it into sections, and serve.

◆Steamed Sweet Potatoes
Ingredients:Sweet potaoes 120 g.
Preparation:
Wash the sweet potatoes, put them in a rice cooker, and steam them until they are soft and done. Serve.
If you prefer chewier sweet potatoes, cook them a little more in an oven set to 280o for 5 minutes.

◆Brown Rice Rolls
Ingredients:Nori 1 sheet Cooked brown rice 1 bowl Asparagus 50 g.
Sweet yellow pepper 30 g. Plum vinegar 1 tsp.
Preparation:
1. Chop the asparagus into about 7-cm.-long sections: parboil them in rolling water for 1 minute.
2. Slice the yellow pepper into thin strips. Mix some plum vinegar in with the brown rice, and set it aside.
3. Clip a whole, square sheet of nori into 2 triangular halves. Place these on a counter-top with the tips of the triangles facing forward.
4. First, spread a suitable amount of brown rice onto the part of the nori that is closest to you: in the center, drop some asparagus and yellow pepper.
5. Finally, hold the nori by the right and left base corners. Roll it towards the center to form a shape similar to a sipping-straw biscuit (crepes roulees). Serve.

Day 19 Lunch
◆Noodle Soup
Ingredients:Carrot noodles 80 g. Cold-processed tofu 1 cake Green garlic 30 g.
Sweet peas 50 g. Healthy Anti-Carcinogenic Soup Stock, or good water 800 cc.
Black vinegar 1 tsp. Soy sauce 1 tsp. Sesame oil a few drops
Preparation:
1. Chop the cold-processed tofu into chunks, slice the green garlic slant-wise, and set them aside.
2. Bring a pot of water to a rolling boil and drop in the noodles evenly: cook over low heat for about 6 minutes.
3. In another pot, bring the soup stock to a boil, and then toss in the tofu and sweet peas; cook them until the soup comes to a rapid boil.
4. Ladle out the noodles and add them to the soup. Now, add in the garlic, black vinegar, soy sauce and sesame oil: mix together evenly, turn off the heat, and remove from the pot.

◆Korean Salad
Ingredients:Carrots 30 g. Small cucumbers 80 g. Kelp down 20 g. Shredded ginger 10 g.
Sesame oil 1/2 tsp. Black vinegar 2 tsp. Soy sauce 1 tsp. Sesame seeds 1 tsp.3.
Preparation:
1. Chop the carrots, slice the cucumbers into sections, and put them on a plate.
2. Parboil the kelp down and let it dry: put it on the plate.
3. Mix together the ginger, sesame oil, black vinegar, soy sauce and sesame seeds to make a

dressing: sprinkle this onto the salad.

Day 19 Dinner
◆Taro Rice
Ingredients:Taro 60 g. Brown rice 2 cups
Preparation:
1. Chop the taro into small cubes; set these aside.
2. Put the brown rice and taro together in the inner pot of a rice cooker, add in 3 cups of good water, steam until done, and serve.

◆Salad
Ingredients:Coral greens [Glehnia ittoralis Fr. Schmidt et Miq.] 20 g. Iceberg lettuce 20 g.
Young soy beans 30 g. Almond slivers 10 g. Lemon juice 1 tsp. Passionfruit juice 1 tsp.
Preparation:
1. Tear apart the lettuce, wash it well, and put it in a bowl.
2. Soak the coral grass in water until it expands, and then ladle it out and let it steep in lemon and passionfruit juice for 30 minutes to alleviate its astringent taste. Put this on top of the lettuce.
3. In a pot of rapidly boiling water, cook the young soy beans; dry them, and then add them to the bowl.
4. Finally, scatter on the almond slivers as a garnish. Serve.

◆Nourishing Soup
Ingredients:Carrots 30 g. Dried Chinese black mushrooms 6 stalks Wolfberries 20 g.
Ginseng beard (the tiny filaments sprouting from the main root: they are less expensive than the prized parent root) 20 g. Red jujubes 15 dates
Healthy Anti-Carcinogenic Soup Stock, or good water 2,000 cc.
Preparation:
1. Chop the carrots, soak the mushrooms until they expand, and then set them both aside.
2. Put the soup stock into a pot, and then add in all of the other ingredients. Simmer over low heat for about 60 minutes, and then turn off the heat.

Day 20 Breakfast
◆Black Bean Drink
Ingredients:Black beans 2 cups Good water 6 cups
Preparation:
1. Pour the black beans into some water: soak them for about 6 hours.
2. Along with the water, pour the beans into a juice blender; blend them until smooth.
3. Place a piece of gauze over a pot, and then pour the bean juice through it - this will strain out the dregs.
4. Move the pot to your stove-top; boil the mixture at a low heat setting for 10 minutes. Serve.

◆Fruit and Veggie Salad
Ingredients:Apples 60 g. Baby corn 50 g.
Black poplar mushrooms [Agrocybe agerita (Brig.) Sing] 30 g. Ginger 10 g.
Preparation:
1. Wash the baby corn and then parboil for 1 minute. Ladle it from the pot, cut it length-wise into halves, and then put it on a plate.
2. Parboil the mushrooms, ladle them out, and let them dry. Add them to the plate.
3. In a grinder, mash the apple and ginger into a paste. When this is smooth, use it as a dressing for the other ingredients.

◆Sweet Potato Brown Rice
Ingredients:Sweet potatoes 80 g. Brown rice 2 cups
Preparation:
1. Chop the sweet potato into small chunks, and set them aside.
2. Along with the brown rice, put the sweet potato into the inner pot of a rice cooker: add 3 cups of good water.
3. Place the inner pot in the rice cooker; add 1 cup of good water to the outer pot, and then steam until done. Serve.

Day 20 Lunch
◆Rice with Braised Veggies
Ingredients:Cooked brown rice 1 bowl String beans 30 g. Carrots 30 g. Western onions 30 g.
Chinese black mushrooms 30 g. Manioc starch 1 tsp. Cassava flour 20 g.
Soy sauce just a dab
Preparation:
1. Put the brown rice in a bowl, and set it aside.
2. Chop the string beans into sections; slice the onions and carrots; chop the mushrooms into small pieces.
3. Preheat a nonstick frying pan over low heat: add in the string beans, carrots, onions and mushrooms. Pour in 1/2 cup of good water and saute lightly; cover the pot and let the ingredients stew.
4. Mix the manioc starch with some water until it has an even consistency, and then whisk it

into the pot. Add some soy sauce, mix, and then turn off the heat. Now, use the braised ingredients as a topping for the rice. Serve.

◆Cold Kelp Threads with Sauce
Ingredients:Kelp threads 50 g. Ginger 20 g. Cayenne pepper 10 g.
Preparation:
1. Lightly parboil the kelp threads and then let them dry; chop them up. Cut the hot red pepper into thin strips. Put these into a bowl.
2. In a grinder, mash the ginger into a paste, and then pour it into the bowl: mix all of the ingredients evenly together. Serve.

◆Vegetable Soup
Ingredients:Baby napa cabbage 50 g. Scallions 20 g. Shredded ginger 20 g.
Bamboo salt a pinch Healthy Anti-Carcinogenic Soup Stock, or good water 350 cc.
Preparation:
1. Wash the cabbage and scallions, and then separate them and slice into sections. Set them aside.
2. Bring a pot of soup stock to a rolling boil, and then toss in the cabbage, scallions, ginger and bamboo salt. Wait until the pot boils again, and then turn off the heat.

Day 20 Dinner
◆Mexican Tacos
Ingredients:Corn flour 100 g. All-purpose flour 150 g. Tomato ketchup just a dab
Warm water 125 cc., at roughly 140o F. Bean sprout greens 80 g.
Preparation:
1. Mix the corn and all-purpose flour together, and then use the 140o F. warm water to make dough. Separate the dough into 50-g. portions: roll these out into round cakes.
2. Pour a little olive oil into a frying pan, heat up the pan, and then drop in the round cakes. You now have Mexican taco shells.
3. Wash the soy sprout greens, and then parboil for 1 minute. Ladle from the pot, and allow them to dry.
4. Lay a taco shell out on the counter-top, spread on a little ketchup, and then put some soy sprouts in the center.
5. Roll up the taco shell, holding the right and left outer edges. Once the sprouts are wrapped up, they are ready.
6. Follow the above procedure and finish making the tacos.

◆Sunshine Salad
Ingredients:Carrots 50 g. Western onions 50 g. Green peppers 50 g.
Lemon juice 1/2 spoonful Honey 1 tbsp. Apple vinegar 1 tsp.
Preparation:
1. Shred the carrots; slice the onions and peppers into thin disks.
2. Mix all of the ingredients together and put them on a plate.
3. Blend the lemon juice, honey and cider vinegar to make a dressing. Sprinkle this onto the salad and serve.

◆Zesty Soup
Ingredients:Kelp sprouts 30 g. Winter mushrooms 30 g.
Healthy Anti-Carcinogenic Soup Stock, or good water 350 cc. Miso just a dab
Preparation:
Bring the soup stock to a boil in a pot. Drop in the kelp, mushrooms and miso: bring the soup to a boil again. Serve.

Day 21 Breakfast
◆Fruit and Veggie Salad
Ingredients:Mangos 60 g. Cabbage 50 g. Small cucumbers 80 g. Walnuts 1 tbsp.
Preparation:
1. Wash the cabbage, and then chop it finely: spread it on the bottom of a platter.
2. Slice the cucumber; peel the mango and cut it into chunks. Place these onto the platter.
3. Finally, garnish with walnuts and serve.

◆Mashed Sweet Potato and Taro Root
Ingredients:Sweet potatoes 100 g. Taro 50 g.
Preparation:
1. Put the sweet potatoes and taro into a rice cooker; steam them until they are stewed to rags.
2. Remove the taro and peel it: mash it into a paste. With a soup spoon, scoop out some paste and knead it into a ball in your palm.
3. Finish off all of the taro according to step #2.
4. Take out the sweet potatoes, peel them, and then crush them into a paste.
5. Now, take a taro ball and coat it with a layer of sweet potato paste; Knead this into a ball by hand.
6. Cover all of the taro balls according to step #5. Serve.

◆Brown Rice
Ingredients:Cooked brown rice 2 cups Vegetarian soup stock 3 cups
Preparation:

Put the brown rice and soup stock into a rice cooker together: steam them until they are done. Serve.

Day 21 Lunch
◆Whole-Wheat Steamed Cake
Ingredients: Wolfberries 60 g. Pine nuts 30 g. Baking powder 15 g.
Sticky rice flour 300 g. Whole-wheat flour 300 g. Good water 450 cc.
Preparation:
1. Pour the sticky rice flour and whole-wheat flour into a large bowl, add some good water, and mix into dough.
2. Knead the dough into a thick, flattened disk and put it on a plate.
3. Put the plate into a rice cooker, steam for about 5 minutes, and then wait until the surface is slightly hardened. Scatter the wolfberries and pine nuts evenly over the dough.
4. Now, cover the pot again and steam for 10 more minutes. When the cake has cooled, slice it and serve.

◆Sweet Salad
Ingredients:Large tomato 1 piece of fruit Broccoli 60 g. Western celery 40 g.
Preparation:
1. Cut the tomato into quarters, chop the celery into thin strips, and set them aside.
2. Chop the broccoli into sections and parboil for 1 minute: let it dry, and set it aside.
3. Put all of the ingredients on a plate and serve.

◆Zesty Soup
Ingredients:Lima beans 50 g. Kelp braids 30 g. Vegetarian soup stock 500 cc.
Preparation:
1. Bring a pot of soup stock to a boil, and then toss in the Lima beans and kelp braid.
2. When the soup has boiled again, turn down the heat to low and cook for about 15 minutes, until the beans are soft and done. Now, add in some bamboo salt to taste, and then turn off the heat.

Day 21 Dinner
◆Nutritious Chinese Dumplings
Ingredients:Low-gluten flour 300 g. Good water 180 cc. Spinach 100 g.
Chinese tuber onion greens 150 g. Dried bean curd 50 g. Ginger 30 g.
Preparation:
1. Pour half of the flour into a large bowl, add in a suitable amount of water, and knead into dough.
2. Put the spinach into a juice blender along with some good water: mix until smooth. Use a piece of gauze to strain out the dregs, and you will have spinach juice.
3. Pour the remaining flour into the spinach juice: knead into dough.
4. Roll the dough into a long, narrow loaf, and then cut it into about 2-cm.-long slices. Use a rolling pin to flatten the slices out into dumpling wrappers.
5. Mince the Chinese tuber onion greens, chop the dried tofu into small cubes, and mix together to make the dumpling filling.
6. Put a scoop of filling onto each wrapper, and use your fingertips to seal the dumplings.
7. Bring a pot of water to a rapid boil, and then toss in the dumplings. When the water returns to a boil, add in 1 cup of good water.
8. When the water boils again, wait until the dumplings float on the surface: ladle them out.
Use the above proportions to extend the recipe. The raw, uneaten dumplings can be put into sealed containers and stored in the freezer. When you need them, just take them out and drop them into a pot of boiling water. They are ready.

◆Multi-Colored Braised Veggie Medley
Ingredients:Olive greens 50 g. Sweet red pepper 30 g. Sweet yellow pepper 30 g.
Purple cabbage 30 g. Dried Chinese black mushrooms 3 stalks Olive oil 1 tsp.
Soy sauce 1 tsp. Rice vinegar 1 tsp.
Preparation:
1. Soak the mushrooms in hot water until they expand, and then dice them into thin slivers. Set aside.
2. Chop the olive greens into sections. Bring a pot of water to a rolling boil and parboil the olive greens with the mushrooms. Ladle them out and let them dry off: put them on a plate.
3. Chop the red and yellow peppers along with the red cabbage into fine strips. Mix them well, and then put them on the plate.
4. Finally, blend the olive oil, soy sauce and rice vinegar together to make a dressing. Sprinkle this over the salad and serve.

◆Thick Corn Soup
Ingredients:Corn kernels 30 g. Carrots 30 g. Potatoes 30 g.
Healthy Anti-Carcinogenic Soup Stock, or good water 350 cc.
Preparation:
1. Chop the carrots and potatoes into small cubes, and set them aside.
2. Bring the soup stock to a boil in a pot. Now, toss in the corn kernels, carrots and potatoes. When the water has boiled again, turn off the heat and serve.

Fruits

When you get hungry between meals, eat fruit - it's the perfect snack snack!

Apples

Due to the fact that apples contain every type of organic acid and are therefore excellent anti-toxins, we have the well-known saying, "An apple a day keeps the doctor away." Apple pectin promotes the proper functioning of the internal organs, and this fruit's fructose relieves fatigue. Besides this, apples also contain a large quantity of anti-oxidants, preventing cell damage caused by free radicals. The potassium found in apples binds with the body's excess sodium ions, so if one eats apples, this will aid in ridding the body of salt and will relieve high blood pressure.

Bananas

Bananas should be eaten along with their skin[1]. Their flesh is excellent for the stomach, while banana peel is good for the heart:: eating this fruit, your system can completely absorb and maintain a nutritional acid-base equilibrium, caring for the heart and stomach, as well. The banana's sugar content is an energy-booster, and its fiber can stimulate intestinal peristalsis, causing unimpeded elimination. Bananas are rich in potassium that can stabilize the body's excess sodium, preventing the incidence of high blood pressure and cardiovascular disease.

Grapes

Grapes are a food that is beneficial for the kidneys, internal secretions and the urogenital system, but the pulp, skin and seeds should be consumed together. The whitish layer of the grape skin known as grape phenol is its most nutritious part, having all sorts of effective anti-aging and sickness-resisting properties: it is one of the finest anti-carcinogens. Besides this, the grape's sugar and iron content can renew physical stamina and prevent anemia. Additionally, grapes aid in ridding the liver, kidneys and gastrointestinal tract of wastes and toxins.

Peaches

Peach juice has a delightful flavor, and besides its relatively high carbohydrate, vitamin and fat content, it is also rich in easily assimilated organic acids which can stimulate the appetite and the secretion of digestive juices; moreover, the peach's fiber and pectin increase intestinal peristalsis, aiding the digestion. Peaches also contain a fair amount of minerals like iron, which functions as a useful blood-building agent, and potassium, that has diuretic properties and relieves swelling.

Watermelon

Of all melons, the watermelon contains the most copious supply of juice. On summer days, a chilled, juicy slice of watermelon is not only cooling and thirst-quenching, but can also compensate for the body's lost moisture. When eating watermelon, be sure to consume both the reddish pulp as well as the white outer skin. The watermelon is also extremely good for you: besides providing important nutritional elements including carbohydrates, vitamins, organic acids and minerals, watermelon juice also contains a type of diuretic that can enhance kidney functioning.

Pears

Widely known by the lovely title "ancestor of all fruits", the pear is light, crisp and juicy to bite into. Since ancient times, it has been utilized as a medicinal fruit to purify the heart and moisten the lungs; it aids in reducing phlegm and stopping coughs, and its peel is beneficial for the liver, alleviating heat in that organ and purifying it of toxins. Not to mention its organic, mineral and fiber constituents, which not only lower cholesterol but also stimulate the intestinal lining, thus alleviating constipation.

Tomatoes

The tomato counts as both a fruit and a vegetable; generally speaking, the larger varieties are better than the smaller ones. Tomatoes not only lessen heat in the body, but are also high in fiber; among their nutritional contents there is an abundance of vitamins and lycophene, providing even greater health benefits. Lycophene is an especially powerful anti-oxidant pharmaceutical which can prevent osteoporosis: most importantly, it can also slow down the ageing process and lessen the risk of cancer. High in potassium, tomatoes can also lower the blood pressure.

Kiwi Fruit

Everybody knows that he sweet-tart kiwi fruit is low in calories and rich in vitamin C, but this fruit also contains vitamin E, refined amino acids, carbohydrates, phenols, copper, iron and other powerfully effective anti-oxidant chemicals that can both prevent and combat cancer and cardiovascular disease, while also promoting the body's immunological defenses. Kiwi fruit also contains a high volume of nutritional fiber, promoting intestinal peristalsis and maintaining the body's healthy internal environment.

Star Fruit

In traditional pharmaceutical botany, the star fruit is known as the "five-fold collection", for it is thought to expel summer heat and reduce the fire element[2], produce saliva, quell thirst, moisten the throat and make qi[3] circulate freely throughout the body. This fruit is quite effective in alleviating infectious respiratory ailments. In fact, star fruit has an abundance of moisture and contains the vitamins A, B1, B2, C, as well as dietary fiber, carbohydrates, organic acids, a trace of fat, protein, etc.; it can also improve poor digestion and helps to relieve flatulence, cases of the hiccoughs and other digestive disorders.

Oranges

When eating oranges, it is best to slice off the outer peel with a knife, and then eat the fruit's pulp together with the white wrapping that lies just between the fruit's inner flesh and peel. This should be done due to the fact that the orange peel's tartness is much too strong, making it unsuitable for consumption. Oranges are rich in vitamin C, zinc and folic acid; not only can they lessen the incidence rate of cardiovascular disease and cause injuries to heal faster, oranges can also aid in the absorption of calcium and iron, helping to maintain the body in good health. This fruit is also provided with biological flavonoids, cancer-combating agents that can suppress the propagation of glandular cancer attractor cells.

Grapefruit

Grapefruit is full of nutrients such as vitamins A and C, folic acid and potassium; moreover, the red-pulped varieties also contain beta-carotene and lycophene. These elements can boost the metabolism, reduce cholesterol and prevent the incidence of cardiovascular disease. Grapefruit pulp also contains a unique variety of flavonoid that can be effective in suppressing the metastasis of normal cells into cancerous ones. Yet another of the grapefruit's outstanding health benefits is that it weighs in with 10 grams of dietary fiber -- twice that of most other fruits. Thus, eating grapefruit is excellent for the elimination of bodily wastes.

Pineapples

Besides containing an abundance of vitamin C, the sweet-tart pineapple also has a fair amount of vitamin B1, which functions in conjunction with cereal-based amino acids to mitigate fatigue. Additionally, the bromelin contained in the pulp of this fruit is, like papaya enzyme (papain), a kind of natural proteinase: besides its ability to aid the digestion, research has also proved that this type of enzyme serves to retard and alleviate the development of artery-blocking blood clots and other disorders leading to heart disease.

The Wax Apple

The wax apple is a variety of tropical fruit: it is small, pinkish-red, and shaped like a bell. The moisture content of this fruit is quite high, and its function in traditional Chinese medicine is to cool the body and mitigate excess internal heat. Since the wax apple lowers body temperature, is high in special-quality dietary fiber and additionally has diuretic properties, it is helpful for weight control and can also reduce swelling. In the traditional Chinese medical pharmacopoeia, the wax apple is considered to have nerve-relaxing properties: it can lighten or cure the short-temperedness that accompanies extremely hot weather conditions.

Mangoes

The deeply fragrant mango is a tropical fruit. Its flesh is a golden yellow color, and it is therefore an abundant source of vitamin A; besides beautifying the skin and complexion, it promotes the body's resistance to disease, improves the eyesight and prevents eye disease. This fruit's vitamin C content is extremely high, hence it is beneficial in lowering cholesterol and preventing hardening of the arteries and high blood pressure. Mangoes are also a relatively good source of protein, dietary fiber and fruit pectin; they help reduce fatigue and maintain digestive regularity.

Persimmons

In terms of good health, the best thing about the orange-colored persimmon is that it contains carotene, vitamins A and C, and the minerals potassium, phosphorus and iron. In particular, its vitamin C content is far higher than that of most other fruits; functioning in conjunction with vitamin A, this can effectively boost the immune system, prevent cardio-vascular disease and ward off the mental confusion attendant upon hardening of the arteries. Besides all this, fresh persimmons are not only high in iodine, but also have diuretic properties.

The Honey Dew Melon

The soft, porous flesh of the honey dew melon contains ten times more vitamin C and fifty times more vitamin A than an apple. It is a light food that is high in nutrition yet low in calories. The honey dew melon contains both lutein and zeaxanthin; it helps to lower blood cholesterol, boost the metabolism, and also has anti-inflammatory and cancer-fighting properties. Chinese medical annals relate: "Eat this fruit on hot days and you will never succumb to heat-stroke." In sweltering summer weather, after having absorbed too much sun one can obtain relief from heat conditions and diuresis by partaking of this fruit.

Loquats

Loquats contain an abundant supply of carotene and vitamin B; they help to maintain good vision, keep the skin moist, and also have the important function of promoting fetal development. Furthermore, besides its medicinal use as a cough inhibitor and phlegm reducing agent, it also contains a substance known as bitter almond extract that is a cancer inhibitor. The loquat has just the proper amount of organic acids, hence can stimulate the digestive glands' secretions and benefit the digestion.

Guava

The moderately sweet, crisp-textured guava contains copious amounts of vitamins A and C; especially in terms of its high vitamin C content it counts as the champion of all fruit, and the wild red-centered species that is native to Taiwan has still more. The guava is excellent for relieving colds, headache, stomach-ache, and so on; since it has an abundance of dietary fiber and is low in calories it makes one feel full, so it is a good choice for people who want to control their weight.

Avocado

Although the avocado does not have a sweet taste, it is particularly high in fat and has four times the calories of other fruits. Nevertheless, due to its low sugar / high energy properties, it is appropriate for diabetic diets. Avocadoes contain lots of oil, but this is all in the form of unsaturated fatty acids that can reduce cholesterol in the blood and prevent the accumulation of cholesterol in the arteries: this is beneficial for maintaining healthy brain cells.

Plums

Plums count among the more acidic fruits, but they contain an abundance of minerals such as potassium, calcium and iron, as well as malic acid and citric acid, carbohydrates and dextrose. They can stimulate the production of digestive fluids, increase intestinal peristalsis, alleviate fatigue, prevent anemia and boost the appetite. Moreover, plums are high in dietary fiber and are useful in relieving constipation.

Strawberries

Strawberries are high in vitamin C, bolstering the body's immune system and protecting the circulatory system. On top of that, because they contain anti-oxidants like tannic acid, carotene and cyanine, eating strawberries can control the production of cancer-inducing agents; hence, the strawberry has assumed a prominent role as an anti-carcinogen. Additionally, this fruit contains a fairly high amount of fibrous elements, so it is effective in reducing cholesterol, relieving constipation and correcting high blood pressure.

1 Eat a banana peel?! In fact, this is easy to do: first wash the fruit carefully, and then cut it into thin round slices, leaving a small ring of peel around each slice. This can be consumed with no problem.
2 Fire in the body: According to Chinese medical practitioners, the body is composed of five elements - fire, wood, earth, metal and water -- that arise in succession and also have mutually restrictive properties.
3 Qi: In Chinese medicine, the physical body is thought to be vivified by a form of energy known as qi, which flows in channels running parallel to the nervous system.

Cooked Vegetable Dishes

01 Sliced Sugared Lotus Root
Ingredients:Lotus roots 100 g. Black sesame seeds A pinch
White sesame seeds A pinch Sugar-cane juice 600 cc. Rice vinegar 200 cc.
Preparation:
1. Wash the lotus roots and slice thinly. Set aside ready for use.
2. Put the sugar-cane juice in a pot and bring it to a boil, then add the lotus root slices and rice vinegar, and let the mixture stew.
3. Simmer over low heat for approximately 30 minutes, until the lotus roots have completely absorbed the liquid ingredients and have become soft and tender.
4. Remove from the pot and place on a platter: sprinkle on the sesame seeds. It is ready to serve.

02 Bean Curd Skin with Tomatoes
Ingredients:Bean curd skin 1 piece Large tomatoes 60 g. Scallions 20 g.
Bamboo salt a pinch Cold-pressed olive oil 1 tbsp.
Preparation:
1. Slice the tofu skin into approximately 1 cm. pieces and cut the tomatoes into small sections. Clean the scallions and dice very fine.
2. Pour the olive oil into a non-stick frying pan; warm the pan. Put all ingredients into the pan and lightly stir-fry. Now add bamboo salt and 1 tbsp. water: cover the pan and stew for 1 minute.
3. Remove the cover and stir-fry evenly, then turn off the stove and serve.

03 Tender Steamed Bean Curd
Ingredients:Soft tofu 1 package Green soya kernels 10 g.

Chinese black mushrooms 10 g. Vegetarian soup stock 50 cc.
Preparation:
1. Wash the mushrooms and chop into thin pieces; set them aside, ready for use.
2. Place the tofu and soup stock into a fruit blender and blend evenly.
3. Pour this mixture into a bowl; sprinkle on the chopped mushroom and green soy kernels.
4. Place this large bowl into a rice cooker and steam for 20 min. until the mixture is fully cooked. Serve.

04 Tasty and Refreshing Tossed Vegetables
Ingredients:Soya sprouts 50 g Soy sauce just a bit Sesame oil just a bit
Chinese black mushrooms 30 g. Rice vinegar 2 tbsp. Chili peppers 10 g.
Chinese Mu'er mushrooms [Edible tree fungus / Auricularia auricular judae] 30 g.
Preparation:
1. Chop the mu'er into strips; cut the black mushrooms into thin pieces; cut the chili peppers into small sections. Set aside for use.
2. Bring a pot of water to a rolling boil, and add the soya sprouts, mu'er and black mushrooms. Once they have been parboiled, scoop them out of the pot and let them drip-dry.
3. Add the rice vinegar, chili pepper, soy sauce and sesame oil. Toss all ingredients evenly, put on a platter and serve.

05 South Seas Curry
Ingredients:Onions 50 g. Potatoes 60 g. Carrots 40 g. Vegetarian soup stock 300 cc.
Curry powder 2 tbsp Cold-pressed olive oil 1 tbsp. Soy sauce just a touch
Preparation:
1. Chop the onions, potatoes and carrots into chunks; set aside ready for use.
2. Pour the olive oil into a frying pan and heat. Add the onions, potatoes and carrots: stir-fry until they are almost done on the outside.
3. Pour in the soup stock, curry powder and soy sauce: mix evenly. Lower the temperature and boil for about 30 minutes. Serve right away.

06 Saltwater-Prepared Tender Soya Pods
Ingredients:Young soya pods 80 g. Bamboo salt 1 tsp. Star anise 2 pods
Black pepper powder 1 tbsp.
Preparation:
1. Boil a pot of water and drop in the star anise and soya pods; boil for about 15 minutes.
2. When completely cooked, scoop the ingredients from the pot and allow them to drip-dry. Add the black pepper and bamboo salt: toss evenly. Serve.

07 Kumquats and Turnip Strips
Ingredients:Kumquats 3 fruits White turnip (daikon) 80 g. Chinese wolfberry 1 tbsp.
Plum juice 1 tbsp. Cilantro 1 stalk
Preparation:
1. Chop the daikon into thin strips and mince the cilantro. Mix together in a bowl.
2. Squeeze the juice out of the kumquats, then cut them into cubes. Along with the juice, stir into the daikon.
3. Now, add the wolfberries and plum juice; blend in evenly, then let the mixture steep for 30 minutes. Serve.

08 Vegetable Jelly
Ingredients:Carrots 30 g. Green soya kernels 30 g. Chinese wild yam 50 g.
Elephant foot powder 50 g. Healthy anti-carcinogenic soup stock 100 cc.
Plum juice 1 tbsp.
Preparation:
1. Cut the carrots and Chinese yam into small cubes.
2. Bring a pot of water to a rolling boil. Drop the carrots, soya kernels and Chinese yam successively into the pot; boil until done. Scoop the ingredients from the pot and allow them to drip-dry, then place them in a bowl.
3. Put the elephant foot powder into the bowl, and then slowly add the soup stock. Blend evenly until the mixture becomes sticky and dense.
4. Pour into a mold and place in the freezer compartment of your refrigerator. Serve in slices, dribble on some plum juice as a topping.

09 Bean Curd Balls ·
Ingredients:Tofu 1 piece Carrots 30 g. Cilantro 10 g. Sweet potato starch 1 tbsp.
Bamboo salt a pinch
Preparation:
1. Mince the carrots and cilantro; set aside, ready for use.
2. Put the carrots in a frying pan and fry over low heat until done.
3. Mash the tofu into a paste, and then blend in the carrots, cilantro, cassava starch and bamboo salt. Blend evenly.
4. Heat up the frying pan again. With a soup spoon, scoop up some tofu paste and form it

into a ball. Fry the tofu balls.
5. Repeat step 4 until all of the tofu paste has been made into balls; fry until the surface turns golden-brown.

10 Sweet and Sour Vegetables to Accompany Rice
Ingredients:Tomatoes 50 g. Pineapple 50 g. Green Peppers 30 g.
Tomato Juice 1 tbsp. Filtered water 1 tbsp.
Preparation:
1. Chop the tomatoes, pineapple and green peppers into pieces; set aside, ready to use.
2. Heat up a frying pan. First, put the tomatoes, tomato juice and filtered water into the pan: mix evenly and fry. Afterwards, add the pineapple chunks and the green pepper. Stir-fry for approximately 3 minutes, and then serve immediately.

11 Easy-to-Make'saka Pancakes
Ingredients:Wheat flour 50 g. Water 50 cc. Western cabbage strips 100 g.
Nori powder 1 tbsp. White sesame seeds 1 tbsp.
Healthy and tasty seasoning powder 1 tbsp. Cold-pressed olive oil 1 tbsp.
Preparation:
1. Put the flour, water and seasoning powder into a bowl: mix evenly until it becomes a paste.
2. After chopping the cabbage into thin strips, stir it into the wheat paste mixture.
3. Preheat a frying pan. First, pour in the olive oil, and then add the wheat paste mixture.
4. Cook over low heat for approximately 5 minutes, then flip it over and cook for another 5 minutes.
5. Test to see if the pancake is done: insert a bamboo chopstick into the middle -- when the chopstick comes out without any paste sticking on it, you can turn off the heat and remove it from the pan.
6. Place on a platter. Finally, sprinkle on the nori powder and white sesame seeds. Serve immediately.

12 Braised Wild Mushroom Mix
Ingredients:Chinese black mushrooms 20 g. Abalone mushrooms 20 g.
Pleurotus geesteranus mushrooms 20 g. Sweet peas 30 g. Ginger threads just a few
Soy sauce 1 tbsp. Olive oil 1 tbsp.
Preparation:
1. Cut the black mushrooms, abalone mushrooms and P.g. mushrooms into thin slices. Set aside, ready to use.
2. Preheat a frying pan. First, fry the ginger strips, and then pour in the soy sauce and olive oil.
3. Toss in the mushroom mix and stir-fry. Now, add the sweet peas and fry for 1 minute. Turn off the heat and remove from the pan.

13 Potatoes with Tomato Sauce
Ingredients:
Red tomatoes 100 g. Potatoes 100 g. Onions 30 g. Garlic 2 heads Vegetarian soup stock 1,000 cc.
Preparation:
1. Cut the potatoes into large sections; chop the tomatoes, onions and garlic into small cubes. Set aside, ready for use.
2. Place all of the ingredients in a soup pot. Cook over high heat until the broth has come to a rolling boil, then turn the heat setting down to low. Continue to simmer the mixture for 30 minutes. Serve.

14 Vegetable Stew
Ingredients:Chinese black mushrooms 3 mushrooms Black mu'er mushrooms 10 g.
Taro root 50 g. Tomatoes 30 g. Cold-processed bean curd 1 piece Black vinegar just a touch
Shandong cabbage 100 g. Vegetarian soup stock 1,000 cc. Bamboo salt a pinch
Preparation:
1. Chop the cabbage into sections, cut the black mu'er into strips, and chop the taro root and tomatoes into pieces. Set them aside, ready to use.
2. Pour the soup stock into a soup pot and turn the heat setting to high. Bring to a boil, and then drop in all of the ingredients.
3. Once again, bring the mixture to a boil, then turn down the heat setting to low: simmer for about 30 minutes. When all of the ingredients are stewed to rags, it is ready to serve.

15 Salty Vegetable Pie
Ingredients:Pumpkin 200 g. Apples 50 g. Carrots 50 g. Sweet bell peppers 30 g.
Asparagus 30 g. Pine nuts 1 tbsp. Whole wheat flour 200 g.
Preparation:
1. Slowly add water to the whole wheat flour. Knead it until it is evenly mixed, and then form a ball of dough.
2. With a rolling pin, roll the dough out into a flat sheet. Lay this out over the bottom of a pie plate.

3. Chop the apples, carrots, bell peppers and asparagus into small pieces. Set aside, ready to use.
4. Steam the pumpkin until it is done, and then mash it into a paste. Stir this into the chopped fruit and vegetable mixture.
5. Pour the evenly-blended mashed pumpkin mixture onto the pie dough. With a scraper, even the top so that it is flat.
6. Preheat the oven to 350_ F. Put the pie into the oven and bake until the top has turned a golden-brown color. Serve.

16 Daikon Slices with Miso
Ingredients:Daikon turnip 150 g. Miso 2 tbsp. Bamboo salt 1 tbsp. Rice vinegar 1 tbsp.
Hot red peppers 1 pepper
Preparation:
1. Chop the hot pepper into thin strips and set aside, ready to use.
2. Chop the daikon into thin strips: do not remove the skin. Put this into a large bowl.
3. Sprinkle on the bamboo salt and let the daikon set for 1 day. Wait until the daikon emits moisture.
4. Take the daikon and stir in the miso, rice vinegar and red peppers. Let the mixture set for another day. It is now ready to serve.

17 Natural Flavored Vegetable Shish-kebab
Ingredients:Green peppers 30 g. Carrots 50 g. Potatoes 50 g. Pineapple 50 g.
Ginger juice 1 tbsp. Soy sauce 1/2 tbsp. Honey 1 tbsp.
Preparation:
1. Cut all of the vegetables into chunks, and put them together in a large bowl. Mix them thoroughly, and then let them set for 30 minutes.
2. Blend the ginger juice, soy sauce and honey evenly: this is the sauce.
3. One-be-one, attach all of the vegetables on bamboo skewers.
4. Place all of the shish-kebab on a baking pan. On the surface, paint a thin coating of sauce on evenly, turning the skewers over from time to time. Bake until the surface shows signs of doneness. They are ready to serve.

18 Multi-Colored Vegetable Box
Ingredients:Italian broccoli 50 g. Brussel sprouts 30 g. Pumpkin 50 g. Eggplant 50 g.
Carrots 50 g.
Preparation:
1. Chop the Italian broccoli, pumpkin, eggplant and carrots into small chunks. Set aside, ready to go.
2. On the stove-top, preheat a frying pan. Pour in the carrot, pumpkin and eggplant; afterwards, add 1 tbsp. water and cook until done. Finally, add in the broccoli and brussel sprouts.
3. Remove from the pan and pour into a box. Before eating, sprinkle on a bit of Healthy and Tasty Seasoning Powder, and then serve.

19 Crock-Pot Vegetables
Ingredients:Vegetarian soup stock 500 cc. Bean curd 1 piece Sesame oil a few drops
Shungikee (Garland chrysanthemum) 50 g. Napa cabbage 50 g.
Enoki mushrooms [Winter mushrooms, Flammulina velutipes (Fr.) Sing] 50 g.
Bean thread noodles 20 g. Green garlic 1 stalk Bamboo salt a pinch
Preparation:
1. Wash the napa cabbage and shungikee; cut the tofu into chunks, and slice the garlic slant-wise into strips. Set these aside, ready to use.
2. Lay the napa cabbage out flat along the bottom of a crockery pot. On top, put the tofu chunks: pour on the soup stock and cook until the mixture comes to a boil.
3. Once the broth has come to a boil, put in the shungikee and bean thread noodles; bring everything to a boil again, and then turn off the heat.
4. Before setting on the table, while the mixture is still hot, sprinkle on the green garlic bits, bamboo salt and sesame oil. Serve.

20 Nutritious Pearl Balls
Ingredients:Sticky rice 50 g. Purple Chinese yam 200 g. Shepherd's purse 50 g.
Preparation:
1. Before starting to cook, soak the rice in water for 2 hours.
2. Put the Chinese yam in a rice cooker and steam until it is thoroughly done. Take it out and remove the skin; mash it into a paste.
3. Peel the shepherd's purse, and then chop it into small cubes. Stir this into the Chinese yam paste.
4. Let the rice dry, and then spread it on a plate. Take a suitable amount of yam paste and knead it into balls. Put the yam balls in the plate and roll them around until they have picked up the rice grains. Be sure that the yam is evenly coated with rice.
5. Put the finished pearl balls onto a platter: place in a rice cooker and steam for

approximately half an hour. Serve.

21 Soft Breeze Perilla and Elephant-foot

Ingredients:Elephant-foot slices 30 g. Perilla leaves (Chinese basil) 2 stalks Soy sauce 1/2 tbsp. Large cucumbers 50 g. Kelp 30 g. Filtered water 1 tbsp. Rice vinegar 1/2 tbsp.

Preparation:
1. Slice the cucumber into thin pieces and set aside, ready to use.
2. On the stove-top, preheat a frying pan. First, put in the kelp and elephant-foot strips, and then add the rice vinegar, soy sauce and water. Cover the pot and let the mixture stew.
3. Finally, put in the cucumber and perilla -- saut_ for about 3 minutes. Remove from the frying pan and serve.

Common Questions about the Detoxification Diet Program

1. Q: For a detoxifying dietary plan, how much food constitutes "one portion"?
   A: Each person's food intake capacity is different, and a detoxification regime will take this into account. I recommend 50-60 g. as a standard portion, which can be adjusted up or down according to individual needs.
2. Q: Besides the types of root, stem, flower and fruit vegetables previously listed in your book as having detoxifying properties, are there any others?
   A: Root Vegetables: Carrots, daikon, turnips, horse-radish, beets, burdock, yukijobi [Smallanthus sonchifolius], yam bean [Pachyrhizus erosus].
   Stalk Vegetables: Elephant-foot [Amorphophalus Konjac C. Koch], taro, bamboo shoots, tender-stemmed lettuce, round-stemmed kale, Indica mustard (salted vegetable root), wasabi, potatoes, Chinese yam [Rhizoma diosoreae], lotus root, asparagus, lily, water chestnut, ginger, onions.
   Flowered Vegetables: Cauliflower, broccoli, day lily, flowering Chinese chives, rue.
   Fruit Vegetables: Tomatoes, sweet pepper, chili pepper, eggplant, Chinese wolfberry, okra, sweet corn, water caltrop, lily flowers, okra, small cucumbers and other types of squash.
3. Q: On this diet, what should I do if my hands and feet start feeling cold?
   A: Cold hands and feet are caused by poor circulation and inefficient metabolism. To correct this condition, use food ingredients with heating properties, such as ginger, scallions and onions.
4. Q: Eating sweet potatoes leads to flatulence: is there any way of avoiding this problem?
   A: Sweet potatoes contain enzymes that produce gasification, so as soon as they have entered the digestive system and begin to be broken down, gases will be produced. If the intestinal tract is in an acidic state at this time, even more gases will be produced: this is the cause of flatulence. It is best to maintain the intestinal tract in a weakly alkaline state, in which case this problem can be alleviated.
5. Q: Does eating detoxifying foods cause the body to produce more secretions?
   A: This is a typical reaction to detoxification. Congratulations - keep up the good work!
6. Q: While undergoing detoxification, why is it that those suffering from acute illnesses are advised not to eat sprouts, legumes or leafy vegetables?
   A: You can eat soy and green lentil sprouts which have been sprouted at home, but be extremely careful about those sold in supermarkets - they are apt to contain bleaching or weed-killing agents. For the same reason, it is also not advisable to eat alfalfa sprouts. Legumes can be a potential problem for those with chronic illnesses like cancer or obesity, since most types of beans contain large amounts of vegetable oil and protein, which can aggravate such conditions. For people with no health problems, however, legumes pose no problem when eaten in moderation. Leafy vegetables should not be eaten raw, as they are more apt to contain remnants of agricultural chemicals than root or stalk type vegetables; they may also host insect parasites.
7. Q: Pumpkin, soy beans and mushrooms are excellent cancer-combating foods: why are they not included in detoxification dietary programs?
   A: From a Chinese medical standpoint, pumpkin and mushrooms are both foods that are apt to induce allergic reactions, and clinical research has shown that soy beans should not be eaten by those suffering from tumors. These three types of food have been excluded from the diet for these reasons.
8. Q: If one does not eat fish, meat, eggs or dairy products, how can the body absorb enough protein?
   A: In a detoxification diet, you can eat seaweed, snow-peas, nuts and coarse cereals, all of which provide the body with the necessary protein.
9. Q: What are some possible detoxification reactions? How can I know if the symptoms I am experiencing are detoxification reactions?
   A: Some examples of possible detoxification reactions are: headache, weakness, general discomfort, sensitive skin, slowed bowel movements, diarrhea, increased urination,

fatigue, inertia, nervousness, irritability, feeling negative and depressed, fever and other cold-like symptoms. Some chronic complaints that have been suppressed by medications but not really cured will become apparent; for example, those prone to high blood pressure may find their blood pressure temporarily heightened, diabetics might discover that their blood sugar level is up -- don't worry, this is actually a good sign! Such symptoms should not be cause for alarm, and will naturally go away in a few days' time. In any case, most people find that these symptoms are bearable, and you should feel pleased about experiencing such "problems", since they are signs that the detoxification diet is working.

Detoxification reactions may last from three days to two weeks, depending upon differences in peoples' physical constitutions.

10. Q: When on a detoxifying diet, what can I do to alleviate uncomfortable symptoms?
    A: When experiencing detoxification reactions, you should take it easy, get more sleep, drink more good-quality water and eat more synthetic plant enzymes: this will lighten such feelings of discomfort.
11. Q: While on a detoxifying diet, is it alright to be taking Chinese medicine?
    A: On this kind of diet, you are allowed to take Chinese medicine. There should be no conflict between the two; in fact, they often have mutually-supportive effects, so don't worry and continue taking your medicine.
12. Q: Will eating a detoxifying diet cause one to lose weight for the duration of the treatment?
    A: At the beginning of the treatment you will lose weight, because the recommended foods contain a generous amount of fiber. This will stimulate intestinal peristalsis, cause an increase in bowel movements, and lessen the amount of oil, salt and sugar in the body; as a result, you will lose weight. However, detoxification plans help the physical constitution regulate itself, so you should not continue to lose weight. Generally speaking, after you have lost a bit too much weight for your body type, you should revert back to your normal weight once again.
13. Q: If your body is chilly and weak, can you go on a detoxifying diet?
    A: Yes, you can. Just boil some ginger broth and take it at mealtimes, or add scallions, garlic or onions to your cooking recipes.
14. Q: Do you have to take synthetic plant enzymes and plant energy supplements (made of kelp) while on a detoxifying diet?
    A: If you take these supplements along with the other recommended foods, the detoxification results will be more complete and more evident.
15. Q: In your book, you say that those with chronic ailments or suffering from cancer should eat foods that have been tested by health specialists. Where can one find this type of specialist?
    A: You can find this kind of professional or volunteer specialist -- people who have gone through special training -- in any neighborhood. For more detailed information, call [Taiwan] 886-02-2920-3986, and have a consultation with the Luke Company.
16. Q: When undergoing chemotherapy, radiotherapy or electrotherapy, can one go on a detoxifying diet? Can you tell me what I should be careful about at this time?
    A: You can go on a detoxifying diet while undergoing these procedures, but be sure to find out if foods have come from a polluted source. For the raw-foods portion of your meals, it is advisable to purchase naturally-grown fruits and vegetables; in addition, these foods should undergo purification in a food detoxifier before being eaten.
17. Q: Is it true that you are only allowed to drink kombu [kelp] broth on this diet?
    A: For the soup portion of your meals it is good to add seaweed and vegetables, among which kelp is included. But you should be careful to eat different kinds of foods: eating the same thing day after day is definitely to be avoided.
18. Q: Is it true that this kind of diet absolutely forbids the use of seasonings?
    A: When you are just getting started on this diet, you can begin by reducing your oil, salt and sugar intake, thus allowing your taste buds to gradually revive and adjust. Having progressed this far, you will be able to forego seasonings and let your taste buds experience your foods' true flavors, simultaneously lessening the burden on your body's internal organs. If you do utilize seasonings, it is best to substitute bamboo salt for regular table salt and use cold-pressed
19. Q: Besides brown rice, what other kinds of cereal foods are you allowed to eat?
    A: You can accompany brown rice with the following grains, which may be boiled along with your rice.
    Cereals: Rice germ, millet, Job's tears, wild rice, semi-refined rice (red, white or black).
    Grains: Barley, wheat, buckwheat, Incan quinoa, rye.
    Coarse cereals: Chinese sorghum, corn, amaranth, Gorgon fruit, tapioca, Western Job's tears, lotus seeds, green lentils, red beans.
    Dried legumes: Hyacinth beans, rice beans [mambi beans; Vigna unguiculata (L.) Walp], black-eyed peas, kidney beans (black or red).

Fresh legumes: Kidney beans, string beans, young soy beans, Lima beans, sweet peas, peas, hyacinth beans [Lablab purpureus (L.) Sweet], snow peas.

Fermented beans: Natto.

20.Q: Must one end this detoxification diet exactly at your book's recommended cut-off time?

A: If you can continue this diet right up to the book's recommended cut-off time, you will experience the optimal results; if you cannot continue and go off the diet, then the result will be in proportion to the amount of time you kept it up. In any case, exceeding the recommended cut-off time is better than never having gone on the diet at all.

21.Q: How can working people keep up this diet?

A: Busy working people can mix one piece of fruit and two types of vegetable in a blender and drink this as a beverage. Even the sweet potato and rice part of the diet can be conveniently boiled before going to bed; in the morning, make these into pocket sandwich rolls or sushi and eat them.

22.Q: How can people who work the night shift follow this diet? Should I add any supplementary foods to my diet?

A: Night workers can follow the book's instructions just as they are, supplementing this with B-complex vitamins and synthetic vegetable enzymes. However, the body's energetic channels move according to fixed laws, so you ought to take into serious consideration the far-reaching effects of this type of work. In fact, you would be better off avoiding the night shift.

23.Q: Is it absolutely necessary to drink 1,260 cc. of water every morning? What if I absolutely cannot drink so much?

A: Right after getting up in the morning and before brushing your teeth, drinking some water is helpful for detoxification. Of course, it is rather hard to chug down seven glasses of water first thing in the morning, so start out with 500 cc. and build up gradually from there. If you drink one piece of fruit plus two types of vegetable that have been processed in a blender in the morning, then taking 500-700 cc. of water will be sufficient.

24.Q: How long must one be on this diet in order to see the desired results? Can it help cancer patients?

A: Actually, this detoxifying diet functions both on nutritional and lifestyle levels. Dietary purification will progressively lead to physical purification. Cancer patients tend to have a long-term acidic pH balance, so when their bodies have been purified by this diet, their internal organs will become healthy. In at least 4 to 6 months' time, this condition can be improved. Let me reiterate, this diet is also a life-style: it is a formula for those who want to start a new life through nutritional means.

25.Q: Can you complete a detoxification program in only 21 days?

A: A 21-day detoxification program is designed to benefit people who are not suffering from any maladies; for people with chronic illnesses or tumors, at least four months will be necessary, and all three daily meals should be planned in accordance with the recommended diet. This should be accompanied by 14 days of extra-strength detoxification, and the "seven daily steps for healthy living" should also be energetically carried out.

26. Q: What is "good water"? Where can this be purchased?

A: 400 years ago during the Ming dynasty, Li Shizhen wrote about "snow water" in his book The Great Compendium of Chinese Materia Medica: this is what I am referring to when I use the term "good water". In his travels, Li discovered that villages where people lived to a ripe old age were located midway up mountain slopes; consequently, there would always be a Heaven-sent supply of excellent water available. But ordinary people can follow the advice in this book and select the best kind of water purification system.

27. Q: Does everybody need to take an enzyme supplement?

A: Enzymes are catalysts that help to set off the body's chemical reactions. They are stored in raw greens, vegetables and fruits. If you can eat enough raw fruits and vegetables every day, taking supplements should be unnecessary -- if not, then it is advisable to take these supplements. For those with no health problems, take a supplement before each of your three daily meals; those with chronic illnesses or tumors should accompany their detoxifying meals with supplements, as described in the book Fresh, Light, Toxin-Free! .

28. Q: Are enzymes the same as yeast?

A: No, enzymes are not yeast - the two are not the same. Most of the body's internal activities and reactions require enzymes in order to operate efficiently. Enzymes can maintain the body's normal functions, digest foods, repair tissues, and so on. They contain an abundant supply of B-complex vitamins and plant proteins, and can improve the condition of those who tire easily, or whose lips tend to crack and split in the corners.

29. Q: If I eat kelp, must I still take a vegetable energy supplement (kelp powder)?

A: This kelp powder is a pharmaceutical health supplement containing minerals which have been extracted from a variety of seaweeds using German high-tech methods, so this is not the same as regular kelp powder. It provides the seven types of mineral that the body requires, and will quickly regulate states of high acidity, causing the body to become more alkaline. Naturally, eating kelp is beneficial, but this will not serve as a substitute for kelp powder.

30. Q: People with kidney disease are not allowed to eat seaweed: is it alright to eat kelp powder?

A: Generally speaking, people with kidney ailments should be careful about their potassium intake. This type of kelp powder is a mineral supplement; it is different than other kelp and seaweed food products, hence people with this problem can take it without worry.

31. Q: I live in central Mainland China, where there is a very limited selection of fruits and vegetables available. How can I go on a detoxifying diet?

A: A healthy detoxifying diet program is a model for healthy eating and drinking habits, as well as for your style of living; therefore, it doesn't matter where you live - anyone can adjust their lives according to the plan introduced in this book.

32. Q: Can children follow this diet plan?

A: For children, the detoxification diet is even more crucial than it is for adults. This program will not only help them, it will also serve as a life-long beneficial influence, as well.

33. Q: What kind of milk should be given to infants?

A: It is best for infants to drink mother's milk; if not, then brown rice, millet, soy or goat milk is suitable. For children above the age of two years, drinking cow's milk is even more unsuitable: their teeth will be well-developed, so they should always eat a balanced diet.

34. Q: While you are on a detoxifying diet, will you start feeling relatively weak?

A: It isn't necessarily the case that you will feel weak while on this diet; in fact, since your body will be burdened with fewer toxins, you should feel refreshed and comfortable.

35. Q: I'm on a detoxifying diet, and always feel hungry. What am I allowed to eat?

A: When you are on this diet, your digestion will operate faster without being a burden on the body. This is why it's easy for you to feel hungry - it is a normal sign. When you feel hungry, you can eat fruit, nuts or sweet potatoes.

36. Q: How can I find out if my body is acidic or alkaline?

A: You can buy the litmus paper that is sold in pharmacies, and use it to test the pH level of your saliva.

37. Q: Is it true that you should eat everything with its peel?

A: Generally speaking, yes, you should. But please keep in mind that the outer part of longan and litchee fruit is a shell, not a fruit peel.

图书在版编目（CIP）数据

21天排毒养生餐／林光常著．－北京：国际文化出版
公司，2006.11
ISBN 7-80173-598-6
I.2...　II.林...　III.素菜－菜谱
IV.TS972.123

中国版本图书馆CIP数据核字（2006）第130099号
版权登记号　图字：01-2006-6142号

林光常21天排毒养生餐

著　　者	台湾/林光常	
责任编辑	臧燕燕	
封面设计	林世鹏	
出　　版	国际文化出版公司	
发　　行	国际文化出版公司	
经　　销	全国新华书店	
印　　刷	北京冶金大业印刷有限公司	
开　　本	965×635　　24开	
	8印张　　　250千字	
版　　次	2007年1月第1版	
	2007年1月第1次印刷	
书　　号	ISBN 7-80173-598-6/Z·098	
定　　价	49.80元（随书附送VCD光盘）	

国际文化出版公司
北京朝阳区东土城路乙9号　邮编：100013
总编室：(010)64270995　传真：(010)64271499
销售热线：(010)64271187 64279032
传真：(010)84257656
E-mail：icpc@95777.sina.net
http://www.sinoread.com

About the Translator:

Lynne Mallinson has had a deep interest in Chinese art, philosophy and culture for most of her life, and for over six years she lived, studied and taught in both Mainland China and Taiwan. Now living in Maryland, she practices Chinese martial arts and yoga, as well as doing Chinese calligraphy and brush painting. Although Ms. Mallinson's formal studies have mainly involved Chinese literature and history, her martial arts experience has given her an understanding of Chinese medicine that was useful in translating this book. Ms. Mallinson majored in Chinese Language and Literature (B.A./Wellesley College, '98), and completed her M.A. in the same field at Washington University in St. Louis, '01.

本书之内容为作者若干年来潜心钻研、历经实践的结晶，属一家之言，绝非是要取代合格医师的诊断与治疗，尤其是婴幼儿、孕妇、病人等特殊群体，在排毒前更须征询医生或专业营养师的意见。而书中所列咨询电话或网站，仅提供如何正确吃排毒餐之咨询，若您有任何身体上的不适，我们建议您先请教专业的医疗人员；生病看医生，但健康靠自己。